The
Eye of Prey

The Eye of Prey: Subversions of the Postmodern
is Volume 9 in the series
THEORIES OF CONTEMPORARY CULTURE
Center for Twentieth Century Studies
University of Wisconsin-Milwaukee

General Editor, KATHLEEN WOODWARD

HERBERT BLAU

THE
EYE OF PREY

SUBVERSIONS OF THE POSTMODERN

INDIANA UNIVERSITY PRESS
BLOOMINGTON AND INDIANAPOLIS

Manufactured in the United States of America

Library of Congress Cataloging-in-Publication Data

Blau, Herbert.

  The eye of prey.

  (Theories of contemporary culture; v. 9)

  Includes index

. 1. Drama—20th century—History and criticism. 2. Experimental theater. 3. Criticism. 4. Civilization, Modern—1950-   . I. Title. II. Title: Subversions of the postmodern. III. Series.

PN2287·B456A5   1987   809·2'04   86-46243

ISBN 0-253-32096-8

ISBN 0-253-20439-9 (pbk.)

1 2 3 4 5 91 90 89 88 87

There is of course the eye. Filling the whole field. The hood slowly down. Or up if down to begin. The globe. All pupil. Staring up. Hooded. Bared. Hooded again. Bared again.

—Samuel Beckett, *Company*

The determination of the pack is terrible and unchanging, but it also contains an element of intimacy. A sort of tenderness for their prey can be discerned in primitive hunters.

—Elias Canetti, *Crowds and Power*

There is a delicate empiricism which so intimately involves itself with the object that it becomes true theory.

—Goethe, as quoted by Walter Benjamin, in *One-Way Street and Other Writings*

Will we manage to escape unscathed from the symbolic game in which the real misdeed pays the price of imaginary temptation?

—Jacques Lacan, "The Freudian Thing"

CONTENTS

FOREWORD

With this collection of essays by Herbert Blau, *Theories of Contemporary Culture* expands from a series of edited books to include single-authored books by critics and theorists whose work has significantly shaped the research of the Center for Twentieth Century Studies. A postdoctoral research institute at the University of Wisconsin–Milwaukee, the Center's commitment is to the study of contemporary culture in its interlacing with contemporary theory, with the understanding that the production of theory is itself a form of contemporary culture. Our stance is crossdisciplinary and collaborative.

Herbert Blau has contributed, brilliantly and provocatively, to many of our projects, including our deliberations on the principle of performance in postmodern culture, aging and psychoanalysis, sexuality and the public realm, feminist theory, and the modern text as the locus of the experience of modernity. Several of the essays in this book were presented at the Center over the past few years to our admiring gaze. In the discriminating ambivalences of their thought (and the poetic complexity of the thinking through), in their stunning range and utter seriousness (including eruptions into hilarity), these words, and their performances, have heightened the permutations of our own thought and deepened our lives as intellectuals.

KATHLEEN WOODWARD
Director, Center for Twentieth Century Studies
General Editor, *Theories of Contemporary Culture*

ACKNOWLEDGMENTS

". . . the discovery of the unconscious is still young," said Lacan, "and it is an unprecedented opportunity for subversion." While these essays have variable feelings about the subversion, their gathering gives me the opportunity to acknowledge with unequivocal conscious gratitude various kinds of support:

I have for some time been working on a book entitled *The Audience,* for which I have received a fellowship from the National Endowment for the Humanities and a summer research award from the Graduate School of the University of Wisconsin–Milwaukee. A promise is a promise, and that book will presently materialize. Meanwhile, some of these essays are either groundwork or spinoff or a kind of peripheral vision, "the eye of prey" being one ominous aspect of the specular consciousness that has obsessed all of my recent thought. I have mostly worked out this obsession at home, but was almost distracted from it by an alluring fellowship and other sightseeing opportunities at Cassis in southern France. There, under the auspices of the Camargo Foundation, I studied the *écriture* on the Mediterranean from three balconies overlooking a lighthouse rumored to be the one that Virginia Woolf really had in mind. I also completed at Camargo—under the attentive gaze of our amiable hosts, Russell Young and Michael Pretina—the preface to this book and its final essay, "Shadowing Representation."

Part of that essay was delivered at a forum on images of colonization and the politics of representation, organized by Kathleen Hulley for the 1984 convention of the MLA in Washington. All of the essays were written in the first half of the eighties, up through the reelection of Ronald Reagan. They were mostly for particular occasions, one of them extended. "Universals of Performance; or, Amortizing Play," published in *SubStance,* was the outcome of a long-term international project on the potential exchange of something more than performance techniques, not only within the theater but between the theater and ritual practice. The project was sponsored by the Wenner-Gren Foundation for Anthropological Research, whose director Lita Osmundsen and program coordinator Willa Appel were tirelessly adept in negotiating across cultures the manifold idiosyncrasies and polyglot needs of actors and dancers—some of them "National Treasures" and some who might be if they weren't performing under circumstances which are marginal or dispossessed—and not only actors and dancers, but shamans, gospel singers, tribal chiefs, clowns, anthropologists, performance theorists, and probably unnamable others.

The other occasions were somewhat less exotic. I was asked by the Beckett Society to talk about Beckett in the troublesome light of deconstruction, and the outcome of that was, as I explain in the essay, "The Bloody Show and the Eye of Prey." It has since been revised and published in *Theater Journal*. Shortly after the death of Roland Barthes, the New York Institute for the Humanities and the Center for French Civilization and Culture at New York University held a festival in his honor and invited me to speak on Barthes and Beckett, from which developed "The Punctum, the Pensum, and the Dream of Love," for publication in *October*. "Disseminating Sodom" was commissioned by *Salmagundi* for a special issue on homosexuality. When I was invited by the University of Stockholm to lecture on contemporary American drama, it seemed a chance to make up for a local injustice by spreading the word abroad about the neglect of Adrienne Kennedy, and to examine the related implications of the ongoing but probably unfulfillable promise of the enormously talented Sam Shepard. That eventuated in "The American Dream in American Gothic," since published in *Modern Drama*, which had previously asked me to write about "Comedy since the Absurd" for its special issue on comedy. The essay which opens this book, "(Re)sublimating the Sixties," appeared in a shorter version in the new journal *Formations*.

There are some minor revisions and some additions to the other essays, and now and then a signpost or afterword indicating that some idea will be taken up elsewhere. In a couple of the essays I have left the visible and vocal traces of the occasions mentioned above, not only because the momentariness or the audience figures in the conception, but also on the assumption that if there is some good reason, as recent theory goes, to "insert the subject" in the discourse, there's no point in revising the most conspicuous evidence of it away. The reader will notice, however, that those essays which were written to be read publicly are not much different in style or density from the others, which have also been read aloud, over and over, in the privacy of my study for the *mise-en-scène* of the page.

Whatever subversive opportunities from the unconscious those soundings may provide, some of the support I've received has also repeated itself. Among those who have been abundantly generous, in response to the work and in diverse other ways, are my friend Ihab Hassan—with whom loud argument over some of the issues is not unabundant either—and his wife Sally, who has with elegance and quick intelligence mediated our intemperance over the finest dinners here and abroad, and in the vast drear and middle of the night. There is also the Dean of the College of Letters and Science at UWM, William Halloran, who has, aside from other encouragement, supported my work by the high priority he has given to the Center for Twentieth Century Studies, which first attracted me to Milwaukee.

If the Center has been my host in the past, it has become in a double sense a sort of second home, since it is directed now by my wife Kathleen Woodward. Beyond the line of duty, she has listened to these ideas in all their recursive insistence, even when she's not listening, because of my compulsive habit of trying them on out loud, as if the look of the words on the page can only be—despite the dreamscape of language as a thing to be *seen*—confirmed in the ear. Actually, she has looked at the essays, too, with a compulsion of her own, an editorial eye, to which I remember more than she does my giving begrudging assent. She has, moreover, prompted me into writing one of them: "The Makeup of Memory in the Winter of Our Discontent" reflects a shared desire for the conceptual energies released by critical theory to be further engaged by something more than the self-mirroring propensities of a discourse about discourse. The mirroring is still there, but with something more (I trust) than the materiality of an absence further attenuated by theory. It's not so much a case of "returning to the text," but—in several of the essays at least—going to and from the text to a "realer," more personal content, formerly disallowed by the older New Criticism and then, in the theoretical critique, the newer discrediting of humanism. Originally written for a symposium at the Center on aging, literature, and the imagination—in a (mostly revisionist Freudian) psychoanalytical context—the essay appeared in *Memory and Desire,* a volume edited by my wife with Murray M. Schwartz, for the series being published by Indiana University Press, of which the present collection is now a part.

Those of us engaged in the myriad activities of the Center are endowed with the assistance of Carol Tennessen and Jean Lile, who share one splendid virtue: when anxiety is really flying, they manage to keep it to themselves. As director's spouse and Senior Fellow, I have had more than the fringe benefits. At the Center's new word processor, Shirley

Reinhold put the essays on the floppy disks with accuracy and good cheer. I also want to thank Ginny Schauble, who typed a number of the original versions on a primitive Selectric before the technological break-through. Past and present graduate assistants at the Center have also, without any labor-saving devices, made the clerical side of postmodern living easier (for me). However sketchy the reference, so promptly have they turned up books and articles on request that I may have forgotten how to use the library. My appreciation, nevertheless, to Mark Luprecht, Rose Both, Jaye Berman, Debra Vest, Jon Erickson, and Laura Roskos. One or another has also, with wary eyes, proofread parts of this and other manuscripts. So has Edward Schelb, my research assistant, who has gone meticulously through the essays and—with an affinity for the ellipses—stayed on the trace of recurring themes to prepare the index.

PREFACE

I am going to approach the subject of this book or its various subjects—
including the problem of talking about *the* subject in a period which has
"valorized" or fetishized the word—by looking back to a period of vast
and volatile *subjectivity* that wanted desperately, or thought it wanted
("*and me, me, what am I doing in all that?*"[1]), to abandon it, along with the
autonomous ego and an authorizing identity, to the decision-making
processes of a participatory ideal. I am referring, of course, to the sixties
which have been undergoing recently, through surrounding condescension and outright assault, a nostalgic reassessment. I try to avoid the
nostalgia, probably without success, in the mixed feelings of the first
essay, but a reassessment is in order, since it is the unfinished agenda of
the sixties which infuses the state of mind not only of these essays but of
the newer critical thought which, if there's any unifying subject, the
essays are about.

One of them begins, however, with a portrait of my dead mother
and another with the birth, after a second marriage in my ending middle
age, of a new daughter. So they are also about more or less personal,
more or less specific subjects—aging, love and mourning, gender and
genre, particularly comedy—all of which become in the context of such
thought just about as elusive as the subject which is, with more or less
critical disapproval, about nothing but itself, an obsession with language
freaked on language. The same might be said of the hybridization of
comedy since the Absurd, which would be a laughing matter if it weren't
so absurd. The obsession arose in part as an effort of the subject, divided
from itself, to circumvent that impasse which, as in the comedy of
Beckett, seemed like the ontological dead end of the Cartesian abyss,
which does not, as Lacan said of the unconscious, "lend itself to
ontology."[2] I confront the impasse of that laughing matter in the second
essay where it can be seen, with the focus on the drama, that postmodern
forms, which distrust the drama, are subversions of the comic as the
comic is—the jokes, the puns, the tautological hiccups, the spastic deferral of the last guffaw—the disruptive substance of postmodern forms.
It is also the destabilizing preface to the pleasure of the text.

According to Barthes, it *is* the text. With no institutional voice
"*behind* what it is saying . . ., the text destroys utterly, *to the point of*

contradiction, its own discursive category, its sociolinguistic reference (its 'genre'): it is 'the comical that does not make us laugh. . . .' "[3] And if—in the lexical and syntactical exuberance of this "new philosophic state of language-substance," which even liquidates all metalanguage—it should *happen* to make us laugh (which Barthes neglects to mention), we're not exactly sure what we're laughing about or at, or whether it is really comical at all, since *we* are likely to be the language-substance.

I take up that possibility in the essay on comedy and return to the obsession with language—which spreads itself over everything like the unconscious which it appears to be—not only in the reifications of theory, but in the work of two dramatists who came of age in the sixties nurtured on the Absurd, but still dreaming the American dream, and with remarkable gifts of language. (The sixties also disrupted categories to the point of contradiction, but they lacked the more extenuating irony which, as Barthes says of the text, "does not subjugate. . . ."[4] That's why it seemed at the time, more often than not, as if the major species of comedy was the slapstick of a querulous farce which forgot what Marx had perceived, that history occurs first as tragedy. But then, the sixties were not big on history.) If there was for Sam Shepard and Adrienne Kennedy no other truth of achievable being except in the sphere of language, that's not only because we live in a world of fictions, jargon, sociolects, and simulacra, with its inescapable infrastructure of thought, but also because they were writing for a theater which is part of the apparatus, the American dream-machine, which encourages no thought. Neither dramatist is in any sense a theorist, but their plays converge on the theoretical issues, and one of them is now a movie star whose crossover from the experimental theater to mass culture —the sublanguages of which had turbocharged his plays—seems like the emblematic fulfillment of the postmodern in its movement from the sixties to the eighties.

There is a similar crossover from theater to theory which is also worth thinking about. In a sense this book is a crossover, since it is the first I have written which is not, principally, a theater book, although I have suggested elsewhere that if my work *in* the theater, now suspended and apparently over, could be sustained on the page, it was never really theater that I was writing about. After thirty years in the theater, I'd pretty much come to believe that if it was ever really theater that the theater was about, it was never more profoundly so than when it was impassioned by the thought of putting an end to theater—precisely the opposite, it would appear, of what the sixties were about, with the diffusion of theater into fashion, therapy, politics, education, and everyday life.

As for the self-abolishing thought of theater, it has become something of a model for theory, with its performative impulse and antitheatrical prejudice, and its Derridean dream of "the closure of representation." I shall say more about that through the book. If it is not, though, a book on theater, there are nevertheless the two essays mentioned on the drama (not to be wholly conflated with theater) and one on universals of performance which, in dissociating itself from the drama, has become something of a universal—as the eroticizing body of the text and the instrumental agency of thought—in disciplines other than the theater, and not only the other arts: one of the more vital examples being Foucault's notion of a *"theatrum philosophicum"* or "phantasmaphysics."[5] There are more conventional, less Artaudian versions of performance in speech act theory or in the anthropology of Turner or Geertz or in the sociology of Goffman, but it is the *subversion of thought* in the other notion of performance that is most germane to the recurring (I almost said blurring) subject of these essays, as well as their own habits of mind.

I *see* theatrically, or so I *understand*, in the grain of my understanding of theater. It is the understanding that interests me, I think, far more than theater. The habits of mind are by now, probably, so inseparable from the many years of perceiving in the theater—that peculiar construct of reflected thought—that I'm no longer sure, when I look at any subject, whether it isn't really the theater I'm thinking about. It's rather like Lévi-Strauss with the Indians of Brazil: the subject *out there,* however fastidiously studied, seeming to be a projected shadow of the structure of my mind. That may not be the only delusion. I said in a previous book, *Take Up the Bodies: Theater at the Vanishing Point,* that if the stagings of my work being recalled were being made up on the page, and had never otherwise occurred, the theory derived from them would be no less true—and my theaterwork was being continued right there.

If I meant it as a serviceable fiction, that fiction has obviously been given a lot of support in recent years—some might say to the point of delusion—by the concept of *writing* as performance and the phantasmaphysics of theory. What we are confronted with there is an idea of performance as multiple, synchronous, and polyscenic, a circuitous torsion of laminated thought, where the masks, costumes, cries, bodies, and the interlacing gestures of limbs and eyes are—as in the "reflective mathematics" of Artaud's vision of the Balinese dancers or the ideographic writing of the unconscious, the dismembered evidence of psychoanalysis, *dream-thought*—an intenser form of ratiocination. While I have been disciplined to such thought by years of praxis in the theater, it is aroused here by the demands and detours of other subjects and by a sort of polyscenic encounter in several of the essays with the diffracted, spiraloid, and dilatory thought, the "singular zig-zag"[6] of style in its most exemplary figures: Barthes, Derrida, and repeatedly Beckett who provided, along with the existential ground rhythm, the decentering momentum of the postmodern and, "quaquaquaqua," its vertigo of theory.

That includes its most subversive tendency, as one can see in the analysis of capitalism and schizophrenia by Deleuze and Guattari, who extrapolate from the *"solar anus"* of Judge Schreber to the bicycle horn of Molloy out the hole in his mother's arse to the amniotic conception of flow-producing machines which encourage, as Foucault has said of schizoanalysis, "the epidermic play of perversity" in which "[a] dead God and sodomy are the thresholds of the new metaphysical ellipse."[7] It is the elliptic of this epidermic play, taken over by radical feminist and homosexual discourse, that I try to think over in "Disseminating Sodom," along with the more liberating and alluring manifestations of an unnerving if not ominous practice. Immersed as they are in this discourse—in that sense a sub*version*—the essays are in their own elliptical way, incrementally, maybe perversely, and at some critical limit or *clinamen* of an alignment, outrightly, subversive in the other sense. They are by no means strictly or formally theoretical, but as a critique of the *aura* of deconstruction and its behavioral implications, they are particularly suspicious of what is most attractive: the apotheosis of play in the "structuration" of alternative structures and the doxology of *jouissance,* the ideological program of "the subject of desire" which, as a matter of "lifestyle," was articulated in the sixties through the nonverbal politics which seemed to have plenty of desire without, as they used to say, an ideological program.

Outside ideology, and a marginal figure in the evolution of the modern (to the master of the Wake, an attendant lord), Beckett surfaced in the fifties when the modern seemed to be running out of desire and, characterized in this country by the Age of Ike, entropically winding down. It was like the return of the repressed, a little indigent and worse for wear, from the fading inscription of the originary trace. If he became, nevertheless, a talismanic force during the sixties for releasing an awakened negativity into a culture biding its time, he was a touchstone after the sixties, with the Movement disillusioned and its projects incomplete, for releasing into the postmodern the flow-producing *aporias* of unfinishable forms. Two of the longer essays in this book are on (im)paired experts of the *in*terminable, Beckett and Barthes, Beckett and Derrida, between and among whom I try to make distinctions in a thickening of aporias, as with the overlay of libidinal discourse in "Disseminating Sodom."

Beckett is also a determining if inconsolable voice in the genotext of my reflections on aging, "The Makeup of Memory in the Winter of Our Discontent," as his plays were like the geriatric ward of an aging culture with its regimen of puerility in the comedy of the Absurd. Despite the stone-sucking autogamy of his characters in a regressive circuit of exchange—which has made him something like the tutelary deity of the new dispensation of *play*—Beckett is a man of immense erudition who can't quite live it down because, with the maturing weight of all that knowledge, he seems to have lived twice, without the contemptible illusion (he would feel) of having been born again. What he is unable to forget—from the derisive tragic outburst of the blinded Pozzo to the contracting dimensions of his latest sepulchral prose—is that we are born astride of a grave, which puts another dreadful complexion on the celebration of play which continues through the disillusionments of the sixties in the game theories of therapy and the therapeutic spinoffs of theory and in the linguistic exuberance of theory itself and, even through the second thoughts on deconstruction, in the "carnivalization" of Bakhtin and the labile unfolding of the Imaginary of the feminine. You might think that play would peter out in the sullen unfolding of academic indifference or the hostility to deconstruction and what it represents. But there are those, say, in every English department who— teaching (for old time's sake) a little Brautigan or Vonnegut or even, upping the ante on the postscripts to the modern, some O'Hara and Ashbery along with Pynchon—continue to play around with it.

"I play," wrote Wallace Stevens in *The Man with the Blue Guitar*. "But this is what I think." Ifucan in ashcans, but in a similar vein, Beckett doesn't merely play around: you're on earth, there's no cure for that, not even "the talking cure." Beckett has been in analysis and studied Freud, and the structuration of his writing is like a demonstration of the definition of thought as a sort of detour or blind alley or the cover-up of the loss in the memory of gratification. What is signified by the memorable *fort/da,* that dramatic structure, turns up in the windings of Krapp's spool. It also initiates the theoretical reflections, in the essay on universals and what I say of representation, on the psychosexual declensions of play in the economy of performance. One doesn't have to read widely through the labyrinthine turnings of poststructuralist theory to realize that if performance has become the paradigm and heuristic body of thought, it also worries itself *in* performance—like any Method actor or the psychoanalysis of Lacan—about nothing so much as whether it contributes in its most subjective exposures to the cover-up of the loss.

It's also what worries Beckett and is worried by him. As if overwhelmed by an intelligence which cancels all possible answers to virtually unstatable questions, he can be as derisive about theory as he is of existence. Yet if he can't avoid the ongoing impulse in the inertia of *Comment c'est,* the aphasic or stuttering pause which begins all over again, he can't help theorizing either. For his work proceeds (or recedes) from that subjunctive condition of thought which, in a ceaseless rehearsal of beginnings, backtracks, reconnoiters, and can't avoid canceling itself, as it sends out interrogative feelers to every lymph node, spinal tap, and ruptured vesicle of thought—doing it so exhaustively in those unnamable operations around the unmentionable that he seems to cancel in the process the inaugurating subject of thought. However you view this subject it was, as Derrida might say, "always already" split; for Lacan, "threading," as he says, his "curved needle through the tapestry,"[8] there is an almost surrealistic transposition into the castrating mirror, where the subject is caught between the eye and the *gaze*—that strange contingency in which we find ourselves thinking thoughts that are not our own—as if thought into being by the Other.

"Who! you know how to think, you two?"[9] Perhaps no words occur in Beckett so much as the words of thought, no end to the mirroring in the thinking, *think! think! think!* with its inevitable divisions and revisions, though it may not be the worst, "to have thought," if you really *had* it or knew where it began. "I'm not a historian," says Gogo,[10] as he loses after a moment the faintest semblance of a thought which may never have had a beginning. The sequence on the variora of the Gospels at the opening of the play—which concludes with the no doubt provisional Darwinian opinion that people are bloody ignorant apes—is like a datum of deconstruction with its scorn of logocentrism. But the play's eccentric returns to the subject of origins also anticipates, by the way of rebuttal or compensation, a whole line of books from Frank Kermode's *The Sense of an Ending,* which wants to affirm a beginning, to Northrop Frye's *The Great Code* or Robert Alter's *The Art of Biblical Narrative,* designed to straighten Didi out. Even as I write, there appears in the mail René Girard's study of generative violence in the Gospels, where he not only demonstrates, as he did with Oedipus and Dionysus, that mimesis is what tears people apart, but suggests that it is the Gospels—with their sacrificial crisis and scapegoat—which might put them together again, as well as mastering the relationship, so troubling in French Freud, between the Symbolic and the Imaginary.

"Biblical interpretation," Girard writes, "cannot explain the *nature* of healing miracles. It can only deal with the *language* used to describe them."[11] In the hermeneutics of Beckett's play, "The scapegoat's agony" appears to be the prison house or excrement of language, that is, a crock of . . . the "hard stool," or "a net," the whole network of berserk thought in the diarrheic monologue of Lucky with its historical rundown of the breaking up of the full presence of the Logos in the metaphysical tradition of the West, for which they beat him up. After which dismemberments (the *sparagmos*), they "Raise him up!" As Didi concedes in the preliminary tropes before that eschatological event, *"(squirming like an aesthete).* There's something about it. . . ."[12] The squirming is a sort of half-assed foreshadowing of the *"actio"* described by Barthes in the famous passage about the blissful text, the body language timidly fleshed out, mimesis unpurged, as Didi tries to pick up the incipience of Lucky's power—the *writing aloud,* "the breath, the gutturals, the fleshiness of the lips, a whole presence of the human muzzle . . . throwing, so to speak, the anonymous body of the actor into [the] ear: it granulates, it crackles, it caresses, it cuts, it comes: that is bliss"[13]—to obliterate all difference between the Symbolic and the Imaginary.

Waiting for Godot is not the only one of Beckett's works which is a reverse gloss on the newer theory, as well as a virtual handbook on narrative as it is being written about today. For what also wavers and disappears, along with the subject, in the filiating membranes of the thinking process, are the objective appurtenances of narrative and its customary appointments that his creatures (one can hardly call them characters) try to keep in keeping up the appearances of a plot, which they do half-heartedly when they are not merely bored to death by the deferrals that fill the waiting or scared out of their wits by the absences or, in a delirium of paranoia, momentarily driven from the stage. *What*

keeps them there? to ask an old-fashioned question posed of the drama by
Arthur Miller when it still seemed worthwhile to think about the idea of
Tragedy and the Common Man. Now that we're thinking about the end
of Man, it's certainly none of the older categorical imperatives of the
drama, Destiny, Fortune, Necessity, those tedious mysteries. What keeps
him there? The *dialogue,* says Hamm, or even less, *lessness,* some residual
memory of the outside possibility of a performance remembering in its
recessions the most minimal performance—the *dromenon,* or nucleating
event?—framed after two thousand years of Western theater by silence,
lights up lights down, a cry perhaps, a breath. Yet even in the expiring
silence, in the recurring absence of informing words, there appears to be
(as in the notorious eighteen minutes of missing tape) a disturbing
discourse—a murmur? a rustle? or the running sore of history with its
semiotic flux?—which, if the actors *are* there, abrades upon their presence, causing them to behave in the undeniably carnal body of performance as if they were linguistic shifters doing their metonymic tricks,
slipping away before our eyes—as if, too, the *looking* itself were a kind of
abrasion in its scopophilic desire.

   I wrote about the subversive nature of this speculative enterprise, and
the dynamics of disappearance, in *Take Up the Bodies* and in another
theorizing book which was fallout from the vanishing, *Blooded Thought:
Occasions of Theater,* in which the occasions were the collusions of postmodern performance with "the scopic drive," the desire to *see,* to see
maybe what should not be seen, the intensely specular consciousness
which, in refusing that prohibition, is another obsession of the theory
which seems to be thinking about itself. When it dwells on the *look* or
(they are not always the same) the *gaze*—as in Lacan's seminar on the
splitting of the subject—it often seems like a revival of Renaissance
doctrine about the light of the mind radiating as energy from the eyes,
with the *jouissance* or baroque ecstasy of more or less twisted eyebeams.
That depends on the course of history and the source of power, as
Donne perceived when the dissidence of his body murmured secrets of
state, (dis)enthroning power to his own erotic desire.[14] The look, to be
sure, is not without a political dimension, the terms of which are established by the Renaissance conceit of perspectival space, where the
look is the Law, all being mirrored in the fixity of its gaze. Which can be
held, it seems, only so long. The eye altering alters all, observed Blake,
keeping up with history even as he refused it. What we're into now are
all the ramifications for perception which Shakespeare had discerned

when—fixed upon the outrageous splitting even in the loveliest gaze—
he made those equally outrageous puns about the eye in the first person
singular. That might be the anthem of what is anathema to poststructuralist thought, sinning in what it opposes, always eyeing the I.

The consciousness of the gaze as the locus of power is most
tendentious, perhaps most abstruse, and now just about catechistic in
film theory, a radicalized offshoot of deconstruction which is trying to
counter the gaze traditionally fastened upon the woman as the object of
desire. As with the films which draw upon this theory or reflect it (often
made now by women), the woman is resituated—sometimes, as in
Duras's *India Song*, outside the frame in a disembodied voice—as the
desiring subject who will disempower the structure in which the gaze is
"in the scopic relation, the object on which depends the phantasy from
which the subject is suspended in an essential vacillation," and whose
privilege derives from its very structure, dominated by the Other.[15] The
voice is Lacan's, but Beckett was on to the whole insidious process, in
something like that prose, as early as his essay on Proust, a subversion of
the postmodern in the double sense: as a sort of premonition or pilot
project of that self-reflexive criticism which is an artform of its own,
nearly preempting the (ap)parent subject, and through the modernist
disease of retrospection shared with Freud and Proust. Still unappeased
in Beckett is the intolerable contradiction of survival and annihilation,
the fetishes of Habit, Memory, and Time, "this Janal, trinal, agile monster or Divinity,"[16] the decantations of whose hours are not mere functions of structure—"the old ego" dying hard in its dream of dissolution,
the homeostatic desire—so that like the narrator of Proust's fable of
remembrance, loss, and lessness, "He must return and re-enact the
stations of a diminishing suffering,"[17] remaining a stubborn holdout in
that extenuating pathos from the secessions of the postmodern and the
easier accessions of the seductive *différance*.

Derrida says at the conclusion of his essay "Structure, Sign, and Play"
that he doesn't believe there is any question today of *choosing* between
the "structuralist thematic of broken immediacy," burdened as it is with
negativity and guilt, and "the Nietzschean *affirmation*"[18] which joyously
embraces the play of the world and the innocence of its becoming. It is
Beckett, however, who affirms or at least represents the splitting difference. Or is it the unsplittable difference? Both at once, or so it appears,
for he remains the haunted and Janal figure of the *undecidable:* the one
who "seeks to decipher, dreams of deciphering a truth of an origin

which escapes play and the order of the sign, and which lives the necessity of an interpretation as an exile" *and* "the other, which is no longer turned toward the origin, affirms play and tries to pass beyond man and humanism, the name of man being the name of that being who throughout the history of metaphysics or of ontotheology—in other words, throughout his entire history—has dreamed of full presence, the reassuring foundation, the origin and the end of play."[19]

I had been exploring this mind-splitting difference in other words and other ways before I read Derrida, since I first directed *Waiting for Godot* and *Endgame* in the fifties (when Beckett was largely unknown in this country), and I return to it again in the essay on Beckett and deconstruction, the writing of which began on an occasion which, turned toward origin, seemed to affirm play, in "The Bloody Show and the Eye of Prey." If the equivocations of Beckett can tease us out of thought, like the labor of birth and the erasures of *différance,* he is nonetheless—like Artaud, who has teased Derrida—a cause by which the mind can think. Such a cause is not, to say the least, exactly restful to the mind, but he has remained with me over the years as an influence made of anxiety, as if he owned the subject. When the postmodern is not achieving "break-throughs," it is in the habit of "beyonding"—beyond this, beyond that, and now and then beyond Beckett. But he adheres to the scene and the time to which he came belatedly, an authorizing power of whom one is not easily, or even desirably, disburdened: "eye of prey," a primal source, about which—as the occasion seemed to require and as I say in the essay—I have my doubts. Those doubts, in one form or another in each of the essays, and including self-doubts measured by the engagement with the newer critical thought, are for me the major concern of this book.

In going over some journals before writing the essay on Beckett and Barthes, for a testimonial occasion after Barthes's death, I was reminded that I met them within a week of each other in the late fifties. It was soon after I had directed Brecht's *Mother Courage and Her Children* (the first production of it in this country, where Brecht was still largely unknown), and Barthes and I conversed in my poor French despite his better English about the *Verfremdungseffekte* of Brecht, under whose influence we both were at the time. It was a little after he had published *Mythologies,* when he was still writing for *Théâtre populaire,* the journal which developed in the orbit of Jean Vilar, and in which first appeared the brief but remarkable essays on Brecht. Barthes was also working then on his semiotics of fashion, and I rather ineptly referred him to Henry James while he referred me to Saussure and Lévi-Strauss (of whom I'd never heard), speaking of himself as a "disciple." Even before I began to read him, it was Barthes who made me aware that something acutely stimulating if not arcane was happening to literary studies—and to a lesser extent to theater studies—in France that was a sharp deviation from the methods of the New Criticism into which I had been initiated by one of its major figures, Yvor Winters, a sharp deviationist in his own right. That right was hard-earned, with a reclusiveness even more adamant than Beckett's and the recidivism of undeterrable convictions, a very long distance from Barthes.

Those convictions are not irrelevant to certain qualities in this book that carry over from my theaterwork, though Winters would no doubt be depressed to hear it. At a time when the performance principle is dominating literary theory, I can't help remembering that among his convictions—shared with Ezra Pound, with whom he agreed about next to nothing else—was that the theater is a form of "third-rate intensity." He never approved of my having anything to do with it and never came to see anything I ever did, though his wife Janet Lewis was faithful. Since this book is—though due not so much to a change of heart than circumstances—something of a turning from the theater, if not exactly back to the criticism he would have had me write, it seems an appropriate time to acknowledge a debt to Winters which I've not done sufficiently before. If any book is something of a testimonial occasion, the dais here is shared by a very strange pair always already there, shadowing my thought, Beckett and Winters, to whose convictions I want to return after a word on Derrida.

I began to read Derrida in earnest not through Beckett, Barthes, or other literary studies—which I continued, as I continued teaching literature, through all my years in the theater—but when I began to realize that in the very *difficulty* of his writing he was theorizing the theaterwork which I had been doing in the seventies. That might be described as a deviation from Brecht through Beckett into a highly allusive, refractory, intensely self-reflexive, ideographically charged process in which we were trying to understand, *to think through,* at the very quick of thought—words, words, words, unspeakably in the body—the metabolism of perception in the (de)materialization of the text. There was also in that process—as there is in the art of acting: *how do I do it? where does it come from? what is IT?*—something of an obsession with the indeterminacy of origin, and the impact of volition on origin, and whether the thought of it comes before it does, whatever it is, or whether it couldn't be thought without it. (For this work, as I've described it in *Take Up the Bodies*, Shakespeare's *Hamlet* was also a textbook, to which I'll refer briefly again:) It's the kind of thought which suffuses Hamlet's thinking on the ramparts and which strikes the mind with all its fine harrowing ambivalence when he says, "What, has this thing appeared again tonight?" (*Ham.* I.1.21). For the actor, as for the play, if it appears it becomes a problem and if it doesn't it's certainly worse. I mean whatever it is that *moves* a performance, and which preserves in the most empirical of acting methods something of a mystery, which can amount to the fantasy by which the subject is suspended in the essential vacillation of the mirroring described by Lacan. In any case, it was the precise indeterminacy of the *thing* in all its semantic ghostliness (Coleridge called attention to the superb credibilizing effect of the word) which gave us a method we called *ghosting*. It was an idea of performance concerned, like Derridean theory, with appearance and disappearance and the following of a *trace* which is the origin of the memory through which it appears.

In that intensification of specular consciousness which is necessarily doubled over in the theater, and redoubled in the methodology of our work, we were possessed *in the activity of performance* by what we could see and what we couldn't and, despite the momentary illusion of the most corporeal realization of thought, what we might never see perhaps because it couldn't *be* thought, and therefore might never appear—as if theater and theory (with their now commonly recognized common etymological root) were to embrace in the vanity of a missing identity. As with the Conceptual Art of the late sixties—particularly that strain of it which jeopardized the body in the self-reflexive activity of thought—the subject of our work, and the danger of its becoming, was *solipsism*. It is a subject which comes up in various parts of this book, but it's certainly a far cry, in its soliciting of indeterminacy, from my own critical "origins," a distance signified now, in the vicinity of Derrida, by the usual reflexive hedging of the word.

That's something which Yvor Winters wouldn't have entertained even momentarily in the mind. No more than the hedging of meaning in the new accommodation to the arbitrary play of the signifiers, all the more hedged if methodological. I came to study with Winters quite by accident

(I didn't know who he was) when the New Criticism was still relatively new (I didn't know what it was) in the late forties, as relief from the oppressive anti-intellectualism of a theater to which I'd come—virtually illiterate with a degree in engineering—not long before. I went through engineering solving problems in physical chemistry or fluid mechanics or thermodynamics with little sense of their origins or meaning or the ideological systems in terms of which meaning is produced even in the sciences, no less the *absences* of meaning that showed up in the empty spaces of the Mendeleyev table and far more now, apparently, in high energy and low energy states or in subatomic and intergalactic spaces, among the quarks or quasars, or in the mathematics of Catastrophe Theory, as if the slippage of the signifiers *were* the model of the universe reflected in the microcosm and the macrocosm, as in the genetic codes of DNA. If Winters had no indulgence for that slippage, forcing us to think of meaning in no uncertain terms, he was nevertheless a man who had exerienced to the edge of insanity—which can be seen in the hallucinatory precision of certain early poems—what he insisted on believing was the illusion of no-meaning. And it was that which he wrote about in the remorseless lucidity of his criticism which seemed at times like an arbitrariness to outdo the signifiers.

Actually, though he did as much as anyone to establish the reputations of Crane, Stevens, and Williams—none of whom lived up to his standards—he was a dissident within the New Criticism and wrote devastatingly about its sacred poets, Yeats, Eliot, and Pound. In the era of the verbal icon and the well-wrought urn and the poetic voice, he refused to allow that paradox, image, tension, and the seven types of ambiguity guaranteed the voice of wisdom. Yet he believed, like the other New Critics, that there was some irreducible authority in the text which came from the (nearly) sacramental power of the word, although he was not interested at all in the Word within a word unable to speak a word since, in a civilization squandering its resources and reprehensible in other respects, the word was in trouble enough without such mystifications and could easily be debased. For him, the cultural achievement of language was probably far better than we deserved, and we owed to that achievement the labor of making words mean what they say, although he had no illusions about our reliability in the matter and would have agreed with William Carlos Williams that "Language/is not a vague province. There is a poetry/of the movements of cost, known or unknown. . . ."[20] He was willing to pay the cost through the most arduous labor of his own, enunciated in lines of stern clarity, no mask, no persona, not the slightest inflection of a performative impulse if he could help it, only the movements of cost, the gain, purchased with pain, and the movements of thought arising from *lack,* as the medieval philosophers he studied knew before Lacan who, with his religious background, might have inherited it from them. Winters was not religious, though a moral absolutist, and if "God knows what all this means!/The mortal mind is slow"[21]—which is why it must all be thought so demandingly, as necessity demands, as if necessity were "The very strength we choose/With what we lose."[22] If there's a distinction between the lack and this *loss*—as we look around us in the faint "stir of age" with our aging senses, at things "Brutal and aimless" or falling "Quiet beyond recall/Into irrelevance,"[23] or at irrelevance which is making a lot of noise—it is that the lack, without the strength, is still moving thought which is lacking.

Well, at least it's not puritan and repressive, one might say. True enough, but not sufficient to Winters's strength. Winters thought within a stricter compass, and before the desublimations of the sixties. His distinction, however, was not simply that he practiced what he preached, many lesser critics and poets, and less devoted teachers, have done that. What was distinctive in what he preached with all its strictures was the exactitude of its passion, and what it required from those who engaged with it or argued with it, as I did unceasingly. He'd take the argument with a seriousness that few of us accord our students because we're unlikely to have a position we take seriously enough to be argued with in what, quite accurately, the newer criticism has attacked as the repressive pluralism of our universities, which Winters saw through and attacked long before. It was during the sixties, in which I was very active politically with my students, that I came to know what he meant when he wrote, "The young are quick of speech./Grown middle-aged, I teach/Corrosion and distrust,/Exacting what I must."[24] (Barthes came to know something similar with his students, which I comment on in the essay on the sixties, but despite his affection for the corrosion and distrust of Nietzsche, he exacts what he must by tact, circuitousness, and seduction.) As for the strictures of Winters, if you were looking at the same evidence you'd be hard pressed to oppose him. If there were certain unverifiable things that he'd refuse to see, he could also look at the evidence hard enough that he almost single-handedly prepared the case against all the apparent evidence—and opposing colleagues, the despoilers of learning, "the insensate, calm/Performers of the hour,"[25]—to acquit a man unjustly accused of murder.

His critical position was so rigorous if uncompromising that even generous deference (of which he received little enough then) by the major New Critics couldn't satisfy him or dismiss him. Most of them seemed—though we blame them now for insisting on the autonomy of a text which is a text of power—like flaccid relativists in comparison, especially when he did what he really did best, and that is to put his impeccable ear to a poem, either dismissing or confirming its power. I want to say something about this against the grain of my own sub-versions, in the theater and these essays, of the ideological text. I've talked of various postmodern obsessions in this preface, and another one of them is obviously with interpretation and reader response, ranging from Burke's dramaturgy to De Man's rhetoric to Iser's phenomenology of the reading process to Fish's interpretative communities within which the reader's activity is identical with the text to Barthes's notion in *S/Z* of the writerly text in which we are not only inscribed but are writing ourselves through the infinite play of the world and, going into orbit, a galaxy of signifiers whose elliptic—entrances and exits and tangents—would go on as far as the eye can reach, and farther, through an infinity of languages were it not for the burnout of the writerly reader in the reentry pattern where, in the earth's ideological atmosphere, the codes which were mobilized narrow and the Critic reappearing on the scene is forced to look at the text *as if* there were something there.

I trust that I've already been sufficiently respectful of Barthes that some facetiousness in this running account will be excused. I believe I understand what he means by the multiplicity of the text and his desire for an unconstrained plural which is not an entitlement to think anything about a text that comes to mind in ignorance or mere caprice. As I've said elsewhere, the desire for a text unimpoverished by representation and its ideological taint has always constituted in the theater, as in literary theory today, what is perhaps the most powerful motive of both theater and thought, and I will be thinking about it again in these essays. I admire as much as anyone the proliferous exactitude of Barthes's readings, the almost dazzling performance of a kind of interpretation where he does pick up copiously if not corrosively the signal from Nietzsche, a reading which assumes that a text is "a network with a thousand entrances. . . ." It is the assumption we made in the theater process to which I've referred. Despite the indeterminacies, we always knew, like Barthes, that there is a vanishing point in such an enterprise. One wanted with a passion, nonetheless, to push that point ceaselessly back, as he says in *S/Z*, until it seemed "mysteriously opened: each (single) text [being] the very theory (and not the mere example) of this vanishing. . . ."[26]

Nonetheless, too, when the vanishing seems to run away with us almost before it begins, I am chastened by the remembrance of Winters's conviction that in "each (single) text" there is something *there*, or *not-there*, which he could define, and insisted on doing, although he might not think much of the substantiality of the absence, or the presence for that matter.

Now, I don't want to rehearse the arguments on either side of this issue, and I'm well aware of the world of difference on the side currently favored in theory. That will come up by indirections as we go along. The point which interests me here is this: what we take from a critic is not only espoused principle but what is made credible. And thus—while I am very much aware too of the multiple varieties of reader response and the subtle forgetfulness that, in making us read, endows the text with polysemous scope—what I see in Barthes I also saw, for all the galactic difference, in Winters, and that is the close movement of thought in language, the naming and renaming, "a tireless approximation, a metonymic labor. . . ."[27] Within this labor, the critical difference is that Barthes was infatuated—until the death of his mother narrowed all desire to the *specificity* of grief for a lost presence—with the metonymic *expanse* of the labor and the mind's buoyant dispersal in the approximation; whereas Winters, like the settlers in his poem on John Sutter, sifted the names to assume *one*.

It was an assumption he'd never quite admit, this identification with the settlers. But if I may read the poem as he would not want me to, there is a splitting off from Sutter—the earth grown "dense with grain" at his desire—to the something ominous gathering in his dreams. What Sutter desired from the earth, Winters wanted from language, whose "clear rivers" were despoiled, however, by what they revealed: first the motive, and then the ruinous looting "from the heart of Time." For what had also grown dense—grained with alchemic change—was "Metal, intrinsic value, deep and dense," gold, which "Dispersed the mind to concentrate the will." As moral perception thickens in the poem, there is an alchemical moment when the intrinsic value seems like Winters's poetry—that hard magnitude, in itself alloyed, the entire concentration of whose will was to understand the mind's dispersion. In any case, it was not, as Barthes had spoken of it in *The Pleasure of the Text*, an *extenuating* labor. Winters saw in the desire for unrefined metal—in those who "Drove knives to hearts, and faced the gold alone"—a parable of the fierce individuality of America's greed. As for his own desire, if it wasn't the evil of the metal he condemned, that thing almost prior to nature, "Preanimate, inimitable, still,"[28] it was the *dispersal*. So far as the mind followed nature in the warp of its desire, that was "the fallacy of imitative form," which in the unwavering doctrine of his theory of poetry was something like a cardinal sin.

He resisted it wherever and to whatever degree it occurred; and throughout his embattled career, if he drove knives to hearts, opposing the easy emotion of false technique, it was on behalf of a poetry deep and dense. It was also—and here he merges with Sutter—part of the lonely labor of trying to purge himself. Which is why when he made his own choice for the early edition of his *Collected Poems* he excluded much of what he had written, especially the extraordinary free verse he had done when he was young. So it wasn't an attenuating labor either. Nor like Donne's image of gold to airy thinness beat, where thought failing into desire takes refuge in an elaborated conceit. He knew very well how the forms of the modern had grown accommodating to disjunctures of thought, but he had no desire to augment them. So far as he could help it, he would not let escaping consciousness take its course with the flux of time or, though he'd never use such an image, the deadbeat escapement of Pozzo's watch. As with Beckett, the lack seemed minor compared to the loss. He had no patience with romantic irony or absurdist evasion or, one of the more facile escapements of the postmodern, parody.

What he was engaged in was the almost killing pursuit of absolutes. He believed in their existence despite all the evidence of modernism against them, including the unilluded intensity of his own corrosion and distrust. In the succinct narrative of his poem "Sir Gawaine and the Green Knight," there is an immaculate sense of the thoughtless force which accrues in an encounter with the feminine—"shapes that I had never known"—whose nature remains unknown because, in order to preserve his own identity, Sir Gawaine rejects it. The poem itself might be rejected by readers looking for evidence of the phallocratic order as less an encounter with the female imaginary than a classical imagination of it by a man. But as I said, that was never imagined by Winters, who never claimed to know it and who, like his knight, left the wood with the considerable knowledge of *what he knew,* the terror and sublimity of an experience which might have "grafted laurel in [his] bone," but led instead to the choice of the poem's end: "I found a road that man had made/And rested on a drying hill."[29] It may be that the laurel was grafted anyhow, for the subsidence is only a respite from the lifelong task of achieving in language—the road that men have made—something graven in the gaze, and unretractable:

> The passion to condense from book to book
> Unbroken wisdom in a single look,
> Though we know well that when this fix the head,
> The mind's immortal, but the man is dead.[30]

Winters speaks of this passion—which moves indivisibly through his criticism and his poetry—as the scholar's heritage, a personal demand that would certainly be a nervous thought at the MLA. It is something quite distinct from what a new generation of scholars is now talking about as *desire,* forgetting in their love of polysemy not only the older excoriations of desire in our literary tradition but its "limited function" in the economy of human possibility, of which Lacan reminded his seminar. Rehearsing "[t]he subject of certainty," he spoke of the "strict relation: by which desire is sustained as such, crossing the threshold imposed by the pleasure principle," which is a principle of homeostasis.[31]

It was that strict relation which Winters labored to understand, the struggle with limits constituting the passion. And I would like to believe—whether it came from him or something in me that identified with him through all the resistances—that a kindred passion was moving through my work in the theater, which he resisted for precisely the reasons which attracted me. What always beguiled me there, as it enraged me, was the stricture of its evanescence, the maddening thing in the form, which I refer to again, as it relates to theory, in "Shadowing Representation." For the theater is a paradigm of escaping consciousness—absolutely subject to time which *is* its subject—out of which I wanted to make a work that would appear with certainty and just as certainly disappear in front of your eyes as if, even in its vanishing, it were intrinsic metal or maybe carved in stone, the impossibility of the thing being its motive. There is a similar impulse (or presumption) in some of these essays. That's especially so where I dwell on what

-prior to any ritual origin, if any—is the source of theater, its *incipience*, some generic irritability in the order of things which seeks its own end, the imperceptible and ineliminable motion that won't be fixed and accounts, against all will and desire, for that proto-universal of performance which I describe in the essay on universals as the amortization of play: the incremental payoff inseparable from its pleasure, the homeostatic movement of cost. The concluding essay remembers that cost again in thinking over the dubious politics in the discourse on representation, including the desire to do away with representation.

In the era of the writerly text, which accepts as a matter of course that you can't fix it or ascertain its origins, we have become accustomed to using the word *text* not only about the written page but other social practices and artifacts, as well as the inscriptions in the unconscious of the person standing before you, "the subject of the enunciation," who also has to be read. Things must not be taken, we're told by the new analysis, at the level at which the subject puts them. On the basis of my earliest reading of Winters, however, there was no question for me, regardless of the ethos of distrust and my affinity for evanescence, that something was decidedly *there,* indelible *in* the text, that no other reading would change. "The mind is formed. Dissuade it, he who can."[32] You knew it was not formed overnight. That was doubly so when he would read himself, which is essentially what he did in class with whole essays from *In Defense of Reason,* standing irrefutably *behind* them, if not as a transcendental signifier, as if what was there were a matter of life and death, as I still think it is.

If what I have learned, then, from countless rehearsals in the theater has been confirmed by the newer theory, that there is something seminal and productive in thought's dispersal of thought—what Winters would have dismissed as mere "associational method" or the wildest variety of "pseudo-reference" or a redundancy of theater: the imitative fallacy imitating itself—I learned from him what I don't often see in those who think they are practicing deconstruction with a sort of ideological purity when they fetishize the "free play of the signifiers" and talk about "closure" as if it were Original Sin. While the dispersal has become for them a kind of natural law, you rarely see it *in their writing,* no less their teaching or their lives, taking the risks of what they preach—and that can be confirmed in the quite conventional texts of almost any journal or meeting which concentrates now on one or another version of poststructuralist thought. What is mostly absent in those "texts" is the struggle of dispersal to achieve—even as it resists—another kind of coherence, nor is there anything like the *tension* of the older criticism, before it became a standard practice, without the saving grace of a "sensuous apprehension of thought."

When the newer writing, however, means what it says, putting aside the semiotic exercises and easier demystifications, it is quite another matter. And it is precisely that matter which led me to what is likely to be the most controversial essay here, as it has already been elsewhere, "Disseminating Sodom." What some have felt as the risibility of its critique of homosexual discourse and style, and its radical feminist cognates, is due perhaps to the risk-taking I have admired, however disturbing, in some of it. If the essay seems in any way hostile, that was unintentional. I have not tried to alter unconscious intention here by mitigating the impression. Nor have I revised away the plain statement of a final aversion which I've been told should have been eliminated if I'm really sympathetic because, whether true or not, such things shouldn't be said on political grounds. This reasoning seemed like another extension—in a far more sophisticated context—of certain affiliated pieties in the correct politics of the sixties, which insisted upon the truth and nothing but the truth, particularly the truth of subjective feeling, except where it was a negative feeling about some excess or other of a group newly privileged by its claim to radical otherness. From Herbert Marcuse's successive prefaces to *Eros and Civilization* through the serial politics of *Tel Quel* to the belated infusion of Marxism in American deconstruction to the latest manifesto on polysexuality, this tendency continues. Yet I am more than sympathetic to the discourse of otherness, and I have felt seriously challenged by its implications, as well as by the lives that are being lived out of what elsewhere seems to be—as Marx had to say of the young Hegelians—just theory.

What I've come to feel in Marx I never felt even remotely before I studied with Winters and rarely since in any teacher (perhaps only in Paul de Man, whom I knew only briefly, and not as a teacher). Winters never read Marx so far as I know, but his ideas similarly drove you back upon your own, if you cared about your own—I was just learning to care—and if you didn't care, he suspected as much. What disturbed him almost more was indifference faking it or free-floating attitudes that substituted for ideas or half-formed ideas unpursued, as if like Gogo's they had no history. For the history of his own ideas, pursued as they were, he paid a price considerably more than the ordinary movements of cost. Men always, he observes in his poem on Socrates, "judge definition the most fierce of crimes,"[33] and I can hear him saying about most of thought's dissemination in the female imaginary, and women too. I happen to be responsive, as indicated, to the discourse of radical feminism as Winters could never have been, but I do take issue with it here. When I have tried in the theater to achieve something like the definition I learned to respect in Winters, I have known—as some readers may be aware—the transposed ferocity of my crimes. I have also come to expect no more leniency from a growing commissariat of theory which allows, through all the free play of the signifiers, only certain definitions.

All I can say of both the definitions and the dispersions of these essays is that I have tried to make the indeterminacies precise and to keep the biases as open and undisguised as my failings allow. As for the use of certain personal material here, my mother, my daughter, I have tried to do that in the manner approved of by the aging New Criticism, without being sentimental about it, and by making them as I've tried to do with Winters, subjects of thought. We are reminded, however, by the poignant last work of Roland Barthes that history *is* hysterical, and that we're not exempt from certain of its sentiments unless excluded by an enforced distance which also has its problems. Which is why we're now confronting, in theory, what Barthes did in his grief or what I did in my aversion or what Beckett's Winnie, up to her "diddies" in the muck of history, called "the old style," those emotions we just want to feel or can't avoid feeling—about which, if we think at all, we inevitably have our doubts.

NOTES

1. Roland Barthes, *The Pleasure of the Text,* trans. Richard Miller (New York: Hill and Wang, 1975), p. 29.

2. Jacques Lacan, *The Four Fundamental Concepts of Psychoanalysis,* trans. Alan Sheridan (New York: Norton, 1978), p. 26.

3. Barthes, p. 30.

4. Ibid., p. 31.

5. Michel Foucault, *Language, Counter-Memory, Practice,* ed. Donald F. Bouchard, trans. Donald F. Bouchard and Sherry Simon (Ithaca, New York: Cornell University Press, 1977), pp. 165–96.

6. Ibid., p. 171.

7. Ibid.

8. Lacan, p. 70.

9. *Waiting for Godot* (New York: Grove, 1954), p. 26.

10. *Godot,* p. 42.

11. René Girard, "Generative Violence and the Extinction of the Social Order," *Salamagundi,* no. 63/64 (1984), p. 224.

12. *Godot,* pp. 30, 27.

13. Barthes, p. 67.

14. See Jonathan Goldberg, *James I and the Politics of Literature: Jonson, Shakespeare, Donne, and Their Contemporaries* (Baltimore: Johns Hopkins University Press, 1983), p. 107.

15. Lacan, pp. 83–84.

16. *Proust* (New York: Grove, n.d.), p. 22.

17. Ibid., p. 43.

18. Jacques Derrida, *Writing and Difference,* trans. Alan Bass (Chicago: University of Chicago Press, 1978), p. 292.

19. Ibid.

20. William Carlos Williams, *Paterson* (New York: New Directions, 1963), bk. 3, p. 133.

21. "A Song in Passing," in *The Collected Poems of Yvor Winters,* intro. Donald Davie (Chicago: Swallow, 1978), p. 185. Hereafter cited as *CP.*

22. "A Testament," in *CP,* p. 177.

23. "To the Holy Spirit," in *CP,* pp. 183–84.

24. "On Teaching the Young," in *CP,* p. 146.

25. "An Ode on the Despoilers of Learning in an American University: 1947," in *CP,* p. 182.

26. Roland Barthes, *S/Z,* trans. Richard Miller (New York: Hill and Wang, 1974), p. 12.

27. Ibid., p. 11.

28. "John Sutter," in *CP,* pp. 159–60.

29. "Sir Gawaine and the Green Knight," in *CP,* p. 163.

30. "Time and the Garden," in *CP,* p. 169.

31. Lacan, p. 31.

32. "Socrates," in *CP,* p. 154.

33. Ibid.

The
Eye of Prey

O N E

(RE)SUBLIMATING THE SIXTIES

With an imperiousness worthy of Norman Mailer and an apocalyptic sealing of the envelope, I had just written President Johnson a letter advising him not to do so, when it was announced that the United States was mining the rivers of North Vietnam. The President admitted the possibility of error—the land might be flooded and people starved—but he stressed (publicly, not to me) the terrible loneliness of decision making and the earnest consciousness behind it. He quoted Truman: "The buck stops here." He quoted Lincoln: "A band of eagles swearing" wouldn't prove him right if he was wrong. He was acting out of a combination, in a single figure, of modernism and populism: an inviolate self, autonomous in its ambiguities and paradoxes, yet guided by consensus and analysis.

Could we complain? In the sixties, a band of eagles swearing thought we must. Did we have grounds for asking any political system that it act with charity and simple humanity, unilaterally, for the sake of charity and simple humanity, especially if those qualities don't exist very widely in individuals? The sixties (despite the participatory pluralism and the overflow into the seventies, one is tempted to use the singular) were not interested in the "moral realism" which was the critical underpinning of a technocracy whose "liberal imagination" (Trilling) was soon to develop "smart bombs" for discreet killing (the rhyme is unintentional) and eventually to develop neutron bombs for discreeter killing, disposing of people so that the artifacts of a dubious culture might be preserved. If we learned to think the unthinkable in the fifties, it was the sixties that made it seem unimaginable to kill wantonly even if the aim is not wanton.

Every such act seemed to narrow the chance of exemption from the horrors we were, in the ecology of slaughter, storing up for ourselves and which—like grain in the other silos, filled to overflowing—are still pending. The president was convinced he was teaching aggression a lesson. The aggression of the sixties was to teach the president a lesson. But does aggression ever learn? On either side of such instruction? The seeds of confusion scatter the dead, and the living seem to grow more lethal or more paralyzed, more exacerbated and more powerless every day—and that continues, the only supply-side theory that really works, depending as it does on chance. The rest is outrage. It is the outrage which gets our attention in literature, as it was the outrage which got our attention in the sixties. The outrage is unappeased but, without recourse in the social structure, it now seems to be sinking, where it's not merely hopeless or amnesic, into a no-man's-land of the anti-oedipal, somewhere between radical feminist theory and a sort of ontological anarchy in the politics of deconstruction.

If it's not exactly the end of man, it seems like the end of modernism. Or maybe we should say its inevitable permutation. "By a much longer and much more unexpected path," wrote Foucault in the last equivocal chapter of *The Order of Things,* "we are led back to the place that Nietzsche and Mallarmé signposted when they first asked: Who speaks?, and the second saw his glittering answer"—as all the saints of modernism did, whether through madness, madeleines, or epiphanies—"in the Word itself. The question as to what language is in its being is once more of the greatest urgency."[1] The seeming anarchy in the urgency is a legacy of the modern and the advent of a history which, in the movement of its signs—whether taken for signs or wonders—can't escape itself. That's why literature's obsession with the thought and experience of language traversed *as* language, *its* ontology and shadow play, "is neither the sign of an imminent end nor proof of a radicalization. . . ."[2] It may be, rather, through the metonymic apparency of man's dispersion, more like the Return of the Same. There was, after all, in the most reactionary manifestations of tradition and its individual talent, an affinity with the anarchic, and even the nihilistic, as we may see in the Sweeney-side of Eliot before history's cunning corridors led to his conversion, or in the villanelles of the Villonesque Pound, before some brainwarp in the corridors led to his fascism. Anarchy was the life force, too, in those antecedents of the postmodern returning like the Same from the classical avant-garde, the Futurism of Marinetti or Mayakovsky and, if not in the piety behind the performances of Hugo Ball, the Dada of Tristan Tzara. Futurism and Dada had, like Pound, political agendas as well—however messianic, demented, or befuddled—in which the formerly passive agent of history, the elitist poet or the proletariat, would no longer be mere spectator at the event but, as they came to say in the sixties, *where the action is*, whether in the cataclysm of paint ungrounding the canvas, the mixing up of the media in the confusion of genres, or the cracked absolutes of the bloody stage of history, with its unabsolving signifiers into which the action disappeared.

The end of the sixties focused these issues which had exploded into the sixties with the eloquence of the body to defray the body counts. There was also the rhetoric of a regressive idealism which, from the Free Speech Movement to the linguistic processes of Conceptual Art, seemed to overleap the margins of all speech, seizing upon, teasing, or abrogating the codes. It wasn't long before the essentially antiverbal energy of all this receded into the logorrhea of body language, fractured and dismembered words, and an eventual recognition of the limiting babel of speech where thought is dispersed, attenuated, extinguished, and the promise of an origin in the idealism begins to recede. What seemed to be left in the recession, along with the new conservatism, was the dispossessed *subject* of the postmodern, reviewing the disenchantments, as if through the solipsistic orifice of a needle's eye. This subversion of the relocated spectator, with a newly acquired awareness of the scopic drive (in the absence of action, the stress on *perception*, but perceiving *what?* the absence itself? or its prohibition? what was forbidden in the beginning: the seeing of the primal scene?) had become the subject of history (which either has no beginning or is always beginning again). It is a subject spurred on, despite its resistance to the corrosive workings of our metaphysical tradition, by what Paul Ricoeur has called the "ethos of suspicion" which is—from Nietzsche and Marx through Kafka and Freud—the most powerful heritage of modernism.

If the connection between politics and ontology still seems vague, we are still very good indeed at diagnosing, with awakened scopophilia, the concealed and exposed horrors of our collective lives. It is one of the means, ironically, of psychically perpetuating them as if, like Raskolnikov with his murder that he wouldn't have appropriated, they sustain our mental energy in a kind of delirium and constitute an identity which is otherwise exhausted by the tautological play of the signifiers against the turning screw of suspicion. With all the ubiquity of play in the ethos of celebration, it was conspiracy theory which dominated perception in the sixties, for good reason or wrong, almost more on the Left than the Right. We were prepared to believe anything, particularly the worst, which confirmed itself sufficiently in a paranoid president in this period of *paranoia*. It was paranoia that seemed to be, as in *The Crying of Lot 49*, the psychological condition of the human condition and by a kind of homeopathic magic endemic to the time, a therapeutic cure as well. For there is a determinism in perception, a seeing which (psychically) kills and which, having drawn blood in exposure, always demands more. (That's the curse of the scopic drive in which, as Kafka knew, the *look* becomes by slow accretions something more than surveillance or distributive justice, a kind of bloodlust of the Law.). Having discovered, for instance, the rationalizing instincts of aggression, we almost take pride in its manifestations. The tradition extends from Dostoyevsky on Raskolnikov to Mailer on the White Negro and later Jack Abbott and Gary Gilmore.

The sixties gave us in America a literature that tried in exhaustion or ebullience or gratuitous play—in writers from Kesey and Vonnegut to Coover and Barth (Beckett's play was a model but never quite gratuitous)—to pull away from the unregenerate demonic of the doubly crippled oedipal tradition. Some never really believed it could be done, though they were not untouched by the dissidence and desire: Robert Lowell, for one, whose personal demons confirmed the "mortmain" of history, its dead hand, even as he brought a lumbering grace to the scene in which they were going to levitate the Pentagon; or John Hawkes, who forced the brutality into the psychopathology of every glamorizing dreamscape of his baroque and decentering prose. What beasts, we say, ethologically, and then—enforcing that aboriginal nature—what *holy* beasts, like the phallocratic thug in *The Lime Twig* who tends a war-wrecked Shadow like an angel of mercy and slits elegantly an innocent wrist.

That's why it seemed a kind of poetic justice, if not a belated coda to the sixties, that the members of the Weather Underground accused of the Brink's robbery and murder were tried in Rockland County, epicenter of Ginsberg's *Howl*, which proclaimed as an ecstatic preface to the period that "the soul is innocent and immortal [and] should never die ungodly in an armed madhouse. . . ."[3] When *Howl* was confiscated in San Francisco, in the late fifties, I testified as an "expert witness" at its trial. As usual, when the charge of obscenity is made, the defense was not exactly literary quality but "redeeming social value," hardly exact either, but asked by the lawyers to locate the poem in the history of modern literature, I tried to redeem it thus in an accompanying affidavit: I spoke of the "furious negation" of its hysterical cadence as part of a "literature of disorder, psychosis, and fear and trembling," perhaps the most honored tradition of the modern, "a sustained elegy to the loss of power in a time of power" which made an affirmation of its perversions "out of motives so intensely serious that the placidly conformist mind cannot even feel them," no less question "the legitimacy of the intent, or its right to an open hearing. . . ."

The hearing, we know, has been so open since then that even the placidly conformist mind has experimented with some of the perversions, the legitimacy of which needs no justification in certain advanced stages of post-Sartrean thought. There are those who have outlived the piety which Sartre found attractive in the demonism of Saint Genet. And they couldn't care less for redeeming social value because of an irredeemable aversion to the power which certifies it. Genet seemed born into the necessity of somehow confessing his perversions and making of them a chalice, requiring guilt along with the piety in order to canonize it. There is little or no place for guilt, however, in the spreading dominion of the anti-oedipal. As for Ginsberg, he was a nice Jewish boy who had to make his way through Columbia and Lionel Trilling to the Beats and William Blake. And even so, for all the rage of *Howl* and the revolutionary charisma, Ginsberg was still of a generation which thought it could conduct negotiations—whatever the unnegotiable demands—with the representatives of power, as a raising of consciousness. At the time of *Howl* he was not yet a guru, that came with the sixties. But if he wasn't a holy prophet he was surely a moralist and never—when the protests escalated and others were out for burning—incendiary. Now rabbinical at Naropa playing mantras on the harmonium, he was courageous and exemplary as a pacifying figure. Other immortals of the period were not so innocent. And some of them like the rest of us are relieved—through an occasional twinge of longing for the power and the glory and the LOVE that pitched its mansion in the place of excrement, trashing—that the Days of Rage are over.

As we go on living, however, in the armed madhouse, which extends its dominion by "staying the course," it's hard not to think of the sixties without being tempted to misrepresent it—that singular period of communal desire—by overstressing its spectacular excesses along with the unnegotiable demands. There were obvious examples, from the earliest sitdowns on, of quiet valor and waiting dissent—the energizing passivity of which, the negative capability, was anticipated by *Waiting for Godot,* by no design whatever, but still, the most important *political* drama of the fifties. But so far as literature is concerned—which doesn't necessarily seek its models in forbearance, unless it is extremist too—it is the *theatricalizing consciousness* of the sixties which has kept it memorably before us and, whatever it does or doesn't do for politics, provides the ongoing momentum for the literature of the postmodern. As for what became *canonical* in the sixties—with its desire for an uninterrupted present wanting the future in the instant—it was not so much in literature as in *performance,* or literature *imitating* performance, which has the virtue of a repetitiveness which rehearses itself away: the canon to end all canons. If carried theoretically far enough, that includes the canonical weapons of a devious and invisible power—which was maybe the reason the Pentagon *couldn't* be levitated. For it is not by any means a "dense pack" which can be thwarted in Congress but, to use a favorite word of deconstructionist theory, an *occultation* of power, which can't quite be located.

The repetitiveness which disappears into rehearsal has become the model for the cyclical behavior of postmodern forms. The doxology of the recursive without closure is not meant, however—as in the older drama or psychoanalysis or the "retrospective hypothesis" which Beckett saw in Proust—to bring repetition into *remembrance.* It is, looked at askance, essentially the doctrine of the sixties that when a work enters the canon it is already reflecting a lost cause. "No more masterpieces!" said Artaud, one of the tutelary spirits of an unteachable time, who was nevertheless studied not only by Grotowski and Peter Brook but by Derrida and Roland Barthes. Derrida wrote two essays on Artaud during the sixties, when Artaud brought to the theater—what he'd brought vainly in the past—that "integrity of flesh" which sought the "unpolluted body" in "a body without a work" which is the excrement of a mind which imposes *separation* and is always already defiled.[4]

To the extent that the canonical cause is alive—and in literary studies it is—it makes life miserable for the established text, as if it were in an intensive care unit (we call it a department) taking its last breaths in a life-support system which is in jeopardy itself, as it certainly is. In new literary history as in experimental theater, the text—like history itself when it isn't simply ignored or epistemically rehearsed—is subject to repeal, contempt, revision, deconstruction. Or, in the valorized act of interpretation (using the rhetoric which puts the curious off, as it also arouses the hostility of invincible ignorance), the polysemous distribution in a galaxy of signifiers through a field of infinite play. It is a hermeneutic circle from which we haven't broken yet.

There was, as we remember, a liberating energy in the libidinal thinking body which—seeking a "body without organs" or instituted power—subverted the repressive text and disrupted, along with the universities, the institutions of literature and theater, which were exposed in their collusion with other instruments and agencies of power. What I am suggesting, too, is that when the radical activism of the sixties abated or went underground it surfaced again in *theory* as a new erotics of discourse. The lifestyle desires and polymorphous perversity which were celebrated at Woodstock and seemed to be savaged at Altamont also went under, retreating across the Atlantic, and entered the high intellectual traditions of continental thought, given the *ideology* they were charged with *not* having in the sixties, and are being recycled, biodegradably, as an assault on the phallogocentric structure of bourgeois power, with its invisible ideology.

The "desublimated sexuality" described by Marcuse in *Eros and Civilization* has been (re)sublimated, then, in both senses of the word, moving from lifestyle into thought, reified in repression. (There is even anticipation, despite the earlier refusal of a transcendental signifier, of the new emergence of a materialist Sublime.) What we see, too, in poststructuralism and the schizoanalytical aftermath of Lacanian feminist and homosexual thought is a further reification of performance in the quest of *jouissance*. The model here is not Goffman's presentation of the self in everyday life—since the self is a delusion of bad acting theory—but Artaud's truer theater, the naked sonorous streaming realization he believed Plato had perceived in the Orphic Mysteries.[5]

If you ask, then, of literary theory what Stanislavski asked of actors who were building a character or Freud asked of women who were eluding ego psychology: *What does theory want?*—it wants, at the simple level of living (the nuclear fission or dissemination of the oedipal momentarily aside) what the students used to want, or thought they wanted, as they turned our politics into theater which has, through the conservative backlash, kept the performance going in theory. Unfortunately, living is not simple, nor theater, not to mention the theory. There is something in the theater itself which recoils from its own image as appropriating the world and insists, at the uttermost extremity of performance, when it seems to be overtaking or overtaken by life, upon remaining the illusion which it *is*, *as theater*, which is only inseparable from theory (they share a lexical root) when it sustains its critical and alienating (originary) distance from life. For all his desire to abolish the theater as we know it, Artaud knew the imposing and unnegotiable limit which Derrida was constrained to concede at the end of his essay on the Theater of Cruelty, the "gratuitous and baseless necessity of representation" and "why it is *fatal* that, in its closure, representation continues,"[6] and with it the insidious theater that separation imposed.

The theatricalization of the sixties—from the Love-Ins and Be-Ins and dramatic confrontations to confessional poetry and imaged politics—was self-revealing, self-confirming, presumably dialogical and participatory, but eventually exclusionary, self-negating or—at the margin of survival, as with current solo performances or Performance Art, inevitably and in a Pop/parodistic/post-Conceptual way—*solipsistic,* as I've already suggested. It was also at certain crucial moments in the Movement, in the desire, say, for *Paradise Now,* as with the Living Theater at the living end of its communitarian idealism, which refused an aesthetic in favor of a politics, *politically* inept, but whether in any way avoidable no one really knows. That paradise is over for now could be woefully seen in the pathos of the Living's recent performances in New York, an enfeebled return of the Same after years of exile abroad.

Yet, all honor to the Living! Nobody was adequate to the sixties which, for any thinking person, was a period of noble aspiration and apocalyptic dimensions built into a double bind. It is that double bind, with its universal paranoia and ethos of performance, which is reflected in certain talismanic works of the period from the anonymous legions of the Trystero to the clamorous Armies of the Night. If one is moved by the ardor of the period and caught up in the memory of its radical objectives, there was the reverse Catch-22 in the derision of Law and Order which insisted upon due process, in the disruption of the very courtroom, to keep the revolutionary spirit alive.

I suppose the real *scandal* of the sixties—to use one of the melodramatic buzzwords of new critical thought—was not so much Watergate, which got rid of the paranoia of Nixon, but the demagoguery which derogated the normal and brought us Reagan. Now what we have instead of paranoia is imperturbable self-satisfaction. The liability of democracy—at best a disappointing system of governance—is that it invariably confronts you, as socialists in this country have always been confronted, with the desires and predilections of the political *Other,* those who, through the upped ante of the scopic drive, don't see it and don't *want* it the way you do, and who choose to register *that* dissent with all its undeniable mental hangups as a majority, whether or not moral, at the polls. As for the cleansing terror of reflexive rage—what can one say?—only those inside the terror can speak for the terror, and the justice of its cause. The rest of us have no alternative, given what we've learned in the twentieth century, from life, from literature, of the ordinance of terror, except to oppose it with the most resolute memory of every dis-membered limb.

It was not the aesthetic minimalism but the political reductivism of the sixties that one regrets, although I suppose each was in fear of the other, the falsifying afflatus of a mind-blowing consciousness. It's one thing to say it's possible, as Robert Frost once did, to wish a reality into being, and quite another for those who've not experienced much reality to do the wishing (and Frost's luck ran out of gas with the New Frontier). For all the admirable idealism of the period—I wince at the phrase, not wanting to sound like those who always wanted it to fail—there was a radical fault on the radical Left. Not everybody shared it, obviously, but there was the mean-spirited binary thinking that made it tortuous to endorse the politics, as one had to in all conscience. You did it knowing it was a self-canceling politics, unstable and with little endurance, and with an inability to sort out—as nostalgic academics still can't—the undeniable instances of oppression from the stereotyping of authority, the abuses and bluster of bureaucracy from a callow distaste for useful hierarchy. It's not only aging liberals suffering from existential bad faith who came to this impasse. We see it in Roland Barthes on the verge of poststructuralism in his remarkable testament to the discomfited end of the sixties, "Writers, Intellectuals, Teachers," published in 1971.

"Yet is it not the case," he says, plaintively, after acknowledging the necessity of "the giddying whirl of speech" in the voice-over vertigo of the teaching space, "that the teacher has a fixed place, that of his *remuneration,* the place he occupies in the economy, in production?"[7] After providing, as others of us did more or less, the theoretical grounds for the unseating of authority, he can only suggest with a certain neo-Marxist delicacy that he is paid to represent it. Barthes reminds his students that in "a society locked in the war of meanings"—which has led us to think more arduously about control not of the means of production but of the signifying systems—"the liquidation of the old criticism can only be carried forward *in* meaning (in the volume of meanings) and not outside it" (p. 208).

Baudrillard has since scoffed at that in his Borgesian allegory of simulation which replicates a discourse of the unconscious which can never be retrieved or unmasked because there is nothing behind it, nothing true or false, nothing in the precession of simulacra, the poly-saturated miasma of images—which bears any relation to any reality whatever, nothing but a mirror of assimilated madness, hyperreal, with "dead and circular replies to a dead and circular interrogation."[8] For Barthes, the interrogation of criticism is meant to bring things into crisis but—despite Marx's call for a critical ruthlessness about everything existing—nothing so bleak and devastating as all that. When Barthes wrote his essay, the urgency of ideological criticism was such that it seemed to require "a certain semantic enterism." If the "exemption" of the signified was the foremost materialist task, the intellectual might have to accept, precisely, condemnation to various "operations of theft," depending on the pickers and stealers of thought (with Artaud and Genet as exemplars, but . . .) which recognize that the signified may be "more easily 'lifted' in the *illusion* of meaning than in its destruction" (p. 208).

In all this sleight of hand/mind and ideology, one may see a pivotal shift in Barthes away from the more politicized pleasure of his earlier Brechtian text to the lubricious forgetfulness of *jouissance* and the later vestiges of a disgraced humanism in the raptures of the *punctum* (which I explore, along with *A Lover's Discourse,* in the essay on Barthes and Beckett, whose humanism seems incurable while he dreams of the end of Man). Assessing Brecht's assurance of an "axiomatic field" where interpretation of the facts will move the proletariat into action, Barthes observes "that a certain number of objects do not directly concern the proletariat (they find no interpretation within it). . . ." Since the class situation of the proletariat is quite obviously not that of the intellectual, it is "a real headache of a problem" for the intellectuals to establish them-selves as "*representatives*" or "*oblates* who devote themselves to the pro-letarian interpretation of cultural facts." The cultural fact is, besides, that what speaks in the proletarian discourse is "still bourgeois language, in its degraded petit-bourgeois form. . . ." The solace of the intellectual may be, in view of this, that while the proletariat is silenced in that language, it may still speak in "the discourse of the intellectual, not as canonical founding voice," however, "but as unconscious" (p. 210). In the section on "*Writing as Value,*" where he remarks that there is no critical putting into crisis without *evaluation,* Barthes is moving toward a

notion of "peaceable speech" which mediates with an impacted eloquence, his virtuosity on the edge of sophistry, a distaste for the excesses
of academic insurrection (p. 213). But if he acknowledges the repressive
discourse of liberal conscience, he sees an escalation of that conscience,
similarly bourgeois, in the "terrorist discourse" of his students, whom he
wants to defend as having at their disposal no other access to justice than
the free force of the word, or as he puts it in semiotic phrasing which
seems comic in a high-voltage political context, "the lucid adequation of
the enunciation with the true violence of language . . ." (p. 208).

Comic or not, we are still quite familiar, in the sublimations of the
sixties, with "certain small-scale terrorisms" of the larger discourse
which, wanting to destroy stereotypes, function "above all by stereotypes
themselves," as anyone knows who has followed the infighting of film
theory, certain feminisms, and the liaison of Marxism and deconstruction in undoing the colonization of the psyche where the stereotypes are
oppressively spawned. In the more polysemous discourse of recent
theory, there is the insistence on the absence of closure which, as Barthes
remarks of any discourse of good conscience, forecloses "the other
scene" and refuses *writing,* giving off the odor of seriousness which arises
from the commonplace itself (p. 209).

The irony is that this does not necessarily arise from commonplace
minds, which would be hard pressed to enter the discourse. If one is
critical of the discourse, as Barthes is (as I am), one assumes the good
conscience, as well as the likelihood that it is not a matter of going after
paper tigers. There are some very good minds in a warp or lapse of
perception who enunciate a politics in theory that they cannot possibly
live with in reality, there being no lucid adequation between them.
Barthes was addressing the escalated violence at the end of the sixties
when, despite the high IQs among the dissidents and what I have just
said of the best and brightest, there were also a lot of dopes. There has
been much said of the obliviousness to history in the exciting improvisation of praxis which amounted to a wanton disrespect for the rigors of
ideological analysis and the concrete work needed to understand the
Power Structure, no less to achieve its dismantling, as the escalated
discourse is still talking about it today. Whatever that structure is, it is not
a slogan. And it was never seriously threatened by the Movement, as it is
not now by the politics of deconstruction with its sometimes facile in-
vocations of history as a sort of accrediting agency in the discourse, lest
politics be the slogan. (One version of history, which keeps slipping in

the polyvalencies of the discourse, is the narrative of the annunciation of the long pregnancy of truth, in the spirit of *différance* a pregnancy without birth, which I will come to later in Beckett and Derrida.) Long before literature caught up with the dispersion of its authorizing text, the exchange mechanisms of bourgeois capitalism had grown immensely diversified and multinational, so that the invisible network of power which Genet had dramatized in the panopticon of *The Balcony* and which Foucault theorized in his studies of surveillance may be apprehended but not contained.

Meanwhile, if power corrupts, so does naiveté about power, so far as it is encoded in language. That was the major lesson, I think, of the manic aggressiveness of the sixties, which is now in danger of encoding itself in the labile and alluring discourse of the subject of desire. Bespeaking this danger is, I should add, no warrant for those knowing nothing of the discourse—the most engaging if labyrinthine we have around—to continue with what was business as usual even before the sixties began.

With its attempted subversions of power by parody and its millenarian investments in the Absurd, the sixties led through the licensing of Love's Body to the apotheosis in theory of the inflated currency of play which, like the aging subject of comedy, is always devalued by time. I will come back to this subject in the next essay, the reifications of play in what is now the hybrid genre of comedy. From the *Short Organum* of Brecht to the style of schizoanalysis—what Foucault describes as the surge of libido in its antirepressive politics—comedy has become the only tenable and (ideologically) allowable genre in a postindustrial world where the mystifying inevitabilities of the older tragic form are mere vitiating *appearance,* a logocentric vestige which, when not turning the screw of suspicion, is putting the screws to desire, and deterrent to social change.

NOTES

1. Michel Foucault, *The Order of Things: An Archeology of the Human Sciences* (New York: Vintage, 1973), p. 382.
   2. Ibid., p. 383.

3. Allen Ginsberg, *Howl and Other Poems*, intro. William Carlos Williams (San Francisco: City Lights, n.d.), p. 19.

4. "The Theater of Cruelty and the Closure of Representation" and "*La parole soufflée*," in *Writing and Difference*, trans. Alan Bass (Chicago: University of Chicago Press, 1978).

5. Antonin Artaud, *The Theater and Its Double*, trans. Mary Caroline Richards (New York: Grove, 1958), p. 52.

6. Derrida, *Writing and Difference*, p. 250.

7. Roland Barthes, *Image-Music-Text*, trans. Stephen Heath (New York: Hill and Wang), p. 206. Further references to the essay "Writers, Intellectuals, Teachers" will be in the text.

8. Jean Baudrillard, *Simulations*, trans. Paul Foss, Paul Patton, and Philip Beitchman (New York: Semiotext[e], 1983), p. 17.

T W O

COMEDY SINCE THE ABSURD

We need to start, in approaching the subject of comedy today, by parsing out the comedy from the laughter. We can hardly think of comedy without laughter, but we have learned to think of laughter without comedy. There is also the problem of identifying the subject of comedy which, while it may seem to bring them together like the dancer and the dance, separates the laugher from the laugh. There is the subject you may remember and never can forget, the gravity of the laughing matter. Since the incursion of the Absurd upon a guilty and precarious stage, that subject has been looked upon as inseparable from the subject of language, which seems to have no gravity at all, essentially comic, words flying up, the body remaining below, growing more and more suspicious of the nature of language.

If man is the animal who laughs, it appears that he laughs through language which, according to recent theorists on the agencies and illusions of power, has been making him all the more laughable by making him more powerless as it deconstructs the idea of man. If we think of the deconstruction as subversive and not another agency of power, we arrive at that comic impasse of the postmodern which, replacing the art of the possible with the strategies of the polymorphous, the apotheosis of play, seems to be to play it for laughs: "Spit out yer teeth. Ear pulls. Nose pulls. Pull out a booger. Slow scratches from shoulder to belly. Hitch up yer shirt. Sex, man. Tighten yer ass. Tighten one cheek and loosen the other. Play off yer thighs to yer calves. Get it all talkin' a language."[1]

By itself, the passage is a decoy. I want to use it as a touchstone, ignoring where it came from, to which I'll return more or less theoretically, in somewhat comic fashion, roundabout. It might be, however, from a hip rendition of that skinnier Falstaff, Ruzzante returned from the wars, another braggart soldier showing off his prowess. Whoever he is, somebody else is being worked over. And he seems to be the conventional object of comedy, a person becoming a thing, the spitting image of everything anal, puppetlike, uptight, automatic, and genitally fixed which, in a quick release of contradictions, contradicted, produces a belly laugh from a double bind. The sequence contains glimpses, as if through the swinging door of the staccato words, of various things we tend to find comic in whatever period, from the animation of the words to slapstick to body humor to mixed signals to parody (say, Marlon Brando as Stanley Kowalski, scratching slowly from shoulder to belly) to the implication at the intimidated end of the laughing matter, of hyper-active self-abuse. Why we should be laughing at that we're still not entirely sure, but if we imagine the actor, bewildered, miming the imperatives of the words, we see an elemental figure in one of the oldest comic routines where—restating Beolco and Bergson through Deleuze and Guattari[2]—we find the desiring subject reduced to reflexive ma-chine.

There was lots of playing around with machines in the acting "games" of the sixties. It was usually for purposes of parody, and the comedy at La Mama or in the campiness of the Judson Church was rarely more than that. There were also the "psychophysical exercises" with their higher motives and carnal methods, of which the ass-to-mouth resuscita-tion also seems a parody, the desire for the full unimpeded body of play, libidinal play, its plenitude, "a flow-producing machine" or "signifier without chains," as they say in *Anti-Oedipus: Capitalism and Schizophrenia*.[3] With Artaud as exemplary figure, the schizziness is honorific, getting "it all talkin' a language," like the barnyard in the belly of the Mother in *The Screens*. While the Mother also seems to be playing games—with her trick valise and unbreakable legs, " . . . Whang! Zoom! Boom! . . . boom!"[4] imitating lightning on the king's highway, dancing with sweat rolling down from her cheeks to her tits from her tits to her belly—they are far less frivolous games, onomatopoeic but also self-punitive, the ideograph-ic documentation of something laughable because flow-producing and savagely repressed.

Let us look at that a little further, keeping the theoretical doxology of body-play in mind: the comedy in the mother's milk is swollen with contempt and laced with bile. Her antics on the royal road are not merely the "carnal stereophony," the language lined with flesh, of Ro-land Barthes's desire in *The Pleasure of the Text*.[5] If there's *jouissance* in the rolling sweat it's because she's dancing on the grave of a colonial order in which "Lunatics are allowed only words" (*Screens,* p. 120), which are also colonized. There is a kind of elephantiasis of dispossession in the con-

ception, an extravagant rite of passage, monstrously comic. She still has
the strength, she says—the "Most High Mother and not yet on the
retired list . . ." (p. 120)—she with her "wrestler's forearms, to cleave the
Red Sea and make a path for the Pharaoh . . ." (p. 113). At the paranoid
margins of the sleeping village in which she is a pariah, she presides with
a sort of gargantuan glee over the snoring prospect of a ferocious
brotherhood rising like laughter out of the earth. "While snoring away,
everyone prepares the nightmare into which he'll plunge on awakening"
(p. 114). The question is, who is being laughed at in these ludic magnitudes of laughter?

Despite the opinion of Beckett's Hamm, an expert in the matter, all
nightmares may not be alike. But it does seem as if the nightmare into
which we plunge on awakening is the historical nightmare from which
we are trying to awaken. And what Marx said of history in *The Eighteenth
Brumaire,* that it recurs as farce, does seem to be happening when the
popeyed Mother with her wrestler's forearms who was dancing on the
royal road comes barking back on stage. When she does, the two nightmares—one from history, one from the sleeping self—seem to meet in
some blinding instant of racing desire like a collision of Marx and Freud.
It's as if the primal action occurred not at the place where three roads
meet but as the highway crossed a heath where the outcast son disguised
as a madman in a play with a missing mother is putting all nightmares
behind him, only to see the bleeding eyeballs of his father advancing—
that wrecked instrument of the torture machine—and "The worst returns to laughter" (*Lear,* IV.i.6). At which point the Mother embraces
her lost son, the Bedlam, who was embracing the "unsubstantial air"
(IV.i.7), like the double illusion of theater which is the comic vision of
Genet.

The unsubstantial pageant fading, it could only leave comedy behind.
It's as if the writing on the screens were being done with Prospero's
broken wand, the bereft instrument of language which, buried by
Shakespeare, was, among Genet's many thieveries, stolen out of the
grave, like the words of the dead by the Mother through the "poor
unhappy Mouth" (*Screens,* p. 54). By the time the barking is heard, the
dead words of the colonizers are getting more "jittery," clearing out fast.
For the Mother seems to be calling up an invisible force also speeding
over the landscape, a "sprint setting in the shape of a rabbit, a flight in
the shape of a bat . . ." (p. 113), a spectral avatar of an absence like a
perpetual motion machine which empowers the revolution in its absence

by disappearing into desire. How comic can you get? The barnyard in the belly hasn't touched bottom yet. Speaking of capitalism and schizophrenia, the Mother wants it all, the *visibility* of laughter in her *own body*, the capitalization of Laughter, its surplus value.

It's a reflex of laughter going back to Jarry's *Merdre!* Planted "on two big feet in the dead of night deep in the countryside," she wants "to be seen more clearly!" So she draws a crescent moon in yellow chalk on a black screen and advances toward the audience, speaking to the paper moon: "Hello! I'm Laughter—not just any laughter, but the kind that appears when all goes wrong." Among the things that have gone wrong, however, is the disposition of laughter in the modern theater which, since Jarry, has confused its subject and object. If the Mother embodies Laughter, to whom does it appeal? or is she still the subject of laughter? "(*She looks at the audience.*) It's the night full of nettles." Are they perplexed by Laughter, or being laughed at? There is never a straight answer, or put-down, in Genet, who knows how *being looked at* can make you feel like shit and who, through the antipathies of regression, may be the stickier subject itself. "Nettles! (*Suddenly lyrical.*) Through the lords of old, go back to the Fairy, back to the Virgin, I, I've known since childhood that I belong—perhaps through the females, and Saïd [her son] through me—to the nettle family. Near ruins, tangled with shards, their bushes were my cruelty . . ." (p. 112). If we follow this lineage of Laughter—like dreams, pronominal, also tangled with shards—through those cruel bushes of the royal road (the term used, by the way, in Freud and Marx for their respective quests, or inquests), what is it that we find? Is it, *near ruins* (of the old phallic order), the mothering source of Comedy? the breaking of the incest taboo? which is to say, all boundaries, all barriers, between the laugher and the Laugh?

After such magnifications, let us go back to the comic reduction, and the worked-over figure of the reflexive machine, ear pulls, nose pulls, trying to talk a language while the teeth are spitting out. I was looking at it various ways before and I want to do a double take on it now through gesticulations of the Absurd as it went nonverbal.

One of the paradoxes of the theater of the Absurd—which was hyperconscious of the repressive, even brutalizing power of words—was that what left it speechless brought it alive. It also became, as a collection of bits, fragments, routines, *bricolage*, a virtual encyclopedia of the comic exercising the abused rites of incapacity in disjunct simulacra of remembered popular forms. These forms are aboriginal and contemporary, from the Atellan farces to the circus to vaudeville to burlesque to *Grand Guignol,* figures of Negative Capability, from two old farts rallying the birds to Emmett Kelly in a vast emptiness gathering up the light. Still, with all the hallowed trickery of the archaic forms, there is the corporeal hilarity of impotence and age and, as with the bloating of the Rhinoceros, the swollen humor of bureaucratic rage. Despite the Gray Panthers, the flesh remains weak and we continue to laugh at that. What the theater of the Absurd accomplished, however, was a cerebral juggling act in which, even more than in ancient comedy—where the incapacity seemed less (and more rewarded)—enervation was inexhaustible, as we see with the tramps in *Godot.* In the long entropic fallout from Pisthetairos and Euelpides to Didi and Gogo, the residues of Myth were, with every tatter in their mortal dress, quickened into mirth, or some demented facsimile, where something irrepressible and protoplasmic, some queer fibrillation of failing luck, excreting language, seemed to fall and rise as on a broken-down carousel of the Eternal Return.

It was both a phenomenological reduction and an archetypal lesson. The lesson was plaintive in Beckett, who has never believed he could be a teacher; and Ionesco, despite his denial of ideology, drove it pedagogically home. So did Brecht, no absurdist he, in *A Man's a Man* (written in the twenties, but part of the scene of the sixties), when Galy Gay, by increments of dehumanization, no longer turning the other cheek, becomes a Human Fighting Machine. But that's not exactly what's happening in the apparently comic figure who is tightening one cheek and loosening the other. In that context, where the body is being exhorted to talk a language, the reflexive machine is a desiring machine resisting the comic reduction, yet wanting something more recurrent and sustaining than a ("Sex, man") libidinal flow. "I got my patterns. Original. I'm my own man" (*Tooth,* p. 61). It's as if some instinct of tragedy is still trying. For the language of body language, in Sam Shepard's *The Tooth of Crime,* is part of a showdown of language in which style is the fatal weapon, but as the styles become the man the man feels like nothing but language and we feel the subject is lost: "Now I'm outa' control," says the rock superstar Hoss in his dread encounter with Crow. "I'm pulled and pushed around from one image to another. Nothin' takes a solid form. Nothin' sure and final." No personality no ego no boundaries no self, not even a ridiculous comic character (is all character comic?) in the old reliable sense. "Where do I stand! Where the fuck do I stand!" (p. 65).

It may be no comfort to Hoss, but there is the tradition of the comic hero with a thousand metamorphic faces for whom, as with the infinite play of difference in Derrida, the sense of incompletion is a ubiquity to be wished. In theory, increasingly behaving like theater, this kind of comedy is policy. In theater, which foreshadowed such theory, we see it as more than a masquerade of character in the dazzling proliferation of self-canceling images as absenting presences in *The Screens*, the principle of Indeterminacy as the figure of Revolution, even in the comedy on the other side of death, where the visibility desired by the Mother (theoretically) dis-appears. For the screens are the screens of language leaving images behind, those historical projections of language—class, race, family, gender, style—from which the image-system takes its power. What we are to imagine now, in a sphere (almost) beyond representation—where nothing takes solid form but the historyless echo of gratuitous play—is disembodying laughter, more or less imageless with more or less speech, since for the newly arrived in death, still stammering (a premonition of laughter), some "bits of time" are still flowing between the teeth (p. 144). The laughter is uproarious to the point of hiccups as identity slips away.

If we shift from *The Screens* to *The Balcony*, it appears to be the same: nothing but mirrors and images where less and less is mirrored back. Among the Allegorical Figures we hear the same protest that we hear from Hoss, but some of the "characters" are willing to go all the way, completely into fantasy, letting the Image take over, like the Chief of Police into the tomb. But he doesn't go without conditions. Aside from the "low mass" to be recited to his high glory, they must—if he is to repeat the whole comic cycle of Western culture—"Notify the kitchens!" to be sure there's "enough grub for two thousand years."[6] Even if it's only a radish, comic heroes never starve. They know they can't live wholly on images. It's the best of impossible worlds, a little spirituality, too, for the mass of laughing matter while it's waiting immortality out.

The metamorphic characters in Genet, saturated with history, seem to be lived untellable times over, born and born again, the natal pipes so clogged with the scum of history that the revolutionary must be a plumber to ratchet or snake them out. As the consummate fantasy in the Brothel, the political illusion has, in the infrastructure of illusion, about the same historical consequence as, say, the plumbers at Watergate in the Morality Play that followed: a Divine Comedy gone to seediness, with its cast of undercover agents, extortioners, hit men, Disney admen, liars, thieves, drunks, perjurers, Quakers in the Oval Office, the pieties and obscenities of paregoric power, even a god from the bureaucratic machine, a mystery figure with muffled throat and, as a sort of comic theophany, "at this point in time," bringing the sacred to the profane, the uproarious hiccup of history in the eighteen minutes of missing tape.

It is like the Queen's embroidery in the Funeral Studio in the cover-up by the Envoy, there and not-there, a "grave problem" (*The Balcony*, p. 69). As the vacancy keeps circling around its empty center, there is an ontological significance in the missing history. The sadomasochistic exercises of the age-old fantasies turn up the same Allegorical Figures, like the archetypal comic hero making the ancient rounds. We recognize the fantasies, old as they are, as forms of infantile regression. Obscene as they are, they are also exhilarating. But if there is something rejuvenating in the cycle, it is also arduous. Irma says of the illusions in her studios and the long-perfected self-exposing roles that they are the outcome of heroic labors. Heracles, we recall, was a comic figure. Comedy, says Northrop Frye, is played for the young men in the audience.[7] Perhaps so. "Young men must live" (*I Henry IV*, II.ii.95), but even Falstaff learns that if the readiness is all it comes with aging, *secondariness*, Part 2, "always already there," as Derrida keeps saying of the "originary trace" in the "phallogocentric" tradition which, along with the grub, the Chief of Police brings into the tomb.

The trouble with Hoss, and Shepard, is that as they grow older they are, unlike Falstaff, prematurely young. The problem for Hoss is that there is very little sense of history around him, things moving too fast, the "Root Force . . . slip-streamin' " his time (*Tooth*, p. 19), "no sense of tradition in the game" (p. 24), the code "going down the tubes" (p. 26) and the Gypsy Marker coming in the Killer Machine, a " '58 black Impala, fuel-injected, bored and stroked, full blown Vet underneath" (p. 31). The linguistic fuel is a synthetic of sci-fi high-tech low funk *Star Wars* gold records and the newest galactic bangs of rock. Actually, aside from all the jive and rhythm and blues, there is some theater tradition as well, though it's an absurdist tradition with a very short fuse.

We know that Shepard picked up his games from the exercises of the Open Theater, which gathered from Beckett that there might be some improvisational advantage in a lapse of memory which disperses *Action* (the title of a Shepard play) into undetermining activities or "tasks" which, inevitably, leave behavior at loose ends. When what you're doing isn't either necessary or probable, it is inevitably comic. But it may be superficial as well or simply, letting it happen, running out of steam. For instance, "A whore's not something you can improvise," says Warda in *The Screens* (p. 19), robes weighted with time, toenails whited an inch thick, the whole back of her mouth in ruins, as by the decay of language. There is in Warda's ex cathedra certainty, undermined by the breaking down of the colonial order, an entirely different image of performance, favored by Genet. Without the weight of that tradition, Shepard always had a lot of things going that he didn't know what to do with, imaginative as they were, once they were there. Eventually, sensing that, he backed away from the open-endedness into a partially borrowed narrative. He seems to have taken the buried child from either Albee or Pinter, along with what we used to call the "comedy of menace." But the menace that Hoss encountered in Crow, the Gypsy Marker in the language game, made, I think, for his most perilous and Genetic comedy, and the one most relevant to postmodern thought. The *"evil-looking black chair . . . like an Egyptian Pharaoh's throne . . ." (Tooth,* p. 3), around which the verbal duel takes place, might have been lifted from the property room at the Brothel. But the affinity with Genet is in Shepard's ear for the outcast, the styles of the subcultures, like punk, which seem to have been formed by Genet even if they never heard of him, though some inevitably had.[8] There is after all—in the little more than pun that makes it punk—a sort of trickle-down function of the Laffer Curve not only in the radicalism of Reaganomics but in the "libidinal economy"[9] too.

What we see in the theater of punk (and postpunk) is like a demonstration (or monstrosity) of recent theory, that the domain of ideology coincides with the domain of signs. As with Body Art—from the anthropometries of Yves Klein's International Blue to Chris Burden's crawling through broken glass—the theory is inscribed not only in the surrogate body of *writing* but, hair screaming purple, nose both pulled and impaled, in the emblooded personal image of the body politic itself. It is what we also saw in Genet, our role model of deviance. There is the self-inflicted elation of a flattening Refusal. The negativity is acidic, caricatured, the imprint of a hilarious exile chosen in the body which, short of an even greater violence, nobody can take away. If punk lacks, except for its merchandising, the dimensions of Genet, it resembles "Genet's gangster pin-ups, just the darker side of sets of regulations, just so much graffiti on a prison wall."[10] That prison wall is the solipsistic confinement of what Fredric Jameson, via Nietzsche, called the prison house of language;[11] or what, via Shepard, we may put through a comic reduction and also call the tooth of crime.

I have no intention of romanticizing punk as a self-confirming art—what Norman Mailer did with the graffiti on the New York subways—while forgetting to put what it defaces in the balance. But it is important to remember that punk, which escalated profanity and illiteracy to scabrous extremes, is also, like Genet, forcing us back to the semiotic, and the operational prostitution of signs in what we call culture, with the necessity of reading the clamorous handwriting on the obscene wall. The music of punk, like the antidrama of the Absurd, is an even more destructive assault on the last semblance of music, partially because so uninstructed. Its aim, according to Johnny Rotten, was not music but chaos. But there is a liturgy in any irreverence, and an irony at its expense, as Genet understood. For what we hear through the emblazoned and farting cacophony of an ideographic style—like the sonorous and ebullient burial of the Lieutenant in *The Screens*—is not so much the death of a social order, but through the fantasy of that death, the imbecilic persistence of the worded codes which are presumably going down the tubes.

As Wallace Stevens suggests in his stylish early poem *The Comedian as the Letter C*—a sort of elegant particle physics of the comic in language, not at all subculture or entirely for the young—there is no way to talk about comedy, *not any more*, without talking in circles, as I've already been doing here. For at the perceptual threshold of the comic, whatever the social codes, the comedy will always escape us, fail, run out, or transform, returning in another guise. For the sad truth is that there was always something wanting in comedy, if not luck a Lacanian *lack,* which we used to think of as tragic, the *fault* in the subject desiring (or the subject desiring the fault?), but in comedy *never enough,* so that it doesn't end like tragedy in an exhaustion of desire but merely keeps desiring until we have come to feel, in the rhythm of our dubious comedies where the comic doggedly returns, that it is not, as Bergson thought, rigidity, automatism, or an "anesthesia of the heart"[12] that keeps it returning, producing laughter from a machine, but the *élan vital* itself, though we're much less sure of the *élan.*

When I say, amidst these recessions of the comic, that there's no way to talk about comedy except as it escapes us, I am also suggesting that there's no longer any way to talk about the drama, or to write it, with any historical perspective that will keep the comedy out. The more rapid the shifts in perspective, the more swiftly the comedy comes in. Even in the seeming stillness of a center, like Hamm pushed back from the hollow in the wall, there's something dripping in the head. The leakage will be more or less mirthful or deflating or—in the splitting tributary of consciousness from Büchner to Brecht and Beckett or the fracturing of perspective from Pirandello to Genet—more or less grim. For the fact is that the comedy which is not merely the alibi of a passing order is an impertinence of mourning for the values originally mocked that maybe never were. If history consecrates the truth by eruptions of laughter, as it did with the sanctities of the old ritual theater, what could we conceivably expect from a camouflaged or vanishing truth? It was the impactedness of history, reading its own entrails, turning over the duplicities of historical fact, which has spread the infection of the comic idea. The tooth of crime is a rotting wisdom tooth.

Which is not to deny that through the adulteration of determinable forms the genres, like written codes, persist. They persist either as modes of selective inattention or, rarely, with rare consciousness, denying nothing that history reveals, as a refusal of the Refusal, the (un)scrupulous negativities of which—like Celestina, Thersites, or Lenny Bruce—the obsessional comic is made. Having said that, I add that it seems like another fantasy, for I'm not at all sure that a comedy of such consciousness is achievable in anything like a conventional form. It would be hard to find anywhere, but for obvious cultural reasons in the American theater, where the shadows of historical consciousness are embossed on the Master Charge and where, as we see in the plays of Jules Feiffer, our permanent adolescence is passing middle age.

What does seem to be true about the most penetrating comedy of our time is that a sense of aging is in the bones. I mean in the bones of the form which, for all its deference to youth, always saw it coming, from the earliest skeletons in the closet of the self-deluding infernal machine to the cosmic jokes about it all at the beat-up and paralytic end of the theater of the Absurd. What we saw undeniably in the disability of the Absurd was something cutting to the brain like the senility of history. "Any life is laughable," wrote Elias Canetti in his book on Kafka, "if one knows it well enough. It is something serious and terrible if one knows it even better."[13] So if comedy followed tragedy in the original festival, in the ceremonials of history it seemed to be reversed. In Kafka himself, who gave us the prophetic modernist vision of a woeful human comedy, the better we know it the harder it is to know how to take it, as when, looking at Felice Bauer, who was to become his fiancée, Kafka first noticed her "entire mouthful of gold-capped teeth." About which he wrote, their "hellish luster . . . so scared me at first that I had to lower my eyes. . . ."[14]

What a festival it was when we saw the hellish luster of those gold-capped teeth multipled a millionfold! If then, as George Steiner declared in the aftermath of the Holocaust, we have experienced the death of tragedy, it should also be apparent that comedy, which was always a function of aging (if not an agent of the Devil), is certainly feeling it now. While it may flex its muscles, pulling a booger now and then, that's also a cover-up. For comedy is not exempt from the Energy Crisis. Since Freud on jokes and the unconscious, we are also more conscious, as the libidinal wealth runs out, of the tightening belt of comedy, "a tendency to compression, or rather to saving." As Freud insists, "It all seems to be a question of economy,"[15] a kind of stringent budgeting around a jeopardized social security in which, with Hamlet as David Stockman, the funeral baked meats are furnishing forth the marriage tables.

That is why our most festive comedy is likely to be occurring in forms which, often, don't look comic at all and may not be comic for long. There is of course precedent in other periods, but the comic may occur in what appears to be a dead serious play, momentarily or in sequences or suffusing the generic spine of an indecisive or unorthodox whole, as in *The Tooth of Crime,* where the language glamorizes and ignites the worn-out narrative of a late-night cowboy movie, as if watched in leather with razors while reading *S/Z* at a turn-on from *S/M*. Whatever the form it takes or whatever pop culture recycled, it doesn't take a degenerate like Genet or carbon copies like the punks to feel that we've circled a long way from the spritelier Comic Spirit that we may think about in Puck or in the verbal dexterity of the comedian as the letter C. If Jan Kott came along to overstress, perhaps, the underbelly of the comic norm, Stevens was judiciously middle-aged when he wrote his poem and, over the years, increasingly felt the impossible lack: behind the notorious elegance, a sonorous emptiness that appalls.

Yet there may be in the "Nothing that is not there and the nothing that is"[16]—that exquisiteness of the Absurd—an excrescence which, even if you're younger, seems unregenerately worse. "This world is a piece of shit," writes David Mamet, one of our now-aging dramatists, like Shepard, in his most recent play. I haven't seen it, but it is apparently, and not unadmirably, a harsh, ugly, and next-to-inconsolable play, with laugh lines that sink into a long and not disreputable comic tradition with moralistic and sacral roots. The one above is a comic sentiment which, even if there are no laughs, unites certain Fathers of the Church and those who hate their fathers, and certain saintly rebels, like Luther, with the satanic rebels, like the punks, Jarry, Witkiewicz, and Genet. "There is no law. There is no history," says the sodomized character of Mamet's play, which may never have been intended as a comedy, although there is that view of comedy in which comedy is the pits. Which makes it tougher for even the comedy which may be in the pits but remembers things as they were, in the old style, like Winnie in *Happy Days*.

So long as desire remembers in that ridiculous way the form will remain circuitous or, in some inconsolable "swerve"—like the *clinamen* of Lucretius appropriated by Harold Bloom—break into atoms or shards, "so as to make change possible in the universe."[17] That would seem to concur with the Brechtian "Short Organum," which favors comedy for keeping things in motion for the sake of progress. But Brecht pulls back from the atomistic, semiotic, or psychoanalytic flux which, like the *élan vital*, seems to be engendering another species of the comic. In either case, we have come to see that comedy, even in its repetitions, can never be the same. Or only the Same capitalized in the Nietzschean sense, like the Mother's Laughter, which is (cybernetically) the same plus (at least) one, or the same doubled over with laughter which may appear to be circling but can never be complete, like Hoss in the game of language or the comedian as the letter C.

Now there seems to be a contradiction, an incompleteness which is more. That's funny. What has been thought about much in recent years is the nature of the *interruption* which, like some inflection of history in the flux, determines the laughter in the circling which never stops, or the incessancy of the cycle of the disrupted desiring machine—the pilot projects for which were worked out through the history of the avant-garde, from the dynamism of the Futurists to the Bachelor Machine of Duchamp, from the utopian constructions of Tatlin to the Taylorism of the Tramp, from the parodies of the Killer Machine in the self-destructing sculpture of Tinguely to the static locomotive in Wilson's *Einstein on the Beach*.

Two things seem to be working off each other, dialectically, in the process, to which Marx, Freud, Einstein, and the ethologists have given us clues. There is the self-reflexive nature of language as a historical construct in the ahistorical continuum of the unconscious which, like space, curves back upon itself, and there is the biological interruption of an originary cry (first the infant's waul, and only later the laugh), that seeming remembrance of/in laughter which is a mnemonic stoppage of breath. It is the mystery of the interruption which preserves something tragic in comedy, since it seems a synopsis of death. This arcane moment is a breach. It reverberates in the most pragmatic behavior of the comic form, as when the actor is waiting out a laugh. It may seem comic to say it, but every laugh you hear in the theater is a semiotic break. Which is to say that *meaning stops for that moment,* as if in homage to more than meaning, which is the millennial fantasy of coherence in language as the play of an ultimate form.

That a play is conscious of this fantasy may get it a lot of laughs. And so it does for Tom Stoppard's *Jumpers,* whose moral philosopher plays with what appears to be "the same propensity to confuse language with meaning and to conjure up a God who may have any number of predicates including omniscience, perfection and four-wheel drive but not, as it happens, existence."[18] In the approximation of language to meaning, he adds, "There is presumably a calendar date—*a moment*—when the onus of proof passed from the atheist to the believer, when, quite suddenly, secretly, the noes had it" (p. 25). It's no secret anymore that the noes have it, history conceding the proof. The calendar date, of course, was *before* the Absurd, as is the nature of Stoppard's comedy (dated after), since what Stoppard says of its setting might be said of the play and—given the wit, high jinks, and name-dropping—the ideological caliber of its audience, whether at the National Theatre in London or on Broadway in New York: *"The general standard of living suggested by the flat owes more, one would guess, to musical comedy than moral philosophy"* (p. 13).

As for the play's being a retort courteous to Beckett, putting the premium on the thief who was saved—"Wham, bam, thank you Sam" (p. 89)—it doesn't seem to be up to the stubborn data of historical experience which he so fastidiously brought on stage. For all the quick passing of the years and atomistic change, it doesn't date quite that fast. It might be nicer to forget it, but the comedy which has really absorbed the noes in Beckett—not to mention the *Angst* that Wittgenstein brought to his analysis of "The world" which "is the totality of facts, not of things"[19]— renders a more painful homage to the confusion of language and meaning and, as it happens, existence, with whatever modifications or—with due respect to the gifts of *Jumpers*—the acrobatics of mental health.

To review: the caliber of the comedy is a measure of existential depth. Whatever the level of comedy, however, there is in the physiology of laughter, as in a *salto-mortale,* a case of arrested breath. If meaning goes dead when the laugh comes, it's deadlier when it doesn't come. Any performer knows that, let meaning follow after. But what we've had to deal with in the twentieth century, not only in Beckett or Genet, is that when the laughter comes the meaning is deadly, or there's just no meaning at all. Nothing solid, nothing final, as for Hoss. In the logorrhea of the postmodern, a continuous laugh. Beyond laughter, no last word. So: "Where the fuck do I stand!" The lesson of the theory which followed upon the Absurd is, as I suggested before, to hypostatize the incompletions. In recent years this has taken a radical feminist swerve into the cruel bushes of Genet. Don't stand, says the Mother, go further, disappearing into the polysemous becoming of the incestuous body of desire. There is an intimation of a purer laughter in the uninterrupted play of language which is, almost beyond breathing, a brainy series of dyings which *defer* the arresting death. One thinks of Artaud's body without organs, pure agency of desire, leading through "the closure of representation" to Derrida's *différance.*[20]

Shepard is hardly theoretical, but the question at stake in *The Tooth of Crime* is what we encounter in poststructuralist thought: to what degree can identity be, in a world made out of words, a mere matter of words? That is why, aside from the razzle-dazzle of Shepard's conspicuous gifts, I have been returning to the play. With an equal bravura but less intellectuality than *Jumpers,* it picks up the liability of the Absurd and does more with the problematics of meaning than play around with the problem to give us—out there on the overstretched existential tightrope—a balanced or hopeful word. What it does give us, inadvertently and against Shepard's previous biases about life style, music, and language, is something like a critique of theory which plays itself out as a kind of comedy.

What Roland Barthes said of the "echo chamber" of textuality may be said of the (comic) figure which allows itself, unlike Hoss, to be pulled and pushed around from one image to another, "tenacious and floating," an unchained signifier. "No doubt the reason for this is that one cannot at one and the same time desire a word and take it to its conclusion; in him"—this is *Barthes by Barthes*—"the desire for the word prevails, but this pleasure is partly constituted by a kind of doctrinal vibration," writing as *excess* but not uncontrolled, and while not dogmatic, doxological too. The idea of writing in Barthes, as we know, is performative. What he envisaged is something like the calligraphy of the body in Callot's drawings of the commedia dell'arte, the lyrically obscene figures of which suggest an "overflow of style toward other regions of language and subject, far from a *classed* literary code"[21] which belongs to no one's body except, maybe, the living dead. Barthes later illustrates the overflow of excess, *"exempt from meaning,"*[22] with *A Night at the Opera,* where "the wild mechanics of the text-on-a-spree explodes"[23] and "manifests its power of subversion. . . ."[24] For Barthes, as for Artaud, the audacity of the Marx Brothers is that, standing words on their heads as Marx did Hegel, they seem to enter the nightmare of history, tapping the primordial energies and disruptive politics of the unconscious.

It is obviously, to be redundant, no Final Solution. For the operations of the unconscious are, in the comedic cycle, another coded system in the recursive linguistic economy which devours all subject matter, if not like the ovens of Auschwitz, then like Ubu's debraining machine. Near which—subject to age, memory, and bias—these thoughts on comedy started. It was after the incinerators of World War II that we came to the indictment of rhetoric, first in the theater of the Absurd and then in the discourse of language. It is hard to read that still self-consuming discourse, which offers no proof but rhetorical pleasure, without thinking of it as comic thought, *thought-as-comedy,* circuitous, allusive, subversive, exploding the authority of the Text, all the more comic for that, like the six characters in search of an Author who is now searching for a character who is searching for an actor who, at one point in this round—the echo chamber of the prison house—preferred to play not a character but an unmediated self if (since there was a psychosexual problem in the psychophysical exercises) s/he could only find it.

But Hoss has had his inimical fill of this metonymical farce. The indeterminacy is unbearable. So is the Killer Machine, with its tape-looped shredder of language. Hoss comes, like Crow, from a line of real cold killers on the American frontier (with its comic tradition of cursing contests where the language is chewed up in an excess of style which is another model for the play). He was once a "sideways killer" himself, hard to keep track of, "a complete beast of nature" (p. 11), but in some last-ditch reflex of humanism insists he's an Original, ego be damned, neither an animal nor a dead letter, and he wants to be shown "how to be a man" (p. 66).

Not even Crow, who knows all the moves, presumes to act anything like that. That's something which may, in or out of the theater, no longer be possible to *show.* "A man's too hard, Leathers. Too many doors to that room" (p. 66)—in which, for all the words, because of the words (another swerve), the doors keep opening and closing, faster and faster, as in Meyerhold's scenography for *The Inspector-General* or on Buster Keaton in *The Navigator*, utterly alone at sea in a sideways tilting ship. It is the very model of a modern equivocal comedy: the desperately accelerating frames of a silent film, the paranoid comic hero, self-pursued, disappearing into the screen (of language), leaving nothing but the murmur of silence in the projector, perhaps the definitive subject matter of the resistless desiring machine. It is the momentum of laughter whose name is history which seems to leave the subject behind. "All that power goin' backwards," says Crow, taking the Maserati with the keys. Hoss is deposed, and dead. He was "right up there," knocking at the door (p. 75), which dissolves, into a lapse of history. There is not even the last alluring door of the indecipherable Law at the end of Kafka's *The Trial*, that apocalyptic comedy about the secrecy of absent power which preceded the waiting for Godot. In the absence of the objective comic wiliness of even a phony Inspector General—"There's movement all around but no numero uno" (p. 15)—what we have imagined in *The Tooth of Crime* is an encircling structure of successive *subjectivities*, power "Changin' hands like a snake dance to heaven" (p. 75).

It is like returning the subject of comedy to the Indians. Shepard's sidewinding occultism momentarily aside, it may be "another illusion to add to . . . [the] confusion," as Hoss said in the opening song (p. 4), even to think of the play as a comedy. But if thinking makes it so, it also causes us to rethink the historical condition of comedy in terms of the recent obsession with language reflected in Shepard's play. There is also the tradition of the comic, defined by Baudelaire, as "a damnable element born of a diabolic parentage" after the Fall, which is (naturally? historically?) the fall into language. As Baudelaire observes, "the Incarnate Word was never known to laugh. For him who knows all things, whose powers are infinite, the comic does not exist."[25] We can see in that, perhaps, that sideways is bothways (though not necessarily lateral). The snake dance to heaven, with down-home music, is all downhill: "Keep me rollin' down/Keep me rollin' down," sings Crow in a tautological round at play's inconclusive end, "Keep me in a state a' grace/Just keep me rollin' down/I've fooled the Devil's hand/I've fooled the Ace of Spades" (p. 76). If we don't know whether to laugh or what, *at* what, that's probably what Shepard wants (although it's just as likely, given his other plays, that for all the sidewinding he doesn't quite know what he wants). We are nevertheless—better than the Devil's game, out-playing chance—in the uroboric mouth of what Baudelaire thinks of as the essence of laughter. This time it's not quite a comic reduction but comedy with teeth in it, the archetypal tooth of crime: "The Being who wished to multiply His creatures in His own image did not give to men the teeth of the lion—but laughter is man's way of biting. . . ."[26]

Laughter had also been thought of from Hobbes to Darwin and after as having fangs instead of teeth. (Even before that, it was doubled up by Hamlet as two adders fanged, as if Shakespeare, anticipating Freud, had objectified the proposition that wit, as with Rosencrantz and Guilden-stern, is a conspiracy of two against one.) But when it comes to the bite in recent comedy—the bite conditioned still by the major dramatists after World War II: Brecht, Beckett, and Genet—certain questions always remain. The questions are ontological questions and political questions. They are a function of the theoretical critique of oedipal power. The drama is a principal target because it seems to be in collusion, particular-ly tragic drama, but bourgeois comedy as well, which is still the dominant comedy today, not easy to laugh off. As for the critical disposition of bourgeois comedy, it is presumably just another deceit taking its cues from the status quo which, after a few unstabilizing laughs, is unalterably restored. If comedy has always been, in one guise or another, the art of disguise, something of a technique of survival, the disguise is now re-jected as a lie or an alibi, an outright threat to survival. From this reversed perspective, if it is natural at all, it is the natural subject of the laughter which is always laughing to save itself.

That doesn't mean that it will. Nor that, in the imminence of nuclear fallout, laughing through the snake dance will grow a second skin. Even if you laugh until you can't stand it anymore, the laughter may not be enough, no more than reversing perspectives in the Alienation effect. Like this: has comedy, which used to dispel illusion and expose fantasies, become an illusion itself? The thing is, it always was. Not only the arrested comic beings who are, as Wyndham Lewis put it, "illusions hugged and lived in, little dead totems,"[27] but the very form in which they live, *subjected*, the generic comedy itself. That really was the im-portance of the theoretical critique: it turned our sluggish attention to the totemic power of apparent forms and the seeming naturalness of their conventions—the play of *appearance* which, whether looking inevi-table or delightful, keeps the deadly comedy alive.

The strategy of deconstruction seems to be if you can't beat it, join it. Since there is no way out of the logocentric order with the metaphysical legacy of its inscrutable Word, the idea is to move within it, as Derrida suggests in his essay on Foucault,[28] at the subversive edge of a metonymic disguise. It's a cerebral twist of the Hamletic mortal coil that seems like the tail end of the snake dance. Jean Baudrillard speaks of it in another context as a kind of suction or propulsion, "the image of that baroque theatricality of flux which makes for the originality of the carcass."[29] The carcass is also a decoy. It is the propulsion of a surface. The carcass is empty, a signifier with no-matter, or like the "ubiquitous protein" of genetics which is merely "information," joining whatever it chances upon, permutating, like the "linguistic shifter." It is with the semiological (re)discovery of that arch trickster of comedy—not this *that* not that *this*—that there is a seeming tilt in the balance of power, for it's the shifting that raises the questions.

But there is a problem in the problematics. It is, I think, the major problem in cultural theory today, as it is the major problem of comedy which may be, in the commutations of language, more ubiquitous than it knows. The questions may be stated in ordinary language about the subject of comedy, but they may also be stated in theoretical language about the subject of power. Either way, as language picks up the trace of its origins like the transformative comic figure, restoring itself to play through an infinite field of substitutions, not that this not this that, it seems to be asking the questions autonomously of itself: *who's laughing now? laughing at what? who's laughing last?* and then, as a kind of nervous laughter arises in the recursive momentum of the cybernetic stream, the question at the beginning which was always a question of power: *why should we be laughing at all?*

Crow smiles. We can't tell if it has any depth. Down to the belly, as Hoss thinks, laughing "with his whole being" (*Tooth*, p. 71)? Scratch him as we will, we can't say. Crow is a surface. Masked. Or so it appears. He said in a song earlier on that he believes in his dance and believes in his mask, and, in his parting song, he says he's "called the bluff in God's own face" (p. 76), confronting His image with nothing but image, nothing *as* image: pure representation, absence, Total Theater, taking over from the inscrutable Word.

It's like a return to the festival, not of the One and the Many, but only a festival of One. It's also like the lying Cretan who says he lies: how is he to be believed? At the center of the circle of indeterminacy is the greatest acting problem of all, a rather slippery totaled version of the comic double bind. To wit: can Total Theater be credible theater or does credibility, as in farce, go out the window of the theater into the theatricalization of life? Or does it—like Yves Klein leaping into the space of the Void—merely remain up in the air like some levitated figure of absurdist comedy? "Credibility is an expanding field," says the philosopher in *Jumpers* (p. 38), not knowing the extent of it. Is the rolling down another stasis?

All of Zeno's paradoxes are comic. They are speculated with in *Jumpers* but amortized in *Endgame,* where, whatever is taking its course, our deepest comedy is stalled. It is the modernist pathos, the nothing to be done. What we think of as postmodern wants to move it. So does Shepard. But in *The Tooth of Crime* he came to sense the seditious cost of moving through nothing as nothing but fantasy, reducing the "ache for the world" to linguistic games, no pathos, "No blame. No guilt" (p. 71). What is significant about this play of language, in which the slipping subject is pushed and pulled by images, is the pulling back. If Crow is beyond guilt, he is not beyond representation, nor is the actor playing Crow who, in order to do it *totally*, would have to do what Hoss refused, eat Crow, cannibalize himself in images and lose all semblance of self.

Not that actors didn't try. *The Tooth of Crime* was written at the end of a period when the denudation of the ego, the apparent subject of desire, took an autistic turn, as in recent solo performance or the human marionette shows of Richard Foreman or the postserial redundancies of Lee Breuer's *Shaggy Dog* or the Sufi whirling within the stasis of Robert Wilson. It was a period in which pure theatricality was celebrated only to abate with political disenchantment and then rise again (re)sublimated in theory and unsublimated in punk. What is chastening about Shepard's play is its limiting perception of the reifications of "desire in language"[30] and the ceaseless primacy of the play within the play, as well as the criminalized mimicking in punk of the ahistorical delusions of a perpetually self-imaging and exploitative power. In short, what we have in the play is a fine line of refusal of too much theater by theater, *unactably comic,* like Zeno's arrow. Or: biting down on the tooth of crime, if not the disguised serpent, the invisible worm that flies in the night.

I summon up the indeterminacy of that force, Blake's worm, not only because in that same period we abandoned character to play *phenomena* without the boundaries of character, but because we have heard in our time (or refused to hear) the "laughter that never sleeps, but is like a malady pursuing its destined way,"[31] as if there were no subject of comedy, only the canonical absoluteness of the comic turning upon itself, the laugh laughing at the laugh. As we see over and over in Beckett and Pinter, it is this *risus purus* that gives us (*Pause*).

No more than it was in Chekhov, the pause is not a respite of silence, but a rupture of the signifying chain, the *staging* of silence. It is the irruption of history in the forgetfulness of words. Thus, when we return to the subject matter that much of our comedy wants to forget, we might almost want to be the laugher who can't laugh, or even smile, like the masklike woman written about in the newspaper the other day, with the rare congenital defect which has made her nerves and facial muscles useless. As if the incapacity for expressing emotion were a topological warp, an exiled interiority or the intensity of a surface with no depth, they call it the Möbius syndrome. The plastic surgeons are going to move three muscles from her ribs to her face so that they'll get it talking a language. She will be able to laugh and smile, they say, and even—one thinks of the paralytic Hamm soliciting the impaired Clov—kiss. (*Pause.*) Why should she want to?

Beckett is not the only stoic comedian to raise the cruel question. We've heard it more recently from Thomas Bernhard, although it is probably inaccurate to think of his scorn as stoic. His laughter is more savage because remorselessly self-inflicted, without even the faintest shadow of the saving grace of Beckett's nostalgia. For Bernhard, the theater can only be a comedy because we are living an obscenity which it can only replicate, obscenity within obscenity, like the pictures in the album of that bizarre scene in *Eve of Retirement* where the retiring Chief Justice dresses up as Himmler in commemoration of his birthday, as if the Judge in *The Balcony*, already an impostor, were to play the Chief of Police infinitely mirrored in the mausoleum of his desire. Lest there be any mistaken innocence or exemption from meaning, "The whole world is one bloody legalism," says the man in Bernhard's narrative "Is It a Tragedy? Is It a Comedy?" who dresses as the woman he killed. "And tonight, let me tell you, in that theater over there, believe it or not, they are playing a comedy, *yes indeed,* a comedy."[32]

It is hard to know where to situate the laughter in *Eve of Retirement*. The vicious risibility on stage seems directed back at the audience, almost demoralizing the subject of comedy. I should imagine it's far worse if you live in Germany, where you must feel you're being laughed at with the most abrasive derision. It is not merely a mordant satire but limitless contempt. It is contempt even for your virtues, your love of culture, what brought you to this handsomely subsidized theater, and for the music that goes with it, like Beethoven's Fifth, that tradition, which is not merely background to the scene, with its self-edifying passion, but a condition of it, a virtual cause. Speaking of the pictures in the album—photos from the concentration camps juxtaposed with lovely moments of childhood and adolescence, and the lyrical beauty of the countryside—the incestuous sister says, "(*After a pause*)," to her beloved brother:

> Oh Rudolf that we have to hide
> and look at this so secretly
> that's really terrible
> And yet the majority thinks like us
> the majority hides that's what's so terrible
> it's really absurd.[33]

Well, if one objects to the charge, nobody ever said that comedy was meant to be fair. And the comic vision of Bernhard is such that nobody escapes what remains in hiding, the malady which goes undiagnosed in the world which is, if you really want a laugh, ruled by the diseased and crippled. It's *really* absurd, humiliating, an evil degradation, of which the comedy is a symptom. And the theater is humiliating because it can do nothing to relieve it, like tragedy, only repeat it, like farce.

When we think of the subject of comedy, then, any time since the Absurd, we may be thinking of a very painful subject—or subject and object appallingly confused, which is the congenital tragic substance of the most incisive comedy since Oedipus breached the confusion with his mother's brooch. It is also the recursive comic substance of the warp of history when the subject turns grotesque. This is the century of intimacy with the grotesque in magnitudes almost unimaginable. As Bernhard insists, we are only too familiar with the kind of historical experience at which we can only too readily laugh, though what we're laughing at doesn't seem funny, and the laugh feels grotesque or stillborn. "The world can be comical, or derisory," said Ionesco in a lecture (1976), summing up his own writing and the humiliating situation of comedy, which is still trying to get off the hook; "it can also seem tragic, in any case it isn't funny."[34] It's not funny, then it's funny. Or was it, in Beckett, the other way around? No matter. If habit isn't the great deadener, maybe it should be. There is a protective insensitivity which also gives us pause, causing us to think it's funny; or in a Möbius strip of apprehension, oversensitive, we may be laughing anyhow, not knowing what else to do or unable to control it or—isn't that the living end?—we may be laughing intolerably at ourselves, not knowing where the laughter comes from, or if the spastic noise we're making is really a laugh.

Sometimes we know only too well, the laughter doubling over in disproportion. That's the sort of comedy we see in Edward Bond's revision of *King Lear* to bring it into accord with the major experience of the last half of the twentieth century, the escalation of maximum deterrency and, no doubt, the documentary evidence of Amnesty International. Gloucester has become Warrington and the daughters' names are changed with a slightly Restoration flavor, but what is most striking in the comedy is the particularly deranged form of manic aggressive play:

> FONTANELLE Look at his mouth! He wants to say something. I'd die to listen. O why did I cut his tongue out?
> SOLDIER A 'E's wonderin' what comes next. Yer can tell from 'is eyes.
> BODICE (*pulls the needles from her knitting and hands the knitting to* FONTANELLE) Hold that and be careful.
> SOLDIER A Look at 'is eyes!
> BODICE It's my duty to inform you—
> SOLDIER A Keep still! Keep yer eyes on madam when she talks t'yer.
> BODICE—that your pardon has been refused. He can't talk or write, but he's cunning—he'll find some way of telling his lies. We must shut him up inside himself. (*She pokes the needles into* WARRINGTON'*s ears.*) I'll just jog these in and out a little. Doodee, doodee, doodee, doo.[35]

If the venomous doodee doo is a twisted *fort/da*—an absolute perversion of the pleasure principle which has never been separable from the perverse—it occurs, even after all these years, on the unchanging landscape of political violence which is not a far cry from the ontological ground of those other vocables of the Absurd, Didi and Gogo. For Bond, we've heard it so long it is not unnamable. There is a sense in which the grisly comedy has become even conventional, as we can see from the opening sentence of his preface to the published play: "I write about violence as naturally as Jane Austen wrote about manners."[36] It still remains peculiar how, as we up the ante on violence, we get a laugh.

Of course the violence is about as domesticated as the knitting needles. I am writing, for instance, on the day the Argentines surrendered the Falklands after the British caught them sleeping, snoring no doubt, preparing the nightmare. It is the same day we're being told that thousands of people are being killed by Israeli bombings of Lebanon.

"[T]he majority hides that's what's so terrible"—thank goodness for the comic distance? The grotesque, which never seems to sleep either (like those bombers circling the globe with first-strike capability), is not the aestheticized grotesque which, as conceived by Baudelaire, "combined with a certain imitative faculty [works] on pre-existing elements of nature" to express "the idea of superiority, *not* this time of man over man, but of man over nature."[37] It's almost as if, since Baudelaire, we've been much too successful at that, and closer than he imagined to the essence of laughter, the comic distance narrowing down. What with the population explosion and ecological damage (not to mention triage and genocide in places whose names we forget), there seem to be fewer elements of nature to work on. We are almost by natural right, as the excesses of culture become nature, experts of the incommensurate, which produces from the old ritual pollution not only a metonymical but a new metaphysical farce.

It is a form even more dumbfounding than what Marx had in mind when, revising Hegel, he spoke of the repetition of history in "time-honoured disguise" and "borrowed language. . . ."[38] If there's a remembered eloquence to tragedy, it's the farce that leaves you speechless, which is why the theater of the last generation, even as the words poured out, went nonverbal, aside from the fact that the words used or unused seemed, and still do, part of the pollution. Bond remembers the tragic eloquence but can't avoid the comedy, though as a rationalist and socialist he wants to keep his distance from the principle of the Absurd. "Absurdity," however, as Sartre wrote in *Nausea*, "was not an idea in my head, or the sound of a voice, only this long serpent dead at my feet, this wooden serpent. . . . In vain to repeat: 'This is a root'—it didn't work any more."[39] And because it's still not working, Bond has to contend with it. Thus, his reverting to *King Lear*, that model of metaphysical farce, where the stink of mortality is overwhelming and atrocities of cosmic dimension arise from the stupefying vainglory of a domestic nothing like the gas chambers from the aberrations of a house painter, along with the commemorative laughter of a brainlessly recurring howl.

"A charnel-house! A charnel-house!" said the tramp in Beckett's play, lest we forget, anticipating Bernhard's view that there is something obscene in the theater including the theater, as if the serpent were not dead at all or performing at the end of a stick. Anticipating Handke too, the tramps break the frame of the stage and look into the maw of the audience, looking and being looked at, that scopic landscape of desire stupefied by the enormity of it all. "You can't help looking." "True."[40] One of the more potent accomplishments of the theater since the fifties was to have made the audience whose dominant condition is powerlessness the derisive subject of the comedy, conscious of its inertness, the real live Gross National Product, the matter of laughter the laughing matter, in every sense.

I think again of the Möbius syndrome and the surgery about to be done: "For such an operation as this we can hardly accept the theatre as we see it before us. Let us go into one of these houses and observe the effect which it has on the spectators." We may recognize the voice, which had a large influence on our idea of comedy in the fifties; but let's review the diagnosis, since the operation hasn't been completed and may need to be done again and again, despite the postwar valorization of *Verfremdung* and the ideological savagery of post-Brechtian plays such as Bond's and Bernhard's. "Looking about us, we see somewhat motionless figures in a peculiar condition: they seem strenuously to be tensing all their muscles, except where these are flabby and exhausted. They scarcely communicate with each other; their relations are those of a lot of sleepers, though of such as dream restlessly because, as is popularly said of those who have nightmares, they are lying on their backs. True, their eyes are open, but they stare rather than see, just as they listen rather than hear. They look at the stage as if in a trance. . . ."

Rumor was that Brecht, before he died, was going to write an "answer" to *Waiting for Godot,* which he admired, but what he seems to be doing here, as he looks at the audience, is describing the behavior *on stage* in Beckett's plays—all the more when he adds that "these people seem relieved of activity and like men to whom something is being done."[41] The fact is that nobody has written an answer because it may be unanswerable yet. In the period when we were working on those flabby and exhausted muscles as an alternative to the Absurd, we also valorized the idea of trance as an antidote to the same condition, a form of homeopathic magic. Brecht was never persuaded that the nightmare into which you plunged on awakening was ever much more than a snore because he always distrusted the unconscious, as he also disapproved of the Absurd.

Disapprove or not, when the Absurd first came upon the scene it was almost, as in the clawing comedy of *Endgame,* more than one could take. It was hard to know at those first performances—closer to the wartime obscenities they were replicating—whether to laugh or cry. It also seemed for a while as if it was something you couldn't escape, by trance or dance or primal screams, either the appalling subject or the specular drive, the voyeuristic looking that seemed innate in the form and which—in the paratactical logistics of the postmodern—seemed to be playing itself back, as if the theater was behaving like film. If the seriality of the Absurd seemed in its hysteria like a runaway silent film with a knockabout comic figure chasing himself through receding doors, suddenly, as if through a trapdoor of the unconscious, where you're only being *looked at,* there didn't seem to be any doors. It wasn't a question of No Exit, and it was a metacommentary on Brecht: "You don't see any doors here," say the actors in *Offending the Audience,* alienating the Alienation, and with no action to play. "You don't see the two doors of the old dramas. You don't see the back door through which he who shouldn't be seen can slip out. You don't see the front door through which he who wants to see him who shouldn't be seen enters. There is no back door. Neither is there a nonexistent door as in modern drama. The nonexistent door does not represent a nonexistent door. This is not another world."[42]

That it was the same or seamless world remained moot. For there was something hypnotic about it, though it pretended to be up front, and it soon began to recede into the analogical world which was being denied, like any other duplicity of theater which is subject, even when nonverbal, to the representational power of words. As we approached the eighties and the doors seemed to be going back in place, Handke receded from the theater, not any more sure than Bernhard that the obscenity could be transformed or that, as the vested agency of transformation, the age-old comedy would ever end.

Do we laugh or cry? Despite the ecology of laughter and weeping in Pozzo's global vision, the balance inevitably swings, as in Kundera's novel, to laughter and forgetting. Or: reducing the metaphysical madness to an assimilable zaniness, the safer terrain of a *Cloud 9.* Caryl Churchill's play takes up the exploitable safe deposits of the colonialism of *The Screens* as if it were *The Pirates of Penzance.* It's a barrelful of laughs that would make the Mother howl. Both the political and sexual anxieties are collapsed into welcome laughter by the disingenuous evasions of a communal disengendering out of the fondest legacy of polymorphous play. It seems appropriate that it is being performed in New York in the heart of the heart of the homosexual ghetto where the theater on the streets offers—sideways, bothways, all ways—similar desublimated

entertainment for the insatiable scopic drive. All you have to do is step
out the door, though once again, for other reasons, we're not sure who's
laughing at whom. *Cloud 9* is an accommodating comedy lacking the
astringency of the Absurd and—in a world where the oppressed become
oppressors too, Cubans, Africans, Iranians, Israelis, all—it relieves the
uncertainty about laughing and crying by whooping up the devastation,
as if the sleepless laughter were not enough. We've seen the same
tendency in recent years not only in new plays but in certain productions
which do with Beckett (André Gregory's *Endgame*) what they are still
doing with Chekhov (Andrei Serban's *The Cherry Orchard*) since they
discovered he is funny.

True, we each have our tastes in laughter. And there is comedy and
comedy—that chameleon and quenchless form—as there is not quite
tragedy, which exhausts in its irreversible and stifling cadence the power
to bring about change. I suppose, too, that we can ask too much of any
comedy. When we're confronted with the more distressing aspects of the
wilder laughter, it is quite understandable that we might simply prefer
the comedy which makes us forget. It seems humorless not to. Everybody loves a good laugh. And the good laugh is not *that* laugh, manic as
it is, entropic, sometimes almost berserk. Who needs it? For, like the
masochistic subject of history, it seems irreversible too. What most of us
think of, frankly, is something more humorous, and not the distemper
of the old humor psychology. I said before that bourgeois comedy is still
the dominant form. Actually, the almost comic truth is that the more
jaundiced we are about the world the more sentimental we are about
comedy. I am not speaking of sentimental comedy, although the tradition of sentimental comedy may be so deeply inscribed in the fantasy text
of bourgeois power that we've come to overvalue humor or, as we say,
good-natured laughter. In order to keep up to date, it has taken on a
tinge of the Absurd, like the Friday night versions of *Saturday Night
Live,* which came out of a generation reading *MAD* comics and growing up Absurd. We'll forgive almost anything to a sense of humor until,
however, the humor gets out of hand, like the overdosing of John
Belushi.

As for the comedy of writers like Bond or Bernhard, it seems almost
too ferocious to be believed, the rictus, "the pure orthodoxy of
laughter,"[43] too disappointed with the world which is changeless only in
the comic versatility which is still resistant to change. How we laugh
about that depends on how we remember. There is also the pallid

laughter of amnesia, which has become the chronic condition of much of our humor, as of our conventional drama, which has forgotten what it forgets.

NOTES

1. Sam Shepard, *The Tooth of Crime,* in *The Tooth of Crime and Geography of a Horse Dreamer* (New York: Grove, 1974), p. 68. Subsequent references to this edition of *The Tooth of Crime* will appear in the text, abbreviated as *Tooth.*

2. Gilles Deleuze and Felix Guattari, *Anti-Oedipus: Capitalism and Schizophrenia,* trans. Robert Hurley, Mark Seem, and Helen R. Lane (New York: Viking, 1977).

3. *Ibid.,* p. 5.

4. Jean Genet, *The Screens,* trans. Bernard Frechtman (New York: Grove, 1962), p. 16. Subsequent references will appear in the text.

5. Roland Barthes, *The Pleasure of the Text,* trans. Richard Miller (New York: Hill and Wang, 1975), p. 66.

6. Jean Genet, *The Balcony,* trans. Bernard Frechtman (New York: Grove, 1958), p. 116.

7. Northrop Frye, *Anatomy of Criticism: Four Essays* (Princeton: Princeton University Press, 1957), p. 164.

8. Genet provides the behavioral and theoretical model for Dick Hebdige in his study of punk, reggae, teddy boys, and skinheads, *Subculture: The Meaning of Style* (London: Methuen, 1979).

9. Jean-Francois Lyotard, *Économie libidinale* (Paris: Minuit, 1974).

10. Hebdige, p. 3.

11. Fredric Jameson, *The Prison-House of Language* (Princeton: Princeton University Press, 1972).

12. Henri Bergson, *Laughter,* in *Comedy,* ed. Wylie Sypher (New York: Anchor, 1956), p. 64.

13. Elias Canetti, *Kafka's Other Trial: The Letters to Felice,* trans. Christopher Middleton (New York: Schocken, 1974), p. 103.

14. Franz Kafka, letters 405 and 406, *Letters to Felice* (New York: 1973), as quoted in Canetti, p. 54.

15. Sigmund Freud, *Jokes and Their Relation to the Unconscious,* vol. 8 of *The Standard Edition of the Complete Psychological Works of Sigmund Freud,* ed. James Strachey (London: Hogarth Press and Institute of Psychoanalysis, 1960), p. 42.

16. Wallace Stevens, "The Snow Man," in *The Collected Poems of Wallace Stevens* (London: Faber and Faber, 1955), p. 10.

17. Harold Bloom, *The Anxiety of Influence: A Theory of Poetry* (New York: Oxford University Press, 1973), p. 14.

18. Tom Stoppard, *Jumpers* (New York: Grove, 1972), p. 24. Subsequent references will appear in the text.

19. Ludwig Wittgenstein, *Tractatus Logico-Philosophicus,* trans. D. F. Pears and B. F. McGuinness, 2nd ed. (London: Routledge and Kegan Paul, 1963), p. 7.

20. Jacques Derrida, "The Theater of Cruelty and the Closure of Representation," in *Writing and Difference,* trans. Alan Bass (Chicago: University of Chicago Press, 1978).

21. Roland Barthes, *Roland Barthes by Roland Barthes,* trans. Richard Howard (New York: Hill and Wang, 1977), pp. 74, 76.

22. Ibid., p. 87.

23. Ibid., p. 80.

24. Ibid., p. 81.

25. Charles Baudelaire, *The Essence of Laughter and Other Essays, Journals, and Letters,* ed. Peter Quennell (New York: Meridian, 1956), p. 112.

26. Ibid., p. 113.

27. Wyndham Lewis, "Inferior Religions," as quoted in Hugh Kenner, *The Pound Era* (Berkeley: University of California Press, 1971), p. 242.

28. Jacques Derrida, "Cogito and the History of Madness," in *Writing and Difference,* pp. 31–63.

29. Jean Baudrillard, "The Beaubourg-Effect: Implosions and Deterrence," *October,* 20 (1982), 3.

30. See Julia Kristeva, *Desire in Language: A Semiotic Approach to Literature and Art,* ed. Leon S. Roudiez, trans. Thomas Gora, Alice Jardine, and Leon S. Roudiez (New York: Columbia University Press, 1980).

31. Baudelaire, p. 117.

32. Thomas Bernhard, "Is It a Tragedy? Is It a Comedy?" in *Eve of Retirement and The President,* trans. Gitta Honegger (New York: Performing Arts Journal Publications, 1982), p. 214.

33. Bernhard, *Eve of Retirement,* in *Eve of Retirement and the President,* p. 204.

34. Eugène Ionesco, "Why Do I Write? A Summing Up," in *The Two Faces of Ionesco,* ed. Rosette C. Lamont and Melvin J. Friedman (Troy, New York: Whitston, 1978), p. 15.

35. Edward Bond, *Lear* (New York: Hill and Wang, 1976), p. 15.

36. Ibid., p. v.

37. Baudelaire, p. 121.

38. Karl Marx, *The Eighteenth Brumaire of Louis Bonaparte,* in Karl Marx and Frederick Engels, *Selected Works,* no trans. (New York: International, 1968), p. 97.

39. Jean-Paul Sartre, *Nausea,* trans. Lloyd Alexander (Norfolk, Conn.: New Directions, 1959) p. 129.

40. Samuel Beckett, *Waiting for Godot* (New York: Grove, 1954), p. 41.

41. Bertolt Brecht, "A Short Organum for the Theater," in *Brecht on Theater,* ed. and trans. John Willett (New York: Hill and Wang, 1964), p. 187.

42. Peter Handke, *Offending the Audience,* in *Kaspar and Other Plays,* trans. Michael Roloff (New York: Noonday, 1969), p. 13.

43. Baudelaire, p. 116.

THREE

THE AMERICAN DREAM IN AMERICAN GOTHIC

The Plays of Sam Shepard and Adrienne Kennedy

If the drama in the text, as we're always told, is to be realized on the stage, even on the stage there is something unrealized in American drama. Whatever the cause in our disheartening theater, there is a certain improvidence in our social history. From his earliest plays to his last, it troubled the imagination of Eugene O'Neill, still by sheer ambition our greatest playwright. He put the case against America when he was canonized by Henry Luce on the cover of *Time*[1] which—right after World War II, from which we emerged as a superpower—was announcing the imperium of the American dream. On the contrary, said O'Neill, this nation is the greatest failure because it has betrayed the greatest promise. He put the case against himself in the enormous pathos of *Long Day's Journey into Night*, which almost transcends the limitations by the exhaustiveness of their confession, the obsessive massing of the desire to have it all out.

O'Neill knew what the impediment was, the failure in the confession reflecting the failure in the promise. He said he lacked the language. It is a recurring lack in our major dramatists, as we see in Arthur Miller when, for all his social and moral passion, he denounces the improvidence and asks for attention to be paid. Tennessee Williams had the language, but his lacks were of another kind, an insufficiency through the sensationalism (inherited by Albee) that makes one think of stage fright, a lurid necessity through the lyricism that betokens faintness of mind. The verbal and intellectual deficiencies of our theater were by no means diminished or compensated for by the tactile experimentation of the sixties and seventies, despite the claims made for an irreversible impact on our drama. Actually, there were innumerable plays written in this antiverbal period of assaults upon the text, when the actor at times seemed to be going it alone. If there was an impact of body language on the written drama, it released for the most part minor constellations of atomized banality, a plethora of the unmemorable. The truth is that our best writers, granting a rare indulgence, pretty much stay away from our theater.

I want to speak in this essay, however, of two writers who, while representative of the last generation of American dramatists, are so distinct among them, so evocatively gifted, that we can only regret the absence of an active literary environment *in* the theater for their more substantial development. One is white and a man, his gift widely acknowledged here and abroad; the other is black and a woman, and mostly neglected, even at home, and even by blacks. (By last report she is either so discouraged or exhausted she may not be writing anymore.) Neither of them lacks the language. If they still suffer from faintness of mind, that seems by now to come with the territory. What I want to talk about, mainly, through the work of Sam Shepard and Adrienne Kennedy, is the persistence of desire in language to overcome the failed promise. It is what we also saw in the logorrheic stutterings of O'Neill: how the American drama remembers through every disenchantment the loose and elusive features of the American dream, attached to the endlessly retreating image of a lost innocence.

Now I realize that the waning of the American dream has been so endlessly studied in American scholarship that it has become a banality of American thought. It is no less alluring for that—the dream so fractured, however, that it looks surreal or gothic, like a stained glass window in a suburban tract where Edgar Allan Poe still lives—as they used to say of the Bird—not drunk, but freaking out on acid or high on speed. At the same time the endangered heroine (no pun intended) of gothic melodrama has turned feminist with a vengeance and, in the radical critique of the American family, has threatened our very conception of sexuality and, by a kind of toxic shock upon the incest barrier, may change the nature of *what* we dream.

Adrienne Kennedy is not your ordinary feminist—if she is one at all—but the problem of sexuality is caught up in her drama in a confusion of gender with all the desiring shades of gray between black and white. In Sam Shepard—his major limitation perhaps—rebellion is mostly male, macho, and while he is turned on by the image of the cowboy, he rather treats his facsimile of a woman as if he were John

Wayne on a bender or Humphrey Bogart on a bronco. The fact is that Shepard, who is multiply talented, a rock musician as well as a playwright, has become a movie star too, and it remains to be seen, for all the virtuosity of his plays, the right stuff, whether he can portray the female body as something other than the old stuff, camouflaged, concessive, evasive/passive, as a sort of tomboy overcoming the curse or a bitchy cipher from the Hollywood dream machine.

There are times when the domination of American reality by the dream machine—the whole cinematic apparatus, including television— seems like an amendment to the Constitution, if not its natural consequence, like the image of the cowboy in the White House. It is an image that might have been improvised by Shepard who shares with Ronald Reagan a sort of frontier nostalgia and—if not a vision of a little house on the hill, borrowed from our earliest fantasies—then a bird's eye view of the landscape of the American dream from the aerie of Los Angeles, "city of the future," as the Europeans say, if there is a future. Which is what the writer Austin wondered about in Shepard's *True West,* when he left his wife and children up north in San Francisco and went to live in his mother's house in Los Angeles—as if the movies were the mother nurturing fantasies of the father—trying to write a screenplay about the American West. If the true West was lost we lost it, as they say of virginity, at the movies, from which we gathered all our images of the West when, at the frontier of fantasy, the future seemed guaranteed.

It even seemed guaranteed during the Depression, when our president's optimism was seeded by FDR and the New Deal, the future only looking bleak then on economic grounds. Today we worry about the future on other grounds: gratuitous crime, pollution, international terrorism, and—to adapt a phrase from the upbeat forecasts of supply-side theory—the trickle-down illusions of nuclear power, the massive anxiety in the massive deterrents that we *will* realize the desire to have it all out, the overkill of the American dream. "I'll track her down and shoot them in their bed," says another Shepard character from the *Curse of the Starving Class:*

> I'll splatter their brains all over the vibrating bed. I'll drag him into the hotel lobby and slit his throat. I was in the war. I know how to kill. . . . It's no big deal. You just make an adjustment. You convince yourself it's all right. That's all. It's easy. You just slaughter them. Easy. . . . He doesn't know what he's dealing with. . . . He's not counting on what's in my blood. He doesn't realize the explosiveness.[2]

The same blood flows through the body politic as flows through the psyche, which seems to be in nature too, the explosiveness. You are very conscious of nuclear power if you find yourself in California living perilously on the San Andreas Fault. If there is no Original Sin in America, only the endlessly alluring image of a beckoning fiction, it stubs its toe on this unfortunate fault—the long line of slipping tectonic plates below the ground running the whole vertical length of California, south to north, causing earthquakes. The prediction is that a large one is inevitable.

Sam Shepard grew up on this fault. He was born in the Midwest—Fort Sheridan, Illinois—but he was raised in southern California, in an atmosphere like that of the film *American Graffiti,* made by the director who later made *Star Wars,* that infantile sci-fi parody of a future which we also see in Shepard's plays. It was a world of drive-ins, hot rods, surfers, freeways, tight jeans, bikinis, junk magic and neon culture, electrified guitars, biking to Vegas back over the rainbow, the whole kandy-kolored tangerine-flaked streamlined ethos, dragstrips and Muscle Beach, superstars, land's end. There were some very scared people in California, even before Charles Manson and the crazier cults, in the days of the counterculture; there still are. They thought it was going to break off with the next earthquake or nuclear slip of a breeder reactor, and topple into the sea, like some awful consummation of the continental tilt. For those less paranoid it was hard to think about all that danger when you could reach out the window, as I could when I lived there, and pick an avocado, with its lusciously soft lemon-green succulent flesh, very sexy. There are so many avocados in California that with the triumph of Reaganomics they are—according to a recent newspaper report that might have been written by Shepard—mashing them up as the other crops fail, to feed the cows. There may be drought and the fruitfly and fear and trembling in California, and John Birch residues of frontier rage, but the compensating mechanism is, I suppose, the Human Potential Movement which flourishes there as nowhere else, Esalen, Rolfing, Co-Counseling, ESP and est, therapies for every purpose, the hanging loose, laid back, massage, the pacified martial arts, marijuana by the swimming pool. Shepard knows the scene, the coke and the contradictions, the jeopardy in the greenhouse, the agribusiness in the avocados, the sunburnt nightmare of the American dream.

The starving class in Shepard has an orchard-full of avocados. But if they're not mashed up, they're either cramming the fridge or—the male avocados, the inedible kind—hanging hapless, mostly withered on the

bough, like the lamb testicles on the roof in the *Curse of the Starving Class,*
"those fresh little remnants of manhood," castratos, prey for birds. Or
rather, in that play, one spectacular bird which comes on for the testicles
like a nuclear explosion, a savage power, like a wild and hungry force of
nature, classless, something remembered from the raw and original
rapacity of the American dream. When that eagle rips down, "screaming
like a bred mare," dive bombing the testicles "like the Cannonball Express" (p. 184), it's like a seizure from the unconscious, both frightening
and exhilarating. And it seems to come out of some legacy of American
myth with all its equivocal violence, as if it were the screaming mutation
of the bird which the pagan Tashtego nails to the mast with "archangelic
shrieks" in the sinking vortex of the Pequod at the end of *Moby Dick.*

Or did that bird survive with Ishmael, the wanderer, who should have
drowned but came back to tell the story, out of the black bubble upward
bursting, as a way of averting his own death? Shepard is also a wanderer
who almost drowned, as if he were seeking his own death. As the rock
star Patti Smith, for whom he wrote *Cowboy Mouth,* tells us about him, he
had the high-risk habit of living too dangerously, taking off wild and
often going too far, totaling his red Renault while stoned on benzedrine
or slipstreaming Salinas and plunging off a cliff. He "clawed the sky" as
if he were the eagle in some mad desire "to exorcise his racing spirit
from the limiting/shell of his body,"[3] like those culture heroes of the
fifties, James Dean and Jackson Pollock, glamorously suicidal.

That racing self-destruction is what we often see in Shepard's characters who, careening wildly toward some deeply unutterable end, are
always telling stories. It's a way, paradoxically, of stopping catastrophe in
its tracks. That's why long stretches of his hurtling drama are reined in
by narration. The characters take a deep breath and let it all out. It is not
the brooding confession of an O'Neill, but rather the Whitmanian flecks
and flashes of a performing self, the body leaping through a sluice of
disjunct images to some other dimension, going with the flux of words, a
long jazz riff of images reaching toward an identity. Or, when they're
not telling stories, like the one about the eagle, just plain actor's energy
coming thick and fast, not a narrative but a routine, sometimes
clamorous, a standoff of screaming words:

> That was my chicken and you fucking boiled it! YOU BOILED MY
> CHICKEN! I RAISED THAT CHICKEN FROM THE INCUBATOR
> TO THE GRAVE AND YOU BOILED IT LIKE IT WAS ANY OLD
> FROZEN HUNK OF FLESH! YOU USED IT WITH NO CONSIDERA-

TION FOR THE LABOR INVOLVED! I HAD TO FEED THAT
CHICKEN CRUSHED CORN EVERY MORNING FOR A YEAR! I
HAD TO CHANGE ITS WATER! I HAD TO KILL IT WITH AN AX! I
HAD TO SPILL ITS GUTS OUT! I HAD TO PLUCK EVERY FEATH-
ER ON ITS BODY! I HAD TO DO ALL THAT WORK SO THAT YOU
COULD TAKE IT AND BOIL IT! (*Curse,* pp. 140–41)

"Great language," says one of the characters, as the "demonstration"
(and it is that, an acting improvisation) rages over the kitchen. So far as
the language goes, there's nothing spectacular here, just the energy.
Elsewhere, however, the language can be dazzling, since Shepard has a
fantastic ear for all the subcultural vernaculars of American life and the
polyglottism of regional speech: blacks, gays, rockers, rappers, jazz side-
men and Rotary Clubbers, drifters, gangsters, Holy Rollers, drug freaks
and rodeo riders, the New Wave and the Old Frontier, the voice of the
urban cowboy and the voice we just heard, the lumpen voice of the rural
suburbs which—even with a chicken in the pot and the fridge stuffed
with artichokes (also glutting California) is part of the starving class.

For the characters in Shepard, chewing up words, are always stuffing
their mouths out of a kind of spiritual hunger. And what comes out of
their mouths, in their manic and self-identifying stories, sometimes
vomited, is the old American fear of an empty incognito. As for Shepard
himself, it's as if he were juggling *his* identity with a Pacman full of jokers
and the libido running wild. Rootlessness is the theme and also the
aspiration, in a rhythmic self-exorcism playing all over the landscape of
the body of the dream, restoring energy to an absence yet refusing to be
fixed. It is a mythicizing space in a personal oral tradition. There is also a
theory of acting in a drama of splitting characters and bizarre comic-
strip cognomens like Frank Zappa's daughter Moon Unit who sang
about the speech of the (San Fernando) Valley Gals: Geez, Wong, Shooter, Jeep, Sloe Gin Martin, Kosmo and Yahoodi, Star-Man and Galactic
Jack. They are names making up for the nick of anonymity with the
knack of theatrical hunger, everybody seeking stardom and nobody
knowing his role, cut off, in the loneliness of the tabula rasa which is the
painful stage of the arrested adolescence of the fading American dream.

Here is Shooter, somewhat subdued, in a play called *Action,* speaking
in a staccato second person about the kind of performance required of
an actor who finds himself in a play with nothing specific to be done,
where you can't tell subject from object, in a very uncertain setting, even
when it looks like home:

> You go outside. The world's quiet. White. Everything resounding. Not a
> sound of a motor. Not a light. You see into the house. You see the candles
> . . . . Warmth. People. Conversation. Everyone using a language. Then
> you go inside. It's a shock. It's not like how you expected. You lose what
> you had outside. You forget that there even is an outside. The inside is all
> you know.[4]

In the process of being with the others, finding out how to behave, "You
act yourself out." The simple language transcribes exactly the actor's
dilemma, as it might have been experienced at the extremity of the
Method, when it became a symptom of the wider self-estrangement—the
solipsism seeking an unmediated solution, as in the acting of the sixties.
As I've suggested, the acting out of a self sometimes has the features of a
jam session or, more stridently, a rock concert, and sometimes an aria or
a gospel chorus. Since the dialogue between nonpersons, even of the
same family, however energetic, is likely to go nowhere, the soliloquies
and monologues take over the burden of a roto-rooting self. The speaking voice is sought in the audacity of the story which may be the merest
fiction, the pleasure of an outright lie.

In this respect, Shepard's stories are like the Tall Tales of the Mis-
sissippi riverboatmen or, closer to home, the irreverent standup comedi-
ans of the period of radical activism, the ontological rebels of comedy,
making their scene, often obscene, like Lenny Bruce. Because the other
characters are often not even listening when the imagination takes off
like a wild bird, what we have, then, right in the center of the dramatic
action as a strategic impediment to the action is an array of solo performances, a hip or punk Whitmanianism, incantatory and narcissistic, a
manic and updated *Song of Myself:*

> I could smell the avocado blossoms. I could hear the coyotes. I could hear
> the stock cars squealing down the street. . . . I could feel this country like it
> was part of my bones. . . . Even sleeping people I could feel. Even all the
> sleeping animals. Dogs. Peacocks. Bulls. Even tractors sitting in the wet-
> ness, waiting for the sun to come up. I was looking straight up at the
> ceiling at all my model airplanes hanging by all their metal wires.

And in the floating regression of these fictive wires, decals peeling off
the wings, the Jap Zero seems to be reconnoitering. "Taking pictures of
the enemy. Me, the enemy," listening like a cornered animal, in the
space of paranoia like a widening black void, the dreadful thing
approaching (*Curse,* p. 137). And with a big Packard coming up the hill
out of a grade-B movie, the feeling sinks, like the squashy male avocados
falling to the ground, dinner for the worms.

There are a lot of images in Shepard's drama which, through all the verve, come out like that, a moldy superfluity, signs of an economy of abundance grown maggoty, glutted with its own excess—a sort of overgrowth of nature gone to seed. "Everything," says Ella in *Curse of the Starving Class*. "The beat-up cars, the rusted out tractor, the moldy avocados, the insane horse, the demented sheep, the whole entire shooting match" (p. 173). And in Shepard it's also a shooting match you have to imagine, somewhere between Atari computers in front of TV—those fierce war games played by children with amazing proficiency in the living room—or the real live thing, played with a kind of infantile mania by adults, without gun control. There was a picture in the paper a little while ago of a member of the Moral Majority in California responding to the petition for gun control. They're gonna have to come and take my guns, he said, if they want them, and that ain't gonna be easy. It may not be the true West, but it's the vigilante voice of the Old West, and very much alive.

Sam Shepard knows the voice, and that it ain't gonna be easy. We can see that from the guns laid out on the floor as a fetishistic datum for what may be his most brilliant play, *The Tooth of Crime*, about a fight to the finish between two midnight cowboys, rock superstars. The stage is bare except for an evil-looking black chair with silver studs resembling a pharaoh's throne. Music in the background like the song "Heroin" from the Velvet Underground. The weapons are laid out on a black velvet cloth, "pearl-handled revolvers, pistols, derringers and rifles with scopes, shotguns broken down,"[5] all looking beautiful and clean. Hoss, the threatened superstar, in his black rocker gear with silver studs, fondles the guns as if they are alive.

In his earliest work, Shepard had celebrated music as the nervy embodiment of a restless iconoclasm, the style of risk, "flying in the eye of contempt" (p. 217). By the time of *The Tooth of Crime* (1972), he was listening more nervously, still with admiration, but put off, frightened by something ominous in the sound. What he heard was a sound dispossessed of history, savagely, distorting the rituals of liberation by which the sixties were possessed. There was a rock-bottom violence in the high-tech sound, and it didn't sound liberating at all. At the dead end of the sixties, there was rage mixed in with the disenchantments. After the Love-Ins and the Be-Ins and the instant gratifications—in the movement from the festival at Woodstock through the Velvet Underground to the festival at Altamont—the Rolling Stones embraced the Hell's Angels and there was bloody murder in the LSD. No mere *image* of violence,

no fiction, no pleasurable lie, but the real sordid indescribable thing—
the fucked-up vision of an empty myth.

Shepard felt that it had turned the utopianism of rock culture into the
communitarianism of criminality, with a suburban punk Mafia of its
own. That's what Crow seems to represent in *The Tooth of Crime*, a cool
and vicious stylist, another lethal loner born to kill, like Hoss, but at a
more advanced stage of postmodern sadistic power. In his more recent
plays, like *Buried Child* (1978), Shepard seems to recoil from it
altogether: "I just don't want to have them think," says the young
musician who returns home in dark glasses and cowboy boots, "that I've
suddenly arrived out of the middle of nowhere completely deranged."[6]
Trouble is that the middle of nowhere, in the heartland, seems completely deranged, like Grant Wood's picture of American Gothic, the
farmer and his wife, going berserk, and all their children following after,
like Dick and Jane in the schoolbooks, neurotic from birth.

But the children do follow, and there seems to be in Shepard a desire
to make some last-chance rescue of the family, the past, the discredited
signs of human continuity. At the same time there is a desire to resurrect
the buried child which, in the play, is actually out in the cornfield,
mysteriously killed, it appears, for being the spawn of incest, and thus
the end of the family, which lives on the incest taboo. We can feel in the
drama that Shepard wants to undo the double bind, wanting to have it
both ways: breaking the Law on which the family depends *and* keeping
the institution intact.

Or, *is* it an institution, or something deeper than that, a kind of blood
rhythm? In the *Curse of the Starving Class*, Weston, the father, who was
never at home, never behaved like a father, never gave a damn for the
family, suddenly starts cleaning the filthy kitchen and washing everybody's dirty clothes, as if the clothes were still attached to their bodies:
"Like I knew you through the flesh and blood. Like our bodies were
connected and we could never escape that." The feeling of family was
animal, living under the same roof an urgency of nature, not social, and
he started feeling full of hope. "I'm starving," says his son Wesley (p.
187), staring into the refrigerator full of artichokes, undercutting the
sentiment which, one suspects, Shepard himself may be carrying too far,
like slipstreaming Salinas and going off a cliff. Nevertheless, as the
girlfriend Shelly says of Vince, the musician, in *Buried Child* (written
right after the *Curse*), "I mean [he] has this thing about his family now."
Shelly is visiting the old homestead for the first time. "I guess it's a new
thing with him. I kind of find it hard to relate to. But he feels it's

important. You know. I mean he feels he wants to get to know you all again. After all this time" (p. 86).

The reason Shelly finds it hard to relate to, the family, the past, the sense of continuity, is that she comes from Los Angeles, the place where everything starts from scratch or all over again, as if it had never happened. "Stupid country," says the grandfather, named Dodge, who is dying into the secret of the buried past. But even Shelly begins to feel it: "I don't know what it is," she says. "It's the house or something. Something familiar. Like I know my way around here. Did you ever get that feeling?" Dodge stares at her in silence, then says he never did, refusing both past and future (p. 110).

The truth is that Vince *can't* get to know them all again, not as they were, and he's soon ready—like a Vietnam vet who is being rejected at home for the crimes he was sent to commit—to blow the place up, which he does symbolically by splattering whiskey bottles on the porch. But Shelly now, not as laid back as before, wants some answers, about the family, about the past, about the pictures upstairs hanging on the wall, one of which looks like Dodge. "That isn't me!" he insists. "That never was me! This is me. Right here. This is it. The whole shootin' match, sittin' right in front of you." So far as he's concerned, if there was a past at all, it's not anything Shelly would understand. But she won't be deterred. "There's a picture of a farm. A big farm. A bull. Wheat. Corn." "Corn?" (p. 111). In an earlier scene, the mother Halie says to the older son with whom the incest may have been committed, "What's the meaning of this corn, Tilden!" "It's a mystery to me," he says. And so it is. Sometimes it's there, in the back lot, sometimes it's not, or it depends on who's looking. Halie either doesn't see it or refuses to see it, the old sustaining vegetation myth.

Tilden, however, was walking in the mud and looked up, and there it was, "this stand of corn. In fact, I was standing in it" (p. 75). He hypostatizes the corn, grounding himself in it, because he wants what it represents, the continuity of a myth which offers the possibility of a rebirth of the child he might have fathered, the buried child in the missing person, the life we haven't lived. Despite all the congenital emphasis upon experience in America, there is also the experience we have forgotten, the experience *of* our experience, which is the experience of continuity in a believable self, as well as the human family. I have a feeling, however, that Shepard sees the other side of the corn while trying to undo the double bind. I think he is punning too. There is the corn of myth and there is plain corn. Corniness. It might be overdone, pushed too far, like a bad joke—although the joke can be effective theater, even moving, as when Tilden husks the corn in the living room and gently spreads the husks over the body of his sleeping father, just before Bradley, the other son, comes in on his wooden leg and, with black electric clippers, brutally shaves his sleeping father's head.

Vivid as it is, this ritual perversion, it is the battle between Hoss and Crow that, for me, more memorably sticks in the craw. *The Tooth of Crime* bites right through the punk-rock glitter of its extravagant fiction, the occult/futurist/aboriginal fabulation of American life, with its corrosive exposure of the last-ditch illusions of a virulent frontiered self—a mean and ornery persona, many-tiered, masked, nothing but roles, with all the maniac aggression of the old individualistic desire, willing to kill or be killed, as if the abandoned and fractured ego were nuclear fission itself. I am talking about a rage so deep it's outside of gun control. As Ella says of Weston in the *Curse of the Starving Class,* refusing to believe that he will finally do it, "He's always going to kill somebody! Everyday he's going to kill somebody!" (p. 174). Weston doesn't do it. Some do, some don't. But some that say they're going to do it, do it, some of them very young and starving more than we know, like the rich man's son who shot at President Reagan and nearly killed him.

The screaming eagle is a killer with a desire to live outside the law, breaking all codes. But there is a false bravado in Hoss when he insists he's going to do it. For he is losing his secret power, the Force of *Star Wars,* its balance sheet, the real gold record killing power. The thing is he's hungry for a kill, crazy, he hasn't had a kill for months. Besides, he's a *marked* man, the Eyes tell him, reporting from Vegas. It's a gang shot coming up, the word is out, the Root-Force is slipstreaming his time. Problem is—despite the leather, studs, and Maserati—Hoss is old-fashioned in a world where there's a superstar a minute. He has too much humanistic scruple. He was once a beast of nature, a real "Cold killer Mama," as he says in a song, "powerglide supercharged down the line" (p. 211), but now—as compared to the real Gypsy Killer who's on the way, in "a '58 black Impala, fuel injected, bored and stroked, full blown Vet underneath" (p. 223)—he's relatively tame. As for the true genius killer to end them all, that's Crow, and the young people know it. "The kids are flocking to the Gypsy Kills." The gypsies know the ropes, says Hoss's astrological henchman Galactic Jack. "Rules is out. They're into slaughter straight off" (p. 213). They don't scruple for a moment, the codes going down the tubes.

I am speaking the supercharged demotic language of this flashy fuel-injected play, which is actually how the mortal combat takes place, as a war of style, like the word-wars of primitive tribes or the cursing contests of the Wild West. There is also something more at stake which is a liability to Hoss, and that's the meaning of history, about which Crow doesn't give a damn. The trouble with Hoss is that he partially identifies with Crow, weakening the venom he needs to do him in. No man, said Merleau-Ponty, ever strikes a single living face. But Hoss makes a fatal mistake, he gives Crow a human face not unlike his own. They are both outcasts, sharing a common history, with mutual enemies in the past. In one of the narratives in the play, Hoss tells of a savage fight with the jocks from his high school in the parking lot of a drive-in: "This was a class war," he says, with affluent kids from Arcadia with their T-birds and deuce coupes and chicks in their pedal pushers with bubble hairdos. "Soon as I saw that I flipped out. I found my strength. I started kickin' shit, man" (p. 226).

The gypsies break all the rules, but when the time comes for the two midnight cowboys to meet at High Noon in the OK Corral—or this weird sci-fi/punk equivalent—there is a referee with cheerleaders. It looks for a moment as if the fight is going to be reduced to parody, which is often the coward's way out, but the connections are too serious for that. For this is Big Business, like a heavyweight match at Caesar's Palace promoted by the mob in Las Vegas, all the gold records at stake. It is a matchup prepared by computers, and Hoss was briefed on the data bank. But there is no book on Crow, no signals on the data bank. Only he knows who he is, and we're not even sure of that. When the shit starts flying between them, Crow is immediately ahead on image. He seems an immaculate surface, while Hoss is turning inside out. He is dazzled by the surgical indifference and the cryptic glossolalia of Crow's style, a kind of double-talk of doublethink. The parody is there but honed to the sticking point. "Very razor. Polished. A gleam to the movements" (p. 230).

Hoss soon realizes that the Outside, mere image, *is* the Inside now. All the dazzle is only a mirror. There is a momentary comeback when Crow, his feathers ruffled in a quick exchange, drops his guard and the mirror appears to crack. But instead of taking advantage and going in for the kill, Hoss merely gapes at the mirror as if there were something human in sight: "There! Why'd you slip just then? Why'd you suddenly talk like a person?" (p. 232). Crow refuses to be a person more than once. He accelerates the attack. He takes over Hoss's persona, nothing but a mask himself. About the momentary lapse of power: "Sometimes the skin deceives" (p. 233). Crow dominates Hoss on style, while Hoss feels himself losing control. "Nothin takes a solid form. Nothin sure and final. Where do I stand! Where the fuck do I stand!" "Alone, leathers," says Crow (p. 245). Hoss can't even stand in the corn.

He goes down defeated because, unlike the implacable Crow, he *can't* go all the way. He can't live a lying image and he's not an inhuman machine, without blame or guilt, "Passed beyond tears. Beyond ache for the world. Pitiless" (p. 249). As everything slips away, he decides at last to lose big, true style in the true West, a gesture that can't be copied, reclaiming himself in his death, one clean shot, putting the gun in his mouth (to end this play about language). It seems to be what the world requires as it becomes more barbarous on image, more soulless behind the mask, a scene of galactic indifference whose power is without a name, the power of the Killer Machine. It is Shepard's toughest vision, and it isn't pushed too far. Hoss hasn't denied in losing that Crow is "riding in a state of grace" (p. 249). Shepard doesn't choose one over the other. He identifies with both. Nor does he let history run away into bargain basement myth with the easier shamanism of some other American plays.

"I did him a favor," says Crow. "Now the power shifts and sits till a bigger wind blows" (p. 252). The thought of that wind may cause some of us to sit and shiver, but while we're waiting for the shifting power, there is something to think about:

Crow is a figure of pure appearance who, if he's right in the final song, has "fooled the Ace of Spades" (p. 253). He is an image of Total Theater, what we used to think we wanted (and still do, if we're following, say, the anti-oedipal rhetoric of radical theory or some Performance Art). Some of the better minds of our generation have been telling us there is *nothing but appearance,* and we may be better for knowing that. Yet if so, and we get to like it—looking into the magic mirror of the magic marker—it might also be well to remember Hoss's best moment with Crow, when he can't help but admire the indifference: "I just hope you never see yourself from the outside. Just a flash of what you're really like. A pitiful flash" (p. 250). For, in this century, we have seen the kind of indifference we may never want to see again.

There is not the faintest flash of indifference in what Adrienne Kennedy does, although she does not do it so prolifically as Sam Shepard.

Her plays are fewer and short. So if I do not talk as extensively about her, it's not because I want to contribute to the indifference which persists. On the New York scene, they're now paying attention to women playwrights but still ignoring her. Yet she is surely the most original black dramatist of her generation and, along with Shepard, the most original, black or white.

But unlike Hoss in *The Tooth of Crime*, she put no premium on originality, certainly not in the supercharged risk-taking way that seemed instinctive with Shepard. Wherever the action was, as they said in the activist sixties, he was very much with it. That wasn't the case with Kennedy, whose search for authenticity was more private than that of the more militant and existential blacks. Nor is she entirely sure, as she rehearses the guilt, fantasies, and phobias of her secretly divided world, where sterility seems black, that she wouldn't rather be white. Whiteness is very much engrailed, maybe against her wishes, in her lyrical quest for roots.

She understands the racial pathology involved, the twisted morbidity of self-contempt nurtured by the long shameful history. She was nevertheless out of place in the emergence of Black Power when it erupted as a revolutionary defiance of the Killer Machine with a ruthlessly aggressive style of its own. Nor was she ever at home in the world of black jive, the argot appropriated by rock, that black sounding music made by whites. Her own language, learned in a bourgeois Negro family—her mother was a school teacher, her father a social worker—was more literary, unexplosive, more like litany and prayer, but not the holy rolling kind, the evangelical frenzy, the glossalalia or speaking in tongues. When I approached her about writing a play for us—when I was directing the Repertory Theater of Lincoln Center in New York in the mid-sixties—she reminded me of nothing so much as a kindergarten teacher, girlish and shy, awed by such attention.

The demeanor was deceptive. For she was hardly entirely out of it, neither the agitation over blackness nor the experimental impulse in the theater. In the *Funnyhouse of a Negro* (1962), written before the experiment had focused itself *as* activism, she is very conscious of the political turmoil, as well as the torment among blacks over the questions of religion, miscegenation, integration, black nationalism, the Muslims, the Panthers, Pan-Africanism, and the dubious nature of African roots later celebrated on television. These issues came up in her plays, however, as symbols, by indirection, in a highly idiosyncratic and expressionist style—something like a fusion of Tennessee Williams and Garcia Lorca:

the sensuous helplessness of Williams, the theater poetry of Lorca, with encouragement from Edward Albee, who was her teacher for a while. It is symptomatic of Kennedy's relationship to the black heritage that she never speaks as other black writers do, if only belatedly, of black models.

If it is clear that there was/is nothing militant about her, it is also apparent that powerlessness and death are obsessions. Moreover, she used the word *Negro* somewhat archaically even when white liberals were insisting on black. For the truth appears to be, as she sees it, that her experience is irredeemably Negro experience, *the desire for assimilation,* emotionally, intellectually, psychosexually, something more than integration, surely not the separatist aspect of black. If there is something regressive in that, politically recidivist, there is also, dramatically, something peculiarly moving—and moving in more blacks than would now admit it.

If lost innocence remains the theme of American drama, one has the feeling that Kennedy has never lost it, even at the movies, about which she has written in one of her most recent plays, *A Movie Star Has to Star in Black and White* (1976), in which one of her early characters performs with Bette Davis, Marlon Brando, Montgomery Clift, and Shelley Winters, and other stars alive and dead. "Each day I wonder with what or with whom can I co-exist in a true union?" Clara (Passmore) says,[7] still trying to pass and virtually speaking for Adrienne Kennedy. And if a true union is impossible it's because of the innocence, something virginal about her—though she is actually a dozen years older than Shepard, whom we still tend to think of as a young playwright, promising, even now that he has reached middle age. In Kennedy there seems to be no super-ambition, and only the promise of what she gives, the fragility of an innocence that was felt as a blemish from birth. It is not, however, only the blemish of being black—she is light-skinned, and that seems to be part of the problem—but the blemish of being a woman, a woman and black, so doubly cursed among the confusions of the starving class. The confusions of race and the confusions of gender are doubly doubled over, painfully so, in the fear not only of *being* but of *having been* raped: "Black man, black man, I never should have let a black man put his hands on me," says the Mother in the Funnyhouse. "The wild black beast raped me and now my skull is shining."[8]

I shall say more about the shining skull, the death's head, but it is the mortification of that inheritance which has made Kennedy so insular, I think, without the leaping audacities and dimension of Shepard. Hers is a plaintive, eccentric, and dramatically exquisite voice, recessive and stricken with horror, grave, not so much crying out as crying within. It is a far imaginative cry from the explosive outbursts of, say, Ed Bullins or even Imamu Amiri Baraka when he was still LeRoi Jones in *Dutchman,* the subway parable about the repressed ferocity of the blackness coming out. What comes out in Adrienne Kennedy emerges with reticence. Yet her obsessions are writ large in the confessional mirror of her autoerotic plays. We may find ourselves, however, looking a little askance, eyes squinting, startled by what we see, because it's a distorting mirror too, as in the funnyhouse with tricky corridors and dead ends of endless mirrors reflecting multiply upon the self, a beguiling and frightening time-warp with anachronism as the norm. On the confessional side of the silverless mirrors, there's a glimpse of Adrienne Kennedy in the figure of Queen Victoria at the *Funnyhouse of a Negro,* great ravens flying about her as if they came out of Poe, as she looks into the mirror, another kind of bird, weird, in plays of metamorphosing birds, the ravens changing into canaries, doves, and also into an owl, the solitary bird.

Kennedy has written a play called *The Owl Answers,* but no eagles. Given her obsession with powerlessness, one might suspect that the American eagle which, in Shepard, came swooping down upon the lamb's testicles, would either be an endangered species or already extinct in her. So far as there is a lamb, with its paschal suggestion of the Infant Jesus, that is also quickly distorted. The Jesus seen through Kennedy's warping mirrors is a hunch-backed yellow-skinned dwarf whose testicles are long gone and, like almost everybody in the funnyhouse, his hair as well, which he carries in a red paper bag, while the figure of the Bastard's Black Mother carries a little vial of blood. Blood of Jesus? menstrual blood? pubic hair? images woven into questions in a ceaseless psychic displacement as we remember the shining skull, as well as the old shame of black women who might have kinky hair. It is just such a Jesus, the yellow-skinned dwarf, as might have been imagined by a light-skinned Negress living among pitch-dark blacks who, in a queer distortion of history in the mirror, worship a white Father-God who has deflowered the half-black daughter whose Victorian values, and fear of sexuality, were imposed upon the jungle by a colonizing power.

Think now of the ravens flying around Queen Victoria, that black aviary of swarming desire. If it smells of something gothic, it is not entirely out of Poe, but out of Africa by way of Poe. For "the black man, black man" who is not only the biological father but the assassinated political father as well—Patrice Lumumba, hero of black nationalists and Pan-Africanists—is seen coming out of the jungle and knocking, knocking on his daughter's chamber door. We are once again, as in *The Raven*, back to the germinative incest supporting the American dream. Patrice Lumumba is described in the cast of characters as "One of Herselves," referring to Sarah the Negro who is also Queen Victoria who is also the Duchess of Hapsburg who is also the stunted Jesus. There is a circular crime in the raping of the half-white daughter by the black father. If it suggests the perverted sexuality brought to America by the African Negro, it also reminds us that his American religion was preceded in the jungles by proselytizing missionaries sent by "Queen Victoria Regina, Monarch of England" (*Funnyhouse*, p. 6), who also colonized through her literature the psyche of Adrienne Kennedy. It is a psyche formed by white culture which she finds not contemptible but beautiful, more maybe than black is beautiful, the poetry, the fictions, the achievements in music and art. The presence of Patrice Lumumba constitutes for Kennedy, then, an intimidating political pressure, against her grain, like the surrounding Black Power, invading her privacy, her withdrawal, and calling her back to history, not in the hallowed literary past but in the crude, agitating, and potentially violent present where the culture of the whites, however glorious, doesn't entirely seem to serve. Loving it as she does, it is even hostile, cold, indifferent to her desire.

We see that in *The Owl Answers* (1965) when "She who *is* Clara Passmore *who is the* Virgin Mary *who is the* Bastard *who is the* Owl" is imprisoned in the Tower of London, as was the "Bastard's Black Mother *who is the* Reverend's Wife *who is* Anne Boleyn,"[9] wife of the phallocratic father of the "bastard" Queen Elizabeth who reigned over England's greatest literary age. She who is Clara Passmore etc., including Adrienne Kennedy, identifies with Anne Boleyn who, reversing the designations, is the Reverend's Wife who is the Bastard's Black Mother, which is how the transformations of Kennedy's play proceed.

But "They" do not approve. When She who is Clara Passmore unfathomably visits England—as Adrienne Kennedy unfathomably did—she says:

> We came this morning. We were visiting the place of our ancestors, my father and I. We had a lovely morning, we rose in darkness, took a taxi past Hyde Park through the Marble Arch to Buckingham Palace, we had our morning tea at Lyons, then came out to the Tower. We were wander-

ing about the gardens, my father leaning on my arm, speaking of you,
William the Conqueror. (p. 252)

And because of the black man's distorted relation to the colonizing
power, in the lineage from William the Conqueror to Queen Victoria,
She who is Clara Passmore who is the Virgin Mary who is the Bastard
who is the Owl—the dramaturgy itself following this liturgical formula,
over and over as in a schizophrenic's dream—reaches poignantly into
the past: "My father loved you, William—" Whereupon they interrupt,
They including that other William, the greatest of all poets for Kennedy,
Shakespeare, and Chaucer too. They say, staring at her coldly: "If you
are his ancestor why are you a Negro? Yes, why is it you are a Negro if
you are his ancestor? Keep her locked there" (p. 252).

As Kennedy is locked, in a repetitive litany of unknowing in the
phallocratic Tower, deserted by her literary forbears because of her
kinky hair. It is germane that the word *kinky* has come to mean weird,
peculiar, even perversely erotic. And if there is something illicitly gothic
in Kennedy, it is not only because she is bookish, which she is, with her
references also to Poe, but she is unabatingly tautological, that is, locked
mesmerically, circularly, in the nightmare that for all the incursions of
Black Power simply won't go away—even down in the subway where, in
Dutchman, the repressed animosity came lethally out.

She who is Clara, coming up from the South, haunts the subway for
sexual experience. But when a Negro Man approaches her she rejects
him for the love of God, that white God who is supposed to be "Love
God," as the Bastard's Black Mother who is the Reverend's Wife rejects
the Reverend who is the Dead Father who is also Goddam Father who is
the Richest White Man in the Town, who seduced the Black Bastard's
Black Mother who is the Reverend's Wife but, when he approaches her
sexually, wards him off with a butcher knife which is the knife with
which, through Clara Passmore's "dream of love," is used upon the High
Altar by the Bastard's Black Mother to put an end to it all, the damnable circle of the recursive dream, including the vain looking for answers by She who is Clara who is the Bastard who is the Virgin who is the
Owl who says, "I call God and the Owl answers" (p. 266) with the same
old painful wisdom, that she really is a Negro with kinky hair that
she wants to tear off, an irredeemable screech owl, "Ow . . . oww"
(p. 268).

The subway is no escape for the Negro because, as in Kennedy's scenic conception, its screeching womb—*"sound of moving steel on the track"*—has taken the Negro neither out of the jungle nor away from *"the gates, the High Altar, the ceiling, and the Dome"* which, like St. Peter's and the Tower of London, are *in* the subway, as the sound of the steel on the track also contains at *"the most violent times of her experience . . . Haydn's Concerto for Horn in D (Third Movement)"* (p. 251). Such transformations are, dramaturgically, second nature to Kennedy, as are the surreal happenings and properties of her plays, the masks and skulls and magically metamorphosing birds. *"Objects on the stage,"* she says in her directions for *The Owl Answers, "(Bears, wigs, faces) should be used in the manner that people use everyday objects such as spoons or newspapers"* (p. 251). And when she says immediately after that the Tower Gate should be *black,* yet slam like a subway door, there is an animism in the Tower, an aboriginal impulse in the stagecraft, black magic, that causes us to wonder whether even subways, built by whites in an industrial world, came out of the jungle, too, unregenerately black.

The social analysis seems simplistic when you parse it, but the theatrical sophistication is innate and was conceptually disturbing when the plays were first produced. "You will assume I am trifling with you, teasing your intellect, dealing in subtleties," says the Negro who has stepped through the wall, maybe old maybe young, wild kinky hair, *"a faceless, dark character with a hangman's rope about her neck and red blood on the part that would be her face"* (*Funnyhouse,* p. 7). But we are warned that we are wrong by this hardly disguised avatar of Adrienne Kennedy, denying connections as the heartbreaking connections are made, and also explaining the nature of the play, its absence of cause and effect and elliptical procedures, "refusing to accept the fact that a statement has to come from an ordered force. . . . For the statement is the characters and the characters are my self,"[10] secretive, splitting, elusive, fading in and out of each other, apparitions rather than characters who all tell the same story, over and over, sometimes in unison—like the self-revealing narratives of Shepard's plays but even more compulsive, paradoxical, asking nothing but anonymity, yet confessionally direct:

> I am an English major, as my mother was when she went to school in Atlanta. My father majored in Social Work. . . . I write poetry filling page after white page with imitations of Edith Sitwell. It is my dream to live in rooms with European antiques and my Queen Victoria, photographs of

Roman ruins, walls of books, a piano, oriental carpets, and to eat my meals
on a white glass table. . . . I find it necessary to maintain a stark fortress
against recognition of myself. My white friends like myself will be shrewd,
intellectual and anxious for death. Anyone's death. I will mistrust them, as
I do myself. . . . But if I had not wavered in my opinion of myself, then my
hair would never have fallen out. (p. 9)

Queen Victoria and the others show up in her "small room on the top
floor of a brownstone in the West Nineties" where, playing through all
the transformations, she asks "nothing except anonymity" (p. 8).

The displacements and substitutions are close records of serious mental operations struggling through guilt and confusion to the closest
approximation of a coherence that is logically denied. This disjunct
mental state and the changes of costume, role, sexual identity are like
adulterate racial mixtures in the obsessive stream of thought, a form of
mental miscegenation. The desperate selves of the associative play are
sometimes projected in narrative and sometimes objectively there, but
no sooner does one feel located there are displacements of space and
time. All of what occurs, however, seems to occur in a suspended moment before death, and if there is a passing there is a passing into death,
when the dreadfulness of memory, history, experience are gathered into
the mind as in more aboriginal cultures—say, the *Bardo Thödol* or *The
Tibetan Book of the Dead*—where death is a living state, seamlessly coterminus with life.

There is very little conventional drama or external conflict in the
plays. What we have instead are the obsessional narratives. They move in
and out of focus in a memory flux, in sensibilities presumably black with
fantasies that are white, as if whites are dreaming blacks who are dying
into white. If characters speak alternately, they are not so much com-
municating as communing, in alternate visions of an incessantly divided
and dividing consciousness. The speeches are monologic, semichoral,
autistic, with the effect of ritual and incantation. What really moves in
memory, past the barbarousness of the jungle and the tawdry religious
colonizing, is the royalty and elegance of a remembered (white) past,
garnered from literature, inscribed on black skin. The poignancy comes
from the double irony that the present fantasizing of the Negro is not
the present fantasy of the white, but retrograde, as if inscribed not by
white history but the *romance* of white history, the interminable
bastardizing of the dream.

There is a kind of epigraph to *A Rat's Mass* (1965) which might be voiced in performance:

> *Rosemary was the first girl we ever fell in love with. She lived next door behind a grape arbor her father had built. She often told us stories of Italy and read to us from her Holy Catechism book. She was the prettiest girl in our school.*[11]

Rosemary, too, is an avatar of the playwright, *her* fantasy, in a period when we are busily deconstructing the authorial voice. The innocence is disarming. Rosemary's physical attire tells the hybrid and sordidly miscegenated story. She *"wears a Holy Communion dress and has worms in her hair"* (p. 353).

"Colored people are not Catholics," *asks* Rosemary in a speech of Brother Rat, then answers herself, saying, "Well, I am, I am a descendant of the Pope and Julius Caesar and the Virgin Mary" (p. 354). And then, in the mumbo-jumbled historicism of a surrealistic seance, the Nazis are invoked as something like childhood demons, boogeymen, who persist through adolescence and adulthood and keep us from being our brother's keepers and consummating our loves. There is a mental breakdown in the drama that is not posited in a character but in history itself, so that what is suffered when the war starts is the derangement of persisting love: "Every sister bleeds and every brother made her bleed" (p. 353), going down the childhood (playground) slide like a second Fall, which is also where the babies come forth. Or they would, were it not for the brutalization of the War, which aborts them. About that horror there is a childish purity in the play, finding it incomprehensible, the Communion wine turning to blood and the children hiding in the hospital in order not to be caught by the Nazis. But, like the ominous specters of ghost stories, "The Nazis are going to get you" (p. 354).

Instinctively, Brother Rat and Sister Rat appeal to the image of Rosemary for salvation from the threat of the Nazis and death on the battlefields of unwanted history: "Rosemary atone us," they pray, "take us beyond the Nazis. We must sail to the Capitol. Atone us. Deliver us unto your descendants." It is not African roots, then, that constitute their image of redemption, *at-one*ment, but the archaic romance of Western tradition. Brother Rat and Sister Rat fear punishment for incest as well, but there is no redemption in Rosemary, who says stonily in her Communion dress: "I will never atone you. Perhaps you can put a bullet in your head with your father's shotgun, then your holy battle will be done" (p. 354). Compared to this indifference, Shepard's Crow, for all his iciness, is a man of deep compassion.

There is a painful desire for the renewal of the Holy Music and the return to childhood before the slide, but now it appears "there will always be rat blood on the rat walls of our rat house just like the blood that came onto the slide," with the Fall, the blood knowledge, the menstrual blood in the Bastard's Black Mother's vial. The vision of a new Capitol beyond the rat head also persists, where Brother Rat (Blake) and Sister Rat (Kay) will sing. "But no within my hot head I see the dying baby Nazis and Georgia relatives screaming girls cursing boys a dark sun and my grave. I am damned. No . . ." (p. 355). Here, in the antiphonal agitations of desire for redemption there *is* the evangelistic rhythm of black Baptism, the autisms of dispossession, desire dancing itself in the play of words, over and over, though the words are not dissolved into desire like the speaking of tongues, but rather lyrically sustained with a kind of cultured grace which is a legacy of the other tradition.

Kay is brought home from the state hospital, but Brother Rat cannot get Rosemary out of his mind. He (Blake) cannot be his sister's keeper. "God is hanging us and shooting us," while Sister Rat remembers the time before she bled, "before descending bombs and death on my Capitol we walked the Palatine—we went to the movies [where for blacks and whites alike, that mothering source, all fantasies now arise]. Now the Germans and Caesar's army are after us, Blake" (p. 355)—and the crossed temporality of desire is, indeed, like that of William Blake, without the transfiguring glory, only the Nazis coming, and no more sounds of shooting in the distance. Through all this there has been a Holy Procession, silently watching—Jesus, Joseph, Mary, two wise men, and a Shepherd. The Holy Procession becomes a firing squad, and the pursued rats, squealing, extinct. Only Rosemary remains.

What one may object to in all these transformative visions of Adrienne Kennedy is that her politics exists almost entirely in the unconscious, with its cannibalistic operations of dismembered being. In this politics of the unconscious, the Nazis are not so much an objective historical phe-nomenon as emblems of an anterior demonism, dreadful and final, but going back to childhood, as if arrested there. You may, therefore, admire the passion and imagination of the plays but reject them for this apolitical naiveté. Certainly during the protests of the sixties, and even now, cruder political constructs were preferred; their bolder versions of black and white were more in vogue. Whether it was a superior politics is, however, an age-old question not so easily disposed of, no more than the aboriginal gothic—with its distressing innocence—in the recessively fitful aging of the American dream.

NOTES

1. *Time,* 21 October 1946, cover.

2. Sam Shepard, *Curse of the Starving Class,* in *Seven Plays,* intro. Richard Gilman (New York: Bantam, 1981), p. 171. All further references to the play, in this edition, appear in the text.

3. Patti Smith, "Sam Shepard: 9 Random Years [7 + 2]," in *Angel City, Curse of the Starving Class and Other Plays,* intro. Jack Gelber (New York: Urizen, 1978), pp. 241–42.

4. *Action,* in *Angel City,* p. 133.

5. *The Tooth of Crime,* in *Seven Plays,* p. 206. Subsequent references appear in the text.

6. *Buried Child,* in *Seven Plays,* p. 85. Subsequent references appear in the text.

7. *A Movie Star Has to Star in Black and White,* in *Wordplays 3: New American Drama,* eds. Bonnie Marranca and Gautam Dasgupta (New York: Performing Arts Journal Publications, 1984), pp. 55–56. The play was done as a work-in-progress by Joseph Chaikin at the Public Theater in New York on November 5, 1976, but then was unavailable until the rescue operation of *PAJ*'s "new" play series. The line is also quoted by Ruby Cohn in her section on Kennedy—an exception to the rule of neglect—in *New American Dramatists: 1960–1980* (New York: Grove, 1982), p. 114.

8. *Funnyhouse of a Negro* (New York: Samuel French, 1969), p. 7. Subsequent references appear in the text.

9. *The Owl Answers,* in *New American Plays,* ed. William M. Hoffman, vol. 2 (New York: Hill and Wang, 1968), p. 250. Subsequent references in the text.

10. This part of the Negro's monologue has been cut from the text as published by Samuel French, which I have been quoting from otherwise.

11. *A Rat's Mass,* in *The Off Off Broadway Book,* ed. Albert Poland and Bruce Mailman (New York: Bobbs-Merrill, 1972), p. 353. Subsequent references appear in the text.

FOUR

THE BLOODY SHOW AND THE EYE OF PREY

> Of course, there is no need of a signifier
> to be a father, any more than to be dead,
> but without a signifier, no one would
> know anything about either state of being.
>
> —Lacan, "On the Possible Treatment
> of Psychosis"

I didn't propose the title of this session, "Beckett and Deconstruction," though fortune disposes in ways that might have been foreseen. For I became a father again as I started to work on this paper. I am not speaking, as they do in deconstruction, of the paternity of the text. The major obsession of poststructuralist thought is, to be sure, the question of *origins,* the allure and (re)lapse of beginnings, the illusory *subject* of the instituting trace. But peace to Derrida! The simple fact is that my wife gave birth to a baby. I'm sure it was she, that much at least, and I'm sure I was there, though Saussure and Lévi-Strauss and Lacan and Barthes have taught us to beware of pronouns.

The destined morning began with an image that might have been godfathered by Beckett, who is agonized by pronouns—the unclotting preface to labor they call "the bloody show." And then, like the spastic phrases out of the Mouth of *Not I,* the contractions, and several hours before Thanksgiving, yes, "almost to the tick," the predicted day, "out . . . into this world . . . this world . . . tiny little thing . . . before its time . . . in a godfor- . . . what? . . . girl: . . . yes . . . tiny little girl . . . into this . . . out into this . . . ."[1] But the passage—were I to continue through the recursive strips of its propulsive and aphasic thought—throws up problems, first of all about the echolocation of its "drifting" and labial subject— "what? . . . who? . . . no! . . . she!"—which/who, "if not exactly . . . insentient . . . insentient," nevertheless "came and went," not knowing "what position she was in . . . imagine! . . . what position she was in!" (*Not I*, p. 15). But as you try to imagine you find yourself moving, not altogether voluntarily, into the "thin air" of conjecture between "this world" she came into and "this world"—the signifiers slipping in a site of becoming, *this* world or *her* world or, as the emerging subject is embraced and swaddled in perception, *my* world, perhaps, "without solution of continuity," as the stage directions say of the voices of *That Time* (*Ends and Odds,* p. 28).

It's a little strange to watch a birth with Beckett on your mind. As a fetal monitor he leaves something to be desired. The ontological vigilance is accurate to a fault, true, a chastening asepsis. But once the tiny little thing is out—footprints taken as the assurance of an unexchangeable self—there is the problem of assenting to Beckett's vision, not only the pronominal shifts of an unstable identity, the metonymic corrosions and macerations "up to the mouth,"[2] by which the footprints seem erased, but the clawing and entropic bloody show itself: the running sores, the wounds, the risible mutilations, the excrementa, the paraplegics, the lactating abortions, the stumps, the stanchers, the skulls, the skulls, the leak in the fontanelles, "never but the one the first and last time curled up worm in slime when they lugged you out and wiped you off" (*That Time,* p. 31), the cruelly extorted pensum of a minimal quantum of being. Or even less, as in the purgatorial mathematics of *The Lost Ones,* the combinatory sets of annihilation, "in cold darkness motionless flesh,"[3] if not exactly insentient, still, the annals of *rigor mortis.*

"What I'd like now," said the narrator as far back as *Molloy,* the pages already accumulating in mortification, "is to speak the things that are left, say my good-byes, finish dying. They don't want that."[4] But since the Nobel Prize apparently they do. I remember that time when his plays were first performed and people who now swear by Beckett—including actors in my company who refused to be in *Godot*—were revolted by his vision. Were they right to begin with? "Nothing to be done"?[5] At the political impasse of postmodern thought, one can certainly understand the desire to go "Beyond Beckett"—but not, as in a recent conference, to those who, following after, are derivative and regressive, already passé. There is, however, the sort of feeling suggested by John Ashbery, who concedes with Beckett that there are no new stories and that, while he wants to believe there is "a lot of life to look forward to,"[6] the one who can look forward remains, like Didi and Gogo at the end of each act, or Clov at the ending or the beginning, motionless. Still, nothing to be done. For Ashbery, it is the last humanistic scruple which is useless, the nostalgia, "the difference between now and other hard times [being] that now there was no comfort in remembering scenes of past unhappiness, indeed he was quite sure there had never been any, and was therefore quite content to remain as he had been, staring uncertainly into the fire as though looking for a sign, a portent, but in reality thinking of nothing at all."[7] Here we have a dispassionate postmodern permutation of Beckett—another is a facile postabsurdist parody passing as portent—with the rhythm somehow becalmed.

The difference is the pensum, curled up worm in slime, with the penalty of remembrance ineluctably unnamable and maybe not-I, "but the brain still . . . still sufficiently . . . oh very much so!" (*Not I*, p. 17). As for the earlier revulsion against Beckett, whether by thinking of nothing at all or thinking not at all, over the years the slime has dissolved in deference or reverence and we've become far more accommodating to the crawling or catatonic humor of repetitively dystrophic flesh with its "fatuous little light . . ." (*Lost Ones*, p. 20). If "totalitarians like Lukács," according to Adorno, "hate in Beckett what they have betrayed,"[8] some of us may love in Beckett what, in that fatuous light, we cannot betray because we never deeply believed it, nor had "no notion who it was saying what you were saying whose skull you were clapped up in whose moan had you . . ." (*That Time*, p. 32). Even on the farthest Left, Beckett is almost universally admired now for the elegiac integrity of the inexhaustible gospel of the unexpurgated mess with its liturgy of humiliations. While it may now be taken for granted, often by a ready laughter that simply laughs it off, it is still an appalling vision—as Didi said, "AP-PALLED"—and not even the subsiding logorrhea and glyphic serenity of, say, . . . *but the clouds* . . ., makes it easier to take to heart.

Especially not for the moment, betrayal be damned, with a baby in the crib, who by all rights should be a sign, a portent, though probably of nothing you intended, and about whom you want to forget the "lesson" of *The Unnamable* which may be inseparable from the pensum, "too hastily proclaimed, too hastily denied" (p. 31). Or as Beckett puts it in *A Piece of Monologue*, rubbing the lesson in: "Birth. Birth was the death of him [who? . . . him . . . of her?]. Ghastly grinning ever since. Up at the lid to come. In cradle and crib. At such first fiasco,"[9] or even before.

It isn't that Beckett, who has suffered not only from the brain but from glaucoma, sees errantly with his "eye of flesh" (to which by the way—many years ago, before using the phrase in *The Lost Ones* [p. 31]—he challenged me to "produce" my children whom I kept promising he would sometime meet. It was almost as if he feared they might be a fiction or delusion, like the child out the window of *Endgame*). It is rather that he has an immaculate affinity for the inaugural fault, the child abuse of mere existence. Which is what makes the existentialism of Beckett, or his sense of the Absurd, not merely a passing fancy of which you can say it's time to go beyond. For the Absurd in Beckett, unlike Sartre or Camus, or Ionesco, is neither a dramatized doctrine nor formulaic with intention, but something to which meaning surrenders like the absence of meaning, as in the "breaking of the waters" into labor or the metabolic rhythms of his prose. What is canonical in Beckett, arising from the traumatizing image of the recurrency of birth, is the enfevered famished craving of what's to come, and come again, another kind of contraction, "all part of the same . . . keep an eye on that too . . . corner of the eye . . . all that together" (*Not I*, p. 21), the diminuendo of gratification, not-I, lessness, as if abraded by the eye, the look of being looked at, for the "Sucklings who having no longer to suck huddle at gaze. . . ." Or—another of what he calls "Picturesque detail," keep an eye on that too—"a mite who strains away," mechanically clasped at its mother's breast, "in an effort to turn its head and look behind" (*Lost Ones*, p. 30), as if in some reflexive postnatal longing for what, empowering an impoverished future, remains in the womb of the past. This nesting stare of the scopic drive, the desire to see the dimly remembered, regressive as it is, may be itself the suggestive model, "the axis about which the sensation pivots," of "the model of duplication *(whose integral purity has been retained because it has been forgotten)*," as Beckett says in the essay on *Proust*.[10]

But in the self-opposing annular rings of the "teeming precinct" of the lost, "such tiny ones are comparatively few." As for the lost one within us all, from biblical and romantic tradition, the tinier little thing within, asleep, who remembers what we forget: "None looks within himself where none can be" (*Lost Ones*, p. 30). And the implication seems to be that like the trace of origins itself the wordless child—poorly duplicated, *re*produced—is abandoned at birth to its drifting *appearance* in life, which is to say an economy of death, *always already* (to use the Derridean phrase) in arrears, overdraft, or default. "So true it is that when in the cylinder [birth canal? teeming brain? O world?] what little is possible is not so it is merely no longer so and in the least the less the all of nothing if this notion is maintained." Which notion appears to be the (other) recurrency which is born of death, dominion of *reproduction,* with its "devouring" and "unceasing eyes" (pp. 29, 33) which "suddenly start to search afresh as famished as the unthinkable first day until for no clear reason they as suddenly close again or the head falls" (p. 32).

Even before this notion is maintained, one might have misgivings about reproduction in this world which, like a breeder reactor whose core is toxic waste, has converted the ancient myth of pollution into ecological fact. One might also have second thoughts about what has become, since I last had a child, a new liturgy—in the books on pregnancy and the classes on reproduction—about the lovely experience of the joy of birth. As a very savvy, solicitous, and indefatigable nurse with something of the gaiety of Winnie said when, with great labor of her own, the bearing down had bottomed out, "Let's face it, it's the pits." So, too, there was the appalling moment when the bloody head appeared and instead of a starry *jouissance,* as in the discourse of desire, it seemed hideous and deformed. I took the skull for the placenta, as if the show had grown egregious and the appearance were reversed. I was not at all consoled for that terrifying instant by Derrida's exergue to "Writing Before the Letter," in which we are told that the future "can only be proclaimed, *presented,* as a sort of monstrosity."[11] Nor by the conclusion of his essay "Structure, Sign, and Play," when he points to the irreducible difference between the "structuralist thematic of broken immediacy" with its sadness and guilt about loss, resembling Beckett's, and "the *seminal* adventure of the trace," in which Beckett is engaged, but "which is no longer turned toward the origin" as it maintains the notion of "full presence, the reassuring foundation, the origin and the end of play."[12]

Now that seems an attractive notion, the reassuring foundation, when you've just had a child, the very promise of play supplanting the bloody show which has been, through the entire history of our oedipal tradition, with its archives of power and domination, the remembered legacy of the aboriginal sacred drama. The notion of play has been hypostatized in postmodern thought, not only in deconstruction, as a refusal of power, a sort of new testament of polymorphous being, "outside time without extension," as Lucky says in his monstrous enunciation of the breakdown of Western metaphysics, the apathia athambia aphasia separated from the divine, and the repetition of its redoubtable image. Play is recursive but unrepeated, *presented* not *re*-presented. "[As] a result of the labors left unfinished" (*Godot,* p. 28), and the all-consuming recession of the phallogocentric source, there is the notion of a pregnancy *without birth,* and thus the end of reproduction, the *structure of repetition* which *is* the economy of death.

That other model of repetition, or duplication, whose internal purity has been retained because forgotten, is really the subject not of the postmodernist ethos but of *modernist* desire which may reappear, as for Proust, through involuntary memory. It overcomes as an epiphany "the poisonous ingenuity of Time in the science of affliction" which makes of life, through the initiation of birth, a "retrospective hypothesis." The ego which is deconstructed and *dis*-seminated through a seemingly perpetual present in the gratuitousness of play is, in this hypothesis, suspended in the fluency of its own desire, repressed, "the seat of a constant process of decantation, decantation from the vessel containing the fluid of past time, agitated and multicoloured by the phenomena of its hours" (*Proust,* pp. 4–5). If Beckett, despite himself, is still turned toward origins or the moment *forgotten as an appearance* in the fluid of future time, from things about to *disappear*—like the sails of the herring fleet or all that rising corn, the mordancy rising with the myth of rebirth, all that *corniness*—he turns away in time, like the painter, or engraver: "Appalled."[13] So, within the very dispensation of play into which he has beguiled others, collapsing subject and object—"Me . . . to play" (*Endgame,* p. 2)—he turns away from the simple-minded mythologizing of play, with its apparent relief from too much consciousness, disallowing play as a mode of salvation. Hamm: "Use your head, can't you, use your head, you're on earth, there's no cure for that!" (p. 68). Though it's playful to remember, as Didi does, that one of the thieves was saved, a reasonable percentage, for Beckett, like Clov, the dominant percentage is *zero* and, finally, it is the obsessional play within the play which, actively forgetting, causes us to remember that play, agitated and multicoloured by the phenomena of *its* hours, is inevitably deadly.

So, too, in Derrida, try as he will, there's no relief in the play of mind from the impediment of the Logos, that history of being which desires to be completely history, *as being.* There is no escape from the movement of the *sign,* the mark of consciousness, the rustle, the murmur, the whisper, the tumult, "now this . . . this . . . quicker and quicker," as consciousness erupts metonymically from the Mouth of *Not I,* no escape from "the words . . . the brain . . . flickering away like mad . . . quick grab and on . . . nothing there" (p. 22), except the being "produced as history only through the logos, and is nothing outside of it," as Derrida says; "all this clearly indicates that fundamentally nothing escapes the movement of the signifier and that, in the last instance, the difference between signified and signifier *is nothing*" (*Of Grammatology*, pp. 22–23).

The movement of deconstruction is, then, unavoidably through the remains of a metaphysics that *inhabits* our structures of thought, even when they think themselves exempt, "as the limitation of the sense of being within the field of presence . . . produced as the domination of a linguistic form" (p. 23), even when they think themselves nonverbal. But as with the waiting for Godot on the selvedge of speech, as if it were the circumference of silence, it is not just the inhabiting but *how* the inhabiting, inhabiting "*in a certain way, because one always inhabits, and all the more when one does not suspect it*" (p. 24). That is what Paul de Man means, I suppose, by the blindness of insight which is, as with the Oedipus inhabited by an identity unknown, the insight of blindness.

The enterprise of deconstruction proceeds in a retrospective hypothesis, *against its own desire*, with such insight. It is forced to borrow— without any certainty about their "elements and atoms" (p. 24)—the resources of subversion, strategic and economic (*borrowing structurally*, that is), *from what it inhabits*, and is inhabited *by*, the ontotheology of Western metaphysics. It thus falls prey to its own work, self-subverted, like the structure of Beckett's fiction, which might have been written at the eroding margins of self-observing thought, with afflicted eyes, and the blood on Jocasta's brooch. For it is the incest taboo which, according to Derrida, following Freud (studied by Beckett), may be the source of all thought, that detour from the memory of gratification, "designed to leave in the domain of the unthinkable" the scandal that makes thought possible, "the *origin* of the prohibition of incest" (*Writing and Difference*, p. 284; emphasis mine). Lest the scandal of thought congeal in the blood before it *is* thought, the *activity* of deconstruction requires, like Beckett's fiction, "the necessity of [a] *trick of writing*" (*Of Grammatology*, p. 24) which is irreducible, fluent, yet hesitates, backtracks, erases its own thought, leaving the erasures there *(sous rature)*, with a tremulously caustic indecisiveness. That irresolution is not incoherence. It is an inscription of what Derrida calls *undecidability*. It opens up the structure *to play*, that is, "the structurality of structure" (*Writing and Difference*, p. 278) which, in order "to be thought radically" must play "without security" (p. 292)— that first defensive instinct and last-ditch illusion of power.

So it is that, in Beckett and deconstruction, *powerlessness* is the disseminating proposition and impelling force of the seminal adventure of

the trace. It works by *aporias,* as in *The Unnamable,* but always questioning
whether it can be, as Beckett writes, "[by] aporias pure and simple? Or by
affirmations and negations invalidated as uttered, or sooner or later?
Generally speaking. There must be other shifts" (p. 3) in the infinite play
of signifiers which moves toward meanings that are always receding or
vanishing, and disremembers where it began. What we see in all of
Beckett's writing is the trembling of perception at degree zero on the
edge of its extinction. According to Derrida, the trembling is appropriate to all post-Hegelian thought which, with the scopophilia of unceasing
eyes, *speculating,* inevitably displaces itself and all it gazes upon. The
quest of eyes begins, with suckling and mite (the power of a nonpower?)
at the mother's breast, turning its head and looking as if, having no
longer to suck, the suckling were proleptic and the future came from
behind. It's as if the child were turning on a crack of the dialectic, the
Hinge *(La Brisure),* which in the Derridean usage *articulates* difference,
out of the *imprint* of a language that seems to be prior to speech, which is
"originarily passive," but with an undeterrable passivity that is pointing
to the past *(Of Grammatology,* pp. 65–66).

"*Where and how does it begin . . .?*" asks Derrida. What is disturbing
about the question of origin is that it carries with it a metaphysics of
presence, the illusion of an absoluteness which is only the ubiquitous
trace, always already subverted by the limitlessness of play (p. 50). "The
trace is not only the disappearance of origin—within the discourse that
we sustain and according to the path that we follow [Beckett and Der-
rida] it means that the origin did not even disappear, that it was never
constituted except reciprocally by a nonorigin, the trace, which thus
becomes the origin of the origin" (p. 60). In this self-enfolded and
tautological path, curled up worm in the history of Western thought,
what undoes the fiction of metaphysical presence is *play,* swinging on the
Hinge, "the *pure* movement which produces difference," whose "*(pure)
trace*" is the (in)famous *différance* (p. 62). Derived in part from the
metapsychology of Freud, *différance* is an economic concept of the writing of the unconscious. It has the double meaning of difference and
deferral, putting off closure or cathexis in the sensible plenitude of play,
as in erotic play, *fore*play, that produces meaning which makes of play—
seen in theatrical terms—not the captivated subject of the older bloody
show, and the structure of power that goes with it, but the *condition* of a
postoedipal plenitude. If, then, in Derrida's patricidal aversion to origins, it seems at times as though play itself—displacing the dead letter of
the oedipal text with a dystopia of signs—has become a Law unto itself

like the originary Word, the text in the beginning, quaquaquaqua, he invariably pulls back from that *mis*construction with an erasure. Or in the trace, the slime, the sticking point of play, *equivocates.*

Between the dream of a playful plenitude—that reassuring foundation—and the desire for the unattainable presence of a disappearing origin, Derrida believes there really is no choice. It is rather a question of trying to work out some navigable common ground between absence and presence, the irreducible difference between the exile from origins and the affirmation of play in the odyssey of the trace. Which returns us—as if the Hinge were also a hymen—*to* the bloody show. For here "there is a kind of question, let us call it historical, whose *conception, formation, gestation, and labor* we are only catching a glimpse of today. I employ these words, I admit, with a glance toward the operations of childbearing—but also with a glance toward those who, in a society from which I do not exclude myself, turn their eyes away when faced by the as yet unnamable which is proclaiming itself and which can do so, as is necessary when a birth is in the offing, only under the species of the nonspecies, in the formless, mute, infant, and terrifying form of monstrosity" (*Writing and Difference,* p. 292).

Like the first impression of my child's emerging head. That was a case where apocalyptic metaphor yielded for me, against my usual instincts, to simpler medical prophylaxis. For when they grabbed the inverted slimy body and did wipe it off it was—whether or not this notion is maintained—quite another thing. It was, nevertheless, a sort of postmodern delivery. They gave me the scissors and I cut the umbilical cord. But even with that premature fulfillment of the doxology of desire, cutting it sooner than later, there was no guarantee of the disappearance remembered at the beginning of *Not I.* For, so far so good and so far as I can tell, the parents are known, *he* not vanished, that is, father still here, in the flesh, before you (I think), at least the Name of the Father (as the Lacanian feminists say), and the "speechless infant" is not unloved, not "spared that," but much loved (I think), for the time being, at least, appropriately for a tiny little thing born at Thanksgiving and no older than the Christmas season. Thus far, whatever the broken immediacy, the phallocratic order seems intact. And speaking of Lacan, the famous mirror phase, I can see by looking in her eyes the old oedipal reflection—although both Lacan and Beckett, reflecting this world in this world through the bloody show, locate the mirroring in the mother, a more enigmatic source.

"I am in my mother's room. It's I who live there now. I don't know how I got there" (*Molloy*, p. 7). From the very beginning of *Molloy*, that exacerbation of a beginning—the mother "lived near the shambles" (p. 28), but "It was the beginning, do you understand?" (p. 8)—the rhythms of Beckett's perceptions are insidious. And with that deconstructive trick of writing, there is no chance of a beginning that is not a beginning again. What appears to be the mother is polysemously at the controls. The words fly up, the thought remains below, as in the operations of the unconscious which has no beginning or end: "the within, all that inner space one never sees, the brain and heart and other caverns where thought and feeling dance their sabbath, all that too quite differently disposed" (p. 50). The insidiousness of perception which then seems out of control—as when the Ghost appears in the Closet—affects not only what is being seen but *seen-as-being*, as if *to be* is only to *be seen*. But it's as if it can only happen in the reconstructed vicinity of the originary trace (thus the mother's Closet), as by the involuntary memory of the interpretation of a dream. Beckett observes the valuelessness, for Proust, of voluntary memory as an instrument of evocation. It "provides an image," he says, "as far removed from the real as the myth of our imagination or the caricature furnished by direct perception" (*Proust*, p. 4. This is what makes the assumed clarity of any congregation of spectators, huddled at gaze, a dubious proposition, a caricature of a caricature. The accuracy of an audience in a consensus of perception is to be counted on only if you assume that one error cancels another.) In the essay on Proust, Beckett writes that "our vulgar perception is not concerned with other than vulgar phenomena. Exemption from intrinsic flux in a given object does not change the fact that it is the correlative of a subject that does not enjoy such immunity. The observer infects the observed with his own mobility. Moreover, when it is a case of human intercourse, we are faced by the problem of an object whose mobility is not merely a function of the subject's, but independent and personal: two separate and immanent dynamisms related by no system of synchronisation" (pp. 6–7).

But they are synchronised, to that extent, in the contagiousness of the infection: there is always a wavering in the eye of flesh. If it makes the seeing indecisive, it also causes a waver. Doubled over in the contagion, it impairs the vision too. There is no immunity from the mobility even when, to begin with—before the declensions of the prospect—there is a promise in the air, the distance, "without solution of continuity," between the seer and the seen. "Nice fresh morning," Beckett writes in

From an Abandoned Work, before the precipitation of rage, often sooner than later, in the increments of perception, "bright too early so often. Feeling really awful, very violent. The sky would darken and the rain fall and go on falling, all day, till evening. Then blue and sun again a second, then night." It is the brevity of the sun, the incessancy of the rain, night's plenitude, and the degree of violence, "feeling all this," that causes the narrator to stop and turn, looking with "bowed head" for "snail, slug or worm," the nearly immobile recursiveness of their slimy traces. There is great love in his heart too, he says, "for all things still and rooted. . . ." For there is a dread of motion, "all moving things," drawing us into perception with the cruelty of intrinsic flux, "no, no mercy."[14] Far from the shambles, it appears, it is still the mother who prefigures motion, the pain of indeterminacy, the very frailty of which is intimidating and seductive: "my mother white and so thin I could see past her (piercing sight I had then) into the dark of the room, and on all that full the not long risen sun, and all small because of distance, very pretty really the whole thing," which in its wholeness or seeming fullness endures for only a moment when perception—as it unmercifully does—fails.

"[If] only she could have been still and let me look at it all. No, for once wanted to stand and look at something I couldn't with her waving and fluttering and swaying in and out of the window as though she were doing exercises . . ." (*Abandoned Work,* p. 40). The word is somewhat unexpected, but the exercises are the gestural substance of the trick of writing in the perception of Beckett that is inhabited by and inhabits the activity of deconstruction: "one glimpse and vanished, endlessly, omit," as in *Imagination Dead Imagine.* The omission is an omen in the whiteness of the rotunda which encircles death and birth like "a ring as in the imagination the ring of bone" (*First Love,* p. 63). There is a momentary ring of hardness in the image like the materials of the imagination which, dead, can only be imagined even when, as in the rotunda, it has the apparent exactitude of geometric form. The measures are a decoy like the allure of seeming symbols with which, as invariably as Kafka, Beckett teases us out of thought. He does so with the semblance of ontology or the stuff of subjectivity or the suckling of remembrance— "the white speck lost in whiteness" (p. 66), like some truth in the mother's milk—or the hymeneal romance of nature glimpsed once and then omitted from the imagining of the ring of bone.

Between the disappearance of the "[i]slands, waters, azure, verdure" and "the light that makes all so white no visible source"; between the

binaries thus conceived: nature/culture, light/dark, body/mind, spirit/
matter, hot/cold, male/female, depth/surface, perceiver/perceived and,
in that perceiving, the endless *gradients,* the rotunda, the illusory fabric
of death/birth; between them, "No way in, go in, measure. . . . Go back
out, move back, the little fabric vanishes, ascend, it vanishes, all white in
whiteness [like the mother white and thin], descend, go back in" (p. 63).
What "experience shows" in its repetitions in the prose is that experience
consists of this movement of perception at the meridian of apprehension, the membrane (brain?) in the pelvic ring of bone, where cerebral is
(con)genital, derived from Ceres, goddess of grain, birth, verdure, all
that rising corn: "Such variations of rise and fall, combining in countless
rhythms. . . . The extremes alone are stable" (p. 64) like the *appearance* of
an object in a "temporary calm," always disrupted in the rotunda where
things if not constructed are only as observed. Yet in the exhaustive
enumeration of the appearances between, it is the appearance of an
apparent stability at the extremes which, like the names we give to the
binaries, "makes the world still proof against enduring tumult. Rediscov-
ered miraculously after what absence in perfect voids it is no longer
quite the same, from this point of view, but there is no other" (p. 65).

The sighting of the little fabric, the membranous meridian between
absence and presence—the hymen in the Hinge—remains "quite as
much a matter of chance, its whiteness merging in the surrounding
whiteness" (p. 64), that is, the threshold of being/becoming or the origin
of imagination in the trace of consciousness or the initiatory difference
between memory and desire or—keeping those psychophysical exercises
of the mother in mind—all that is *not* theater, the site of appearance in
the ring of bone, and the waving and fluttering and swaying which *is,* the
incipience of performance. It is this exercise of perception in the deconstruction of appearances which is the subject of expanding consciousness in the most abbreviated of Beckett's plays, which have always
been about consciousness. Nor is there a moment in his fiction that is not
subject to the tireless scrutiny—somewhere between theory/theater, the
little fabric vanishing—of the eye of flesh. The gaze that begins when the
suckling having no longer to suck turns to *speculation* is compulsive and
unrelieved. What he says in *The Lost Ones* of the long period of redden-
ing "in an ever widening glare" of the "eyes blue for preference" is true
of his subtlest enticements to the activity of perception. There is the
seduction of the spoiling gaze, and the graduations of imperceptibility
with which it occurs: "And all by such slow and insensible degrees to be

sure as to pass unperceived even by those most concerned if this notion is maintained" (*Lost Ones,* p. 39). And the notion here is—dilating over the unceasing repetitions of cylindrical thought, the obsessive speculation—"the difference *considered*" (emphasis mine), that is, the *différance.* It is "not one of speed," quicker and quicker, as with the words pouring from the Mouth of *Not I,* but of "space travelled," a harrowing space of undecidability in which the endurance of perception or "cylinder alone are certitudes to be found and without nothing but mystery" (p. 42). But not the mystery of the Logos which keeps the pronouns in place.

For there is in the cylinder, like some protoplasmic irritability, an impatience with repose. It is that certitude of nothing but mystery which, with the speed of subjectivity, keeps identity at bay, as at the moment of my daughter's birth. Is it possible that we were, from that instant, even before, always already loving someone else? And is she, the one we're loving now—"what? . . . who? . . . no! . . . she! . . . SHE!" (*Not I,* p. 23)—other than the one who remained, "begging the mouth to stop" (p. 20) in the painfully loving delirium of the equivocal bearing down— "when suddenly she felt . . . gradually she felt . . . her lips moving . . . imagine! . . . as of course till then she had not . . . and not alone the lips . . . the cheeks . . . the jaws . . . the whole face . . . all those— . . . what? . . . the tongue? . . . yes . . . the tongue in the mouth . . . all those contortions without which . . . no speech possible" (pp. 18–19)—the lifelong labor to bring it into the world?

But here, unavoidably, the pronouns slipping into the figure of speech, I do seem to be speaking of something like a text, as if it were a dubious birthright, as in the opening of *Molloy,* or the ecstasy of "*writing aloud*" at the closing of Roland Barthes's *The Pleasure of the Text:* "the pulsional incidents, the language lined with flesh, a text where you can hear the grain of the throat, . . . a whole carnal stereophony: the articulation of the body, of the tongue, not that of meaning, of language," but rather "the breath, the gutturals, the fleshiness of the lips, a whole presence of the human muzzle," as monstrous in short as *jouissance* can be.[15] It's next to impossible to think of Beckett and not get caught up in the compulsive textualization of displaced bodily parts, the tongue in the uterus, the speechless infant in the mouth, the writing before the letter on the matriarchal wall, going through similar contortions to achieve self-presence in the living present, that pure autoaffection which, like the writing of the unconscious in the libidinal economy of the womb, does not inhabit or borrow from anything outside itself. "This difficulty," says Derrida in his commentary on Husserl, "*calls for* a response. This response is the voice [*la voix*]. The voice is richly and profoundly enigmatic in all that it here seems to answer,"[16] as in *The Unnamable.*

But what exactly is it answering—"Where now? Who now? When now? Unquestioning. I, say I. Unbelieving" (*Unnamable*, p. 3). And: "How could you have responded if you were not there?" says another voice, enigmatic, in *Footfalls* (*Ends and Odds*, p. 48), as you find yourself answering, I *was* there, I thought, or thought *I* was, supportively, as they say—but when the tiny little thing *wouldn't* come out, for all the labor, in a devouring helplessness at the edge of speech, somewhere between prayer and pensum. It was a kind of perceptual prurience, I thought, watching myself watching the bloody show. There I was, the eye of prey, the self-victimizing consciousness which *is* the monstrosity in the vicinity of birth, "the infinitesimal shudder instantaneously suppressed," in the silence of the rotunda after the mirror mists, "Only murmur ah, no more, in this silence," in *Imagination Dead Imagine* (p. 66).

In Beckett we are always looking at what, perhaps, should not be looked at. We're not quite sure why not, since it isn't as if we haven't seen it before—only, like the deepest memory of dream, what we're looking at is something forgotten, and only thus remembered. Thus, too, in the *Ghost Trio,* the faint and impersonal voice which "will not be raised, nor lowered, whatever happens," responds to the difficulty which calls for it by asking us to "Look. (*Long pause.*) The familiar chamber." And we see it ghosting out of remembrance in the faintly luminous light of no visible source, as a video image. There is the intimate estrangement of that voyeuristic medium around which the family gathers, not only the chamber, but the miniaturized chamber drama. It is the old Freudian family romance, elliptically there, *close up*, like the grain of the voice which is always more material as an image on the screen, however impassive, in the image of the voice, seen, in the dust, the floor, the wall which, having seen, as the voice says, "you have seen it all" (*Ends and Odds*, p. 55).

Despite Othello's lust for ocular proof, seeing is not necessarily believing. As we've learned in recent years from the human sciences and literary theory, *seeing is interpreting.* And the problem with interpreting is that the thing to be interpreted presumes an enigma even if seemingly self-evident, like "the kind of wall" in *Ghost Trio* (p. 55). Without any system of synchronisation between the perceiver and the perceived, it seems impossible to know whether it's a thing in itself with an identity of its own or an interpretative subject *preselected* by thought within the tautological enclosure of its self-reflection: eye of flesh, eye of prey, subject closing upon object, hunter and hunted, mirror upon mirror mirroring the bloody show? or *projected* as an object by the perceiving subject in accordance with the logic of its own desire?

All the preying ramifications of perception in Beckett are variations on the blindness which came to focus in the image of Hamm: the blindness of insight of the solipsistic subject, hooded, and supplied with a stancher for emblooded eyes. The consciousness of Hamm is like a camera obscura. The lens, however, is blocked off to our sight, so that what we experience as he looks darkly toward us is ourselves looking at what only meets the eyes but does not, if his eyes *are* sealed, look back. So there we are doubly looking, picking up the obscurity on which our eyes seem to rest, *un*-enlightened. "I see my light dying," says Clov (*Endgame*, p. 12), and thus do we, the light of the perceptual system without synchronisation illuminating not the voice that comes from who knows where, but *only a surface that speaks*. All vision is both projective and introjective, and what comes back, then, from the seductive blankness of Hamm like an empty signifier over the stream of the look is what, projected there, is deposited back, as in film. What settles on the imaginary plane of perception is marked, as Christian Metz observes of the identification of spectator with camera in the cinema, by "our relation to the world as a whole and . . . rooted in the primary figures of orality."[17] As we gaze upon Hamm, he seems to be—through too much historical consciousness in a play which never forgets—an arrested version of orality, no more than a figure of speech.

"Who perceives, who enunciates the difficulty?" asks Derrida in his essay on Foucault, the "Cogito and the History of Madness" (*Writing and Difference*, p. 37), into which my daughter, tiny little thing, is with the infinitesimal shudder of the eye of prey instantaneously caught up. I should have said shutter, if you'll forgive the pun, because they now let you take pictures in the delivery room. Even now, loved as she is, she is being *stared at*. It is the hauntedness of being the *being-perceived* in the beginning which is in Artaud—whom Derrida has studied as a mirror of thought—the reason for madness. It is also the ontological basis of what for Artaud is Original Sin, the idea of an *audience*, that specular entity whose name suggests the Word, the thing *heard*. The audience—*the ones who look*—is the look of the Law. It is the audited reflection of originary division and primal separation. What occurs in the susceptible body of the speechless infant as fecal matter signifies for Artaud a kind of dismemberment or *sparagmos*. It is a sign of the original bloody show in the ritual drama, the loss of precious parts of ourselves that are only *re*-membered in dreams. It is the preying eye of the specular ego which depreciates us and soils us in the name of a lethal power which steals both word and flesh. It is the insinuating difference in a structure of theft, or rather the double that inserts itself between ourselves and birth, the "subtle subterfuge which," as Derrida says, "makes signification slip" (*Writing and Difference,* p. 177), the nothing that posits itself between us and origins, what comes to be the history whose name is death.

It is in this thievish space of privative being that, in the very deepest sense, the spectator is constituted and—for Beckett as well as Artaud—the theater gives birth to its Double, the self-reflexive subject of thought, the thinking subject stealing thought away, eye of flesh, eye of prey, bringing death to the bloody show:

> *Vladimir:* We must have thought a little.
> *Estragon:* At the very beginning.
> *Vladimir:* A charnel-house! A charnel-house!
> *Estragon:* You don't have to look
> *Vladimir:* You can't help looking.
> *Estragon:* True.
>
> (*Godot,* p. 41)

In Beckett's earliest attempts at drama—deconstructing the well-made play and playing within the play—this holocaustic association was already there. *Eléutheria* foreshadows an equivocal strategy with respect to the theater as an agency of the economy of death which, for the bourgeois audience, gazing on death, is written on the price of its ticket. When, in the last act, Victor has defined liberty as "seeing yourself dead," there is a final curtain in which, reconciled neither to the Krapp family romance nor to suicide, he lies down on his bed after looking long at the audience, *"his thin back turned on humanity."* As for seeing yourself dead, that's the problem of representation which plagues Artaud and deconstructionist thought. "You can't see yourself dead," as Victor says. "That's playacting."[18] Which is the vice of representation in the dominion of death, that death can only be *represented.* Which is to say it can only be theater, falsifying theater, that repeats it over and over, an interior duplication of the division, the *sparagmos*, the originary bloody show—in which we must have thought a little at the very beginning to make a charnel house that seems without end.

"Will you never have done? *(Pause.)* Will you never have done . . . revolving it all? *(Pause.)* It? *(Pause.)* It all. *(Pause.)* In your poor mind. *(Pause.)* It all. *(Pause.)* It all" (*Footfalls*, p. 48). Whatever it is that is being revolved, it seems to steal "the simple presence of its present act from the theater, from life," as Derrida says, rehearsing Artaud, "in the irrepressible movement of repetition" (*Writing and Difference*, p. 247), through which Beckett and deconstruction try to work. It is the structure by which they are inhabited, in order to attain the "repetition of that which does not repeat itself" (p. 250), the prerogative of being in its unrepeatable plenitude, the pure *"present indicative of the verb 'to be'"*—not I, not Other, but *it*, perhaps *it all*, "the pure and teleological form of expression insofar as it is logical," as if an enigmatic *third person* were the real determinant (as Heidegger thought) of the infinitive of being (*Speech and Phenomena*, p. 73). "It is here that *speech* is necessary," writes Derrida (p. 74), and with speech, the inaugurating word, tautological, as in the speechless infant, "the one the first and last time curled up. . . ." One cannot deconstruct this movement of appearance which is the movement of consciousness itself entering history, "without descending," the little fabric vanishing, "across inherited concepts, toward the unnamable" (p. 77), as Derrida says, and as Beckett does.

In Beckett as in the Logos, the beginning is a word, though when push comes to shove, as in the difficulty of my wife's delivery which also called for a response, it seemed a far cry from that. "Astride of a grave and a difficult birth." To bring my daughter into this world, godforsaken world, they had to use the forceps. They were inserted one at a time, "Down in the hole, lingeringly" (*Godot*, p. 58), large shining cusps of surgical steel, as if the Hinge were rounded. They left a mark on my daughter's cheek. It has already disappeared, but as I keep revolving it all it will (I'm afraid), like the "shudder in the mind" in *Footfalls*, be indelibly remembered in its vanishing like the inscription of the seminal trace: "The semblance. Faint, though by no means invisible, in a certain light" (*Ends and Odds*, p. 47). As if it were written, as it now is. And so, as the bloody show continued, that remarkable conception, it was as if an immaculate negation also came forth, but *only as a text*. It came from something unnamable which remained in the womb, like the voice in the first *Fizzle* which gave up before birth, though "birth there had to be," for it's impossible otherwise, "I didn't wail, I didn't see the light it's impossible I should have a voice, impossible I should have thoughts, and I speak and think, I do the impossible, it is not possible otherwise, it was he who had a life, I didn't have a life, a life not worth having, because of me he'll do himself to death, because of me"—what? . . . who? . . . *not* she!—"I'll tell the tale, tale of his death, the end of his life and his death, his death, his death alone would not be enough, not enough for me. . . ."[19]

Nor me. And as the pronouns merge in this reflection, confusing gender and person, slipping from the loving scrutiny of a particular birth to the birth in which love is only scrutiny, the eye of prey, I find myself thinking neither of her nor of him but of *me*, myself my own object in the reflection, an interior space of being where whatever it was that was left behind, the *remainder*, the forgotten part of being, is summoned forth. And as I think of her now, picking her up in thought like the "tender mercies" remembered at the end of *Not I*, "nothing but the larks . . . pick it up" (p. 23), the scrutiny returns again, and the brain, "the beam . . . flickering on and off," scrupling, "starting to move around . . . like moonbeam but not . . . all part of the same . . . keep an eye on that too . . . corner of the eye . . . all that together" (pp. 20–21) repeating, crossing gender and time, becomes me, and I *am* now speaking of the paternity of a text, "the words . . . the brain . . . flickering away like mad" (pp. 22–23) yet something also begging it to stop "unanswered . . . prayer unanswered," keeping an eye on that too, we pray, we prey, words flying up, thought remaining below . . . pick it up:

NOTES

1. Samuel Beckett, *Not I*, in *Ends and Odds* (New York: Grove, 1976), p. 14. Further references to *Not I* and other pieces from this collection will appear in the text under their own titles with page numbers from *Ends and Odds*.

2. *The Unnamable* (New York: Grove, 1958), p. 170. Subsequent references will appear in the text.

3. *The Lost Ones* (New York: Grove, 1972), pp. 15–16. Subsequent references will appear in the text.

4. *Molloy*, trans. Patrick Bowles, with Samuel Beckett (New York: Grove, 1955), p. 7. Subsequent references will appear in the text.

5. *Waiting for Godot* (New York: Grove, 1954), p. 7. Subsequent references to *Godot* will appear in the text.

6. John Ashbery, *Three Poems* (New York: Penguin, 1977), p. 46.

7. Ibid., p. 47.

8. Theodore W. Adorno, "Trying to Understand *Endgame*," *New German Critique,* no. 26 (1982), p. 121.

9. *A Piece of Monologue,* in *Collected Shorter Plays of Samuel Beckett* (London: Faber and Faber, 1984), p. 265.

10. *Proust* (New York: Grove, n.d.), p. 54. Subsequent references will appear in the text.

11. Jacques Derrida, *Of Grammatology,* trans. Gayatri Chakravorty Spivak (Baltimore: Johns Hopkins University Press, 1976), p. 5. Subsequent references will appear in the text.

12. "Structure, Sign, and Play in the Human Sciences," in *Writing and Difference,* trans. Alan Bass (Chicago: University of Chicago Press, 1978), p. 292. Subsequent references will appear in the text.

13. *Endgame* (New York: Grove, 1958), p. 44. Subsequent references will appear in the text.

14. *From An Abandoned Work,* in *First Love and Other Shorts* (New York: Grove, 1974), p. 39. Further references to this story and any other from the collection will be in the text with page numbers from the volume, abbreviated as *First Love.*

15. Roland Barthes, *The Pleasure of the Text,* trans. Richard Miller (New York: Hill and Wang, 1975), pp. 66–67.

16. *Speech and Phenomena and Other Essays on Husserl's Theory of Signs,* trans. David B. Allison (Evanston: Northwestern University Press, 1973), p. 15. Subsequent references will appear in the text.

17. Christian Metz, *The Imaginary Signifier: Psychoanalysis and the Cinema,* trans. Celia Britton, Annwyl Williams, Ben Brewster, and Alfred Guzzett (Bloomington: Indiana University Press, 1977), p. 50.

18. Quoted by Ruby Cohn, *Back to Beckett* (Princeton: Princeton University Press, 1973), pp. 125–26. *Eléutheria* is not yet published.

19. *Foirades/Fizzles* (New York: Whitney Museum of American Art, 1977), a catalogue of etchings by Jasper Johns on Beckett's text, unpaginated.

FIVE

BARTHES AND BECKETT

The Punctum, the Pensum, and the Dream of Love

Pathos has had a bad name in the history of the modern; sentimentality worse. Until the last books of Roland Barthes, they seemed like insipid residues of humanism in the era of the End of Man. An honorable exception was always Beckett—the congenital last holdout of humanism—who couldn't shake the pathos for all its running sores, the laughter of mutilations, and whose cruelty never prevented you from having a good cry, right up the *risus purus,* the laugh laughing at the laugh. If the writing of Barthes—dry, obtuse, *matte,* fatal as he describes it—seems to come from "a gentle hemorrhage"[1] in the discourse of desire, the grotesque comedy of Beckett seems to leak from a defective bypass in the braininess of a bleeding heart. "Nature!" exclaims Hamm, rapturously for a moment *(pause),* forgetting his pain-killer. "There's something dripping in my head. *(Pause.)* A heart, a heart in my head."[2]

Barthes, too, has a heart in his head, as he suggests in his quasi autobiography, *Roland Barthes by Roland Barthes,* in the *pensée* entitled "*L'amour d'une idée*"—Love of an idea. *Love* and *idea:* we might almost say, before loving the idea, a fatal coupling! For at a time when all our thought, and certainly theory, seems infatuated with the sexual, love seems obscene, as Barthes observes in *A Lover's Discourse,* because it prefers the sentimental (p. 175). He prefers it himself with a certain exuberance. "I take for myself the scorn," he writes, "lavished on any kind of pathos: . . . like the Nietzschean ass, I say yes to everything in the field of my love" (pp. 166–67). If sentimentality is still to be thought of as an emotion disproportionate to its motive and somewhat immune to considered judgment, Barthes seems to indulge himself to the point of infatuation, and not only about the idea of love: "For a certain time," he writes in "Love of an idea," "he went into raptures over binarism;

binarism became for him a kind of erotic object. This idea seemed to him inexhaustible, he could never exploit it enough. That one might say everything *with only one difference* produced a kind of joy in him, a continuous astonishment. Since intellectual things resemble erotic ones, in binarism what delighted him was a figure"[3]—as it does in the figurations of love in *A Lover's Discourse,* the goings and comings of love, the ubiquitous plottings, the strivings and contrivings, the measures taken, what keeps the lover's mind racing through all the contingencies, cantillations, and vicissitudes of love. Speaking, however, of Exuberance, the Blakean figure by which the amorous subject negotiates the place of love in an economy of pure expenditure and utter loss, Barthes warns in a parenthesis that "if we would glimpse the transgressive force of love-as-passion," we must remember "the assumption of sentimentality as an alien strength" (*Lover's Discourse,* p. 84).

This strength is what we see in *Camera Lucida,* not only in his refusal to reduce himself-as-subject before the photographs he studies, but in the memorial to his mother in that somewhat Proustian book. He does not weep, he says, in another parenthesis, expecting that Time will simply dissipate the emotion of loss. Meanwhile, he does not refrain from summoning up in bereavement the language of sensibility and irreducible *affect.* He wants to mourn his mother in the untenable words of the ego's old dispensation: as *being, soul, essence,* a quality of life; in a world suspicious of love and substance, the *substance* of the beloved, rather than a reflection of structuralist activity or an illusory Figure of Speech; not the Mother, but *his* mother, the only mother he can mourn. Since the classical phenomenology in which he'd matured had never, so far as he remembers, spoken of desire or mourning, he has to look elsewhere for a way to cross the hysterical division of History—which *is* hysteria, marked and affirmed by Death—in order to recover an Image of his mother which would be immediately steeped in the particularity, the *singularity* of his pain, what would preserve for him the "radiant, irreducible core. . . ."[4] Against his Protestant instincts which refused the Image and his demythologizing past which exposed it, he would give himself up to the solitude of the Imaginary, the Image-repertoire, in order to keep with him, "like a treasure," his desire and grief.

So, too, with the anticipated *essence* of Photography, to which he was drawn as *Spectator* for " 'sentimental' reasons," and which he wants to explore not as theme or question but as a *wound*—a wound which he willingly suffers with nostalgia and a pensiveness which is the recuperative medium of the insufficiency of remembered love. We may have

quite different feelings or amorous sentiments about the details of the
photographs he examines—the sheet carried by a weeping woman, the
black sailor's crossed arms, Bob Wilson's sneakers—but what is undeniably moving in the book is his account of how, when it was impossible "to
participate in a world of strength," appalled by social life, he lived in his
mother's weakness before she died. Nursing her as he did, bringing the
favored bowl of tea to her lips, he experienced her, "strong as she had
been," his inner law, as his feminine child: "I who had not procreated, I
had, in her illness, engendered my mother" (*Camera Lucida,* p. 72).
Barthes had written in *A Lover's Discourse,* not very long before, that he
had learned very early, as a normal person, to endure the loss of a
beloved object, since he was accustomed to being separated from his
mother. But he knew that the separations remained a source of suffering, approaching hysteria. As a "well-weaned subject," he could feed
himself, "*meanwhile,* on other things besides the maternal breast" (p. 14),
but as if in retribution for his having said so the *meanwhile* wasn't long.
Once his mother died he resigned himself to awaiting the remainder of a
life which would be "absolutely and entirely *unqualifiable* (without quality)" (p. 75) before his "total, undialectical death" (p. 72). Which came
much too soon to confirm him in its imbecilic negation, as Sartre said in
his epitaph on the death of Camus.

Like the narrator in Proust, Barthes insisted in *Camera Lucida* not
only upon his suffering but the profundity, the *originality* of his suffering. He was unashamed of its excess, as of the tainted idea of *origin* in
the claim of originality, which in the creed of poststructuralism is as
suspect as pathos. Even if the emotion of loss, amortized, were to van-
ish in time, the gradual labor of mourning would not—he couldn't
believe it—relieve the pain. It is the economics of grief, including a
dialogue with Freud carried over from *A Lover's Discourse,* which is the
perceptual field of *Camera Lucida,* as it is a kind of econometrics of
grief which is the obsession-compulsion of all of Beckett's work, driven
as it is by the desire for what is *not-there* and, chances are, never will
be. It is the immanence of an indecipherable and irrecoverable loss
which is both stochastically and, as in the *Lost Ones,* almost statistically
explored.

Of what Barthes had lost, we have only the reflections on the Winter
Garden Photograph, the sepia print of his mother as a child of five,
which he did not reproduce among the other photographs in *Camera
Lucida.* While it achieved "utopically, *the impossible science of unique being*"

(p. 71)—even the shared values of science couldn't keep the photograph from existing only for him. Were we to see it, he says, it would interest only our *studium,* the term he uses for acculturated concern, for the *studium* is in the category of liking rather than loving. As amenable cultural subjects we might be attentive to the photograph's local color, the little girl's clothes, the period, photogeny, "but in it, for [us], no wound" (p. 73)—which is what he calls the *punctum,* a fissure, sting, cut, hole, tear in the *studium* of a photograph, the eruptive detail, the accident which bruises, the unnamable thing which *pricks* and which, if he can name it, won't prick him at all (pp. 27, 51). In the old semiological jargon, the *studium* is coded, the *punctum* is not. As if the image were launching desire past what we have permission to see, the *punctum* seems to be leading us, in the absence of a transcendental signifier, to "a kind of subtle *beyond* . . ." (p. 59). This, too, is a little shameless in the phenomenological bias of postmodern thought.

Barthes concludes the study of Photography with a summary of the *punctum* as "a sort of link (or knot) between Photography, madness, and something [he] did not know" which—summoning up another sentimental phrase—he ventured to call "the pangs of love." In certain photographs which pricked him, through the action of the *punctum,* which also attests to bodily loss, spoilage, devastation of the autonomy of a pleasurable self, he heard the almost unfamiliar music of an old-fashioned emotion whose name he remembers as Pity (p. 116).

He might have been forewarned by Beckett. "Yes, one day you'll know what it is," says Hamm, in his oracular vision of an infinite emptiness, "you'll be like me, except that you won't have anyone with you, because you won't have had pity on anyone and because there won't be anyone left to have pity on" (*Endgame,* p. 36). It's a prospect of life as utterly unqualifiable because—in the economy of death: even at the start "finished, it must be nearly finished" (p. 1)—the grains of accumulation seem to be nothing but loss, ineluctable and pitiless loss. "It's not certain," says Clov (p. 36), undercutting the apocalyptics, as if he'd pricked the *punctum.* But then, seeing his light dying, he seems to be dying himself as if immobilized with compassion. Something is taking its course, engorged with time, making his body a total wound. Barthes never accumulates anything like the empowering magnitude of this incapacity in the concept of the *punctum,* but as he moves through the earlier affective intention of his book to distinguish a cultural field (the *studium*) from the unexpected flash or hallucinatory rip across it (the *punctum*), he discovers a higher order of *punctum*, the source of Pity, not merely the infectious detail, the charm, but a deadly stigmatum in the brain scan, a definitive click, then *flat Death* in the photograph, "the lacerating emphasis" of Time, the *thing-which-has-been*, not as form, but unfiltered intensity, its "pure representation" (pp. 92, 96).

It is here that the *punctum* is intersected and deepened by what we may feel in *Waiting for Godot* when Didi is gazing at the sleeping Gogo, *being-seen* in his speculation, as if he were sleeping himself, looked at, positioned where his thoughts are, "Astride of a grave and a difficult birth. Down in the hole, lingeringly," as if perception were the grave digger putting on the forceps.[5] So, Barthes, when he gazes at the handsome portrait of the handsome young man waiting to be hanged. What he sees is an anterior future, the *sentencing* of a past, contemplating with horror a subtle *behind* which is appallingly beyond, proleptic, the absolute past of the pose which foretells a future death. "What *pricks* me," he says, "is the discovery of this equivalence. In front of the photograph of my mother as a child, I told myself: She is going to die: I shudder like Winnicott's psychotic patient, *over the catastrophe which has already occurred*" (*Camera Lucida*, pp. 95–96). It's as if through the accretion of remembered loss in the photographs that pricked, Barthes went through the *punctum* and out a black hole to the seminal side of representation, and thus directly into the unconscious whose processes are indestructible and where, as Freud said in *The Interpretation of Dreams*, "nothing can be brought to an end, nothing is past or forgotten."[6] Barthes, who hated dreams and distrusted fantasy and had looked askance through much of his life at the deceits of representation, was now at the imaginary source, possessed by the Image-repertoire. "I entered crazily into the spectacle, into the image," he confesses, "taking into my arms what is dead, what is going to die, as Nietzsche did when . . . he threw himself on the neck of a beaten horse: gone mad for Pity's sake" (*Camera Lucida*, p. 117).

It is this ecstatic burden of the tragic pathos, its madness, abject, stupid, the nearly forgotten, discredited, old-fashioned emotion which brings the Barthes of *Camera Lucida* into the camera obscura of Beckett, the eminent domain where Hamm sits, in his deconstructive blindness, veiled by a kind of Veronica—blood and tears inscribed over the blacked-out lenses of the scopic eyes—as a figure of almost boundless, commiserable, but incommensurable love:

> You weep, and weep, for nothing, so as not to laugh, and little by little . . .
> you begin to grieve. . . . All those I might have helped.
> *(Pause.)*
> Helped!
> *(Pause.)*
> Saved.
> *(Pause.)*
> Saved!
> *(Pause.)*
> The place was crawling with them!
> *(Pause. Violently.)*
> Use your head, can't you, use your head, you're on earth, there's no cure
> for that.
> *(Pause.)*
> Get out of here and love one another. Lick your neighbor as yourself.
> *(Endgame, p. 68)*

It turns mordant, of course, in Beckett, as all humanity (the audience bearing the brunt) takes on the aspect of the beaten horse. But the impossible Pity is impossibly there. As Hamm covers his face with the stancher, ending the play which from the beginning is haunted by the sense of an end, he "remains motionless" (p. 84) as Barthes "remained motionless" (*Camera Lucida*, p. 73) in the inexhaustible commemoration of his mother through the unweeping diminuendo of the emotion of loss, which does not erase the image of what is lost forever, the pain still unappeased.

"Day after unremembered day until my mother's death, then in a new place soon old until my own," says the narrator in Beckett's *From an Abandoned Work*. ". . . I gather up my things and go back into my hole, so bygone they can be told. Over, over, there is a soft place in my heart for all that is over, no, for the being over, I love the word, words have been my only loves, not many."[7] Over and over, trying to mitigate the suffering which proceeds *"from who she was,"* Barthes tries to replenish the sense of banality in his grief, the recurring pathos, "what everyone sees and knows," with the originality of an emotion that belongs only to himself (*Camera Lucida*, pp. 75–76). Overwhelmed by the truth of the image in the Winter Garden Photograph, he would henceforth consent to combine two voices, like Beckett, "the voice of banality" and "the voice of singularity," converting the problem of grief into a problem of language. "Language is my skin:" he had written in *A Lover's Discourse*, "I rub my language against the other" (p. 23). And in *Camera Lucida*, immediately after the assertion that life without his mother would be unqualifiable, he writes, "It was as if I were seeking the nature of a verb which had no infinitive, only tense and mode" (p. 76).

But painful as it is, it is an arduous task, a work in danger of being abandoned. For he cannot transform his grief, it can only be *indulged,* because the photograph, *his* photograph, is without culture, and looked at over and over, it allows him to experience the grief only at the level of the image's finitude, which in photography does not, as in film, move on protensively to other images. Like the death he had predicted for himself, the photograph is undialectical, without the power to redeem the corruptible, converting the "negation of death into the power to work. . . ." What he sees in the photograph is "a denatured theater" where death escapes the gaze and cannot be interiorized. There is in the photograph an "unendurable plenitude" which, instead of being "in essence, a memory (whose grammatical expression would be the perfect tense)," is rather blocked memory, which keeps it from being spoken. What he sees there is "the dead theater of Death, the foreclosure of the Tragic," the pathos, which denies him the catharsis he is looking for, the conversion of grief into mourning (pp. 90–91).

In *A Lover's Discourse,* however, love is another matter in another theater. "Enamoration is a *drama,*" Barthes had written, restoring to the word drama—through Nietzsche on *The Case of Wagner*—the archaic meaning of an enraptured stasis in great declamatory scenes, which exclude action or keep it behind the scenes. For Barthes, the amorous seduction of the lover's discourse *is* such drama, a "pure hypnotic moment," hieratic, "this declamation of a *fait accompli,*" like, you're on earth, the loved one's left you and there's no cure for *that* except the little sacred history—"(frozen, embalmed, removed from any *praxis*)" (*Lover's Discourse,* p. 94)—which you rehearse over and over until through some miracle of mortification it seems to break through the glazed encasement of the mnemonic embalming fluid. It is not merely the alphabetical arrangement of "the great imaginary current, the orderless, endless stream" (p. 7) of *A Lover's Discourse* which causes the enamored figure of Drama to be followed by that of the Flayed Man, "a mass of irritable substance" (Barthes quoting Freud) whose brain and skin are shredded by the rigors of love. Like Hamm. Or Artaud. The origin of the memory of a drama of mysterious origins—the "essential drama" which Artaud remembers and his ravaged body represents—is this irritable substance, whipping its innateness, a jetstream of bleeding image in the cruel service of the violence of thought, not the logical stoppage of thought, but *the cause by which the mind can think.* The thinking occurs, however, as in the *mise-en-scène* of the unconscious, an alchemical space of unremitting desire, through the filiating detour of immemorial dreams. We are reminded by Artaud and Freud that the unconscious—with its ruptures and disjunctures, and bloody eyeballs of the oedipal drama, that *punctum*—is our oldest *mental* faculty. There is, thus, a genetic violence in the lover's discourse, a blindness, a madness, which thinks carnally at every nerve-end of thought "through all the filters and foundations of existing matter" toward the rare and irreducible beauty of a prodigious love, the orderless, endless stream becoming—as Artaud reimagines the Mystery for his alchemical theater—the "complete, sonorous, streaming, naked realization. . . ."[8]

Here, too, the prodigiousness of what's remembered seems a function of what is forever lost. The scale may change, but the violence of thought remains. As Lacan suggests, the aggressivity arises along with the image of the other in the *déchirement,* the tearing, the rending, the laceration, the initiatory splitting off of the self-enamored subject in the drama of the Mirror Stage. We have already seen that Barthes, pensive over the photograph, thinks of it as a kind of theater. If it draws less blood than Artaud had in mind, there is still a violence in the *punctum,* the cut, the tear, as there is in the disorder of repetition that makes Photography, according to Barthes, essentially indescribable. Not the content of the photograph, but its sovereign contingency, the rudimentary Encounter with the Real (Lacan), its irruptive occasion. As Barthes sees it, the photograph is violent because "it *fills the sight by force.* . . ." Realizing that the word violent may be extravagant, he adds: "many say that sugar is mild, but to me sugar is violent, and I call it so" (*Camera Lucida,* p. 91). It's a nuance of his preciosity, this violence, something febrile, over-sensitive, what we used to associate with the nervous system in a case of tuberculosis. Yet one feels he *does* feel as he says, grains on the teeth, just *that,* as the *punctum* of the photograph is just *this,* well-weaned as the subject is.

So—again the scale reduced from the prodigious conception of Artaud's theater, the acuteness of which depends upon an originary and essential separation—Barthes is sitting, alone, at a café on the Piazza del Popolo in Rome. He is on a holiday, part of the spectacle which he is also watching, *feeling watched,* with a sense of pronouncing himself through a fantasy. Everything around him—the bustling world of theatrical Rome whose plenitude is its system—changes value in respect to a function, the

Image-repertoire, which he has entered like a sanctuary, those dismembered fractions of perfected love. There is the streaming realization that he has cut himself off from the world, which seems *unreal,* so that he may surrender himself to the Image. Bereft, withdrawn, he may, as the lover does, hallucinate in a solitary drama "the peripeteias or the utopias of his love. . . ." But there is a second phase which is not quite a fantasy. He is "not 'dreaming' (even of the other)," nor is he deceived. He realizes that "no imaginary substitution will compensate" for the loss of love. (*Lover's Discourse,* p. 90). Speaking of another *punctum,* or syncope, "the noise of a rip in the smooth envelope" of the loved one's Image, Barthes knows that in that rip he may hear the menacing rumble of "*a whole other world,* which is the world of the other"—and no longer the pure amorous field (pp. 25–26). With the horrible ebb of the Image, there is the realization that "the horror of spoiling is even stronger than the anxiety of losing" (p. 28).

We are all familiar with the litany of that spoilage in Beckett, which seems to arise out of nature like the stink of History. "What dreams! Those forests!" says Hamm, after the cracked a—bsolute of his opening yawn (*Endgame,* pp. 2–3), awakening into the nightmare of History from the dream of love, the loss of which can become so intense that even the dream of it disappears. There is a part of the lover's discourse which seems to occur in the zone of zero of Beckett's play or at the freezing point of the rotunda, "a ring as in the imagination the ring of bone," in *Imagination Dead Imagine* (*First Love,* p. 63): "Everything is frozen, petrified, immutable," writes Barthes, not Beckett, "i.e., *unsubstitutable:* the Image-repertoire is (temporarily) foreclosed" (*Lover's Discourse,* pp. 90–91).

But only temporarily. The Flayed Man is too irritable for that. His "exquisite points" are excited by the faintest thought of love, as in *Imagination Dead Imagine* the most minimal sign of life awakens into being against the desire for a stilling of the "countless rhythms" of being, a respite, petrification—"not dead yet, yes, dead, good, imagination dead imagine" (*First Love,* p. 63)—or against the desire for a homeostatic silence, as in *Ping,* where the "Traces blurs light grey eyes holes" are like a polygraph of the *puncta,* "light blue almost white fixed front a meaning only just almost never ping silence," and then before the end of *Ping,* "one second perhaps not alone unlustrous black and white half closed long lashes imploring ping silence over" (p. 72). The pings over the "all known all white bare body" of distilled and humiliated desire, love's body, "Hands hanging palms front white feet heels together right angle" (p. 69) are like the "map of moral acupuncture" over the defenseless body of the Flayed Man in *A Lover's Discourse,* that mythic figure of the most vulnerable love which, even when crushed, still twitches with desire (*Lover's Discourse,* p. 95). It's as if the exquisite points of these two exquisite writers, Barthes and Beckett, were nodes of protoplasmic irritability, the malaise at the selvedge of nonexistence which refuses not to be. It is this refusal of the death instinct *in* the death instinct which Freud tried to understand in *Beyond the Pleasure Principle,* where he also makes the astonishing suggestion that we are more than half in love with death, since death is the *aim* of life. In the circuitous detour of thought which seems to reflect as it reflects upon the circuitous paths to death, Freud surmises that the desire to return to an earlier state of things is so that, with something more or other than pleasure, the organism may die only in its own fashion.[9]

What more can the lover desire? Out of the closet, all known silence over, moving toward the subtle *beyond* of the *punctum,* where he engenders in death a feminine child, without procreation ("Accursed progenitor!" says Hamm [*Endgame,* p. 9], to the amputated remains of the phallic father), Barthes in *A Lovers' Discourse* is also beyond the simpler-minded *jouissance,* the less costly erotic play of *The Pleasure of the Text.* He is at least more equivocal about it, anachronistic, since the lover is not a man of good conscience, who rejects the bait of analogy and the alibi of representation. He is rather entranced by the Imaginary, a *lunar* child, not playful in the old way, but tender, easily bruised in his exquisite points, experienced in anxiety, waiting, and impatient with the arbitrary play of signifiers which seem, in his hypersensitive irritability, worse than an alibi, not only a fissure in the subject like the *punctum,* but a tissue of appalling lies. "One is no longer oneself, on such occasions," writes Beckett, already versed in the failures of love, in *First Love,* "and it is painful to be no longer oneself, even more painful if possible than when one is. For when one is one knows what to do to be less so, whereas when one is not one is any old one irredeemably. What goes by the name of love is banishment, with now and then a postcard from the homeland, such is my considered opinion, this evening" (*First Love,* p. 18).

In a sequence of *A Lover's Discourse* entitled "The World Thunderstruck," Barthes may not share the tone but he shares the considered opinion, the loss of the home of love, the horror of being split off not only from the loved one but from any conception of himself, self-banished, betrayed, abandoned. He articulates the suffering of a complete withdrawal, the vertigo of a terrible absence. "In the first moment I am neurotic, I unrealize; in the second, I am psychotic, crazy, I disrealize" (p. 91). It seems like a kind of death, but if he can manage, "by some mastery of writing, *to utter* this death," *think* about it, as in the pensiveness of *Camera Lucida,* where he engenders his mother in her dying, he can die first in his own fashion, and then begin to live again—although we have seen that there is no guarantee of any real quality to the life before the total undialectical death. "Strange notion in any case, and eminently open to suspicion," writes Beckett in *The Unnamable* of the obligation of the *pensum,* "that of a task to be performed, before one can be at rest. Strange task, which consists of speaking of oneself. Strange hope, turned towards silence and peace."[10]

There is, then, in the craziness of the spectacle where Barthes took into his arms the thing that is dying, something *pensive* in the *punctum* which reminds one of the *pensum,* that curled-up worm of encyclical thought, the mortal coil, the *intractability* of *The Unnamable* which keeps the discourse from coming to an end because the lesson has been forgotten and which—like the stigmatum of the *punctum*—may have been a punishment for the misfortune of being born. No telling what it is, says Barthes, whose last words in *Camera Lucida* speak of "the wakening of intractable reality" (p. 119). "But was I ever told?" asks Beckett (*Unnamable,* p. 30), how intractable it is, the irruption of love in the memory of the dead.

In Beckett, there is an inversion of the sentiment that the dead live on in our memory of them. Reflecting in his essay on *Proust* on Marcel's memory of his grandmother—the involuntary memory which restores what, he then realizes, is *no longer there*—Beckett writes: "The dead are only dead in so far as they continue to exist in the heart of the survivor. And pity for what has been suffered is a more cruel and precise expression for that suffering than the conscious estimate of the sufferer, who is spared at least one despair—the despair of the spectator."[11] It is the despair of the spectator which is, however, introjected in the work of Beckett which is, not only the plays, obsessively and painfully conscious of being observed. There is at the same time disdain for the trust in observation which thinks, like the lover gazing at the loved one, that if you look long enough and hard enough you will really *see.* What you will see, if you use your head, is that there's no cure for that. As for the despair of Beckett, it is thickened by the irony of the *memento mori:* that we seem to be living not only in the memory but the mastery of the dead, who utter without pity for the living the death we think about. "Speak, yes, but to me, I have never spoken enough to me," says the voice of *The Unnamable*, "never had pity enough on me, I have spoken for my master, listened for the words of my master, listened for the words of my master never spoken, well done, my son, you may stop, you may go, you are free, you are acquitted, you are pardoned, never spoken. My master." Whatever's dripping in the head, the heart in the head, "There's a vein I must not lose sight of" (pp. 30–31).

It's a vein which Barthes did lose sight of now and then, understandably, as we see in *Barthes by Barthes,* as he speaks of his childhood, the dead father's name on the blackboard, "the figure of a home socially adrift: no father to kill, no family to hate, no milieu to reject: great Oedipal frustration!" (p. 45). Which is why the Imaginary of Barthes is ever so different from that of Sartre, to which he pays homage in *Camera Lucida.* Sartre's father also died early, but he thinks of that death in *The Words* as a fortunate disburdening, so much so that he claims to have been told by a psychiatrist that he has no superego. Barthes does, which accounts for the frustration, as well as the earlier allure of *jouissance,* anti-Oedipus, schizoanalysis, the feminine, and the infinite galaxy of signifiers in a field of lubricious play, that absolute flow of becoming in the libidinal economy of an imperium of Desire. But if there's madness in *Camera Lucida,* it is the madness of a final realism. This realism is "absolute and, so to speak, original," and nevertheless *bespoken,* that is, spoken *before.* It accedes, then, "to the very letter of Time: a strictly revulsive movement which reverses the course of the thing" (p. 119), as it also keeps its distance—which has wavered in Barthes before—from the clamor of anarchisms, marginalisms, polysexualisms, radical feminisms which want to abolish the images in order to rescue desire from the phallocratic grasp of logocentric mediation—"you are free, you are acquitted, you are pardoned, never spoken"—without which, the *being-spoken,* painful as it is to say, there wouldn't be any desire.

As Beckett has always known, even when kicking against the pricks. "It follows," says Barthes, "that in any man who utters the other's absence *something feminine* is declared: the man who waits and suffers from his waiting is miraculously feminized" (*Lover's Discourse,* p. 14). It may not, as in Beckett, be the best of all possible miracles, but the feminine shift, drift, or habitation is always there, as when Molloy finds himself in an originary longing somehow in his mother's room. Yet, as we see in the feminized figure of *Enough,* the feminization is not enough, for there's still the fatal couple, his old hand on her old breasts: "I did all he desired. I desired it too. Whenever he desired something so did I. He only had to say what thing. When he didn't desire anything neither did I. In this way I didn't live without desires. . . . When he was silent he must have been like me" (*First Love,* p. 53).

The Unnamable and the amorous subject have this in common: they cannot be reduced to the subject as describable symptom. And if one is forced to make fine distinctions about them, as in the present discourse, that's because they are forever making fine distinctions about themselves, tautological, over-subtle, reversing the amorous field—even when, as in Beckett, they seem desperate to hold within the alienation of language their ontological ground. "I was so unused to speech," says the garrulous narrator of *First Love,* "that my mouth would sometimes open of its own accord, and void some phrase or phrases, grammatically unexceptionable but entirely devoid if not of meaning, for on close inspection they would reveal one, and even several, at least of foundation. But I heard each word no sooner spoken." Which is the problem, hearing it, undoing the undying love. For, as they say in the discourse about discourse, as the signifier approaches the signified, becoming the *thing-heard,* it seems to shake the foundation, and becomes in the very logorrhea the bereft and helpless comedy of the originary constipated Word. In this sequence of *First Love,* the narrator awakes from the observation about the word no sooner spoken with the woman renamed Anna beside him, naked, a stewpan she gave him as a bedpan in his grasp. "It had not served," he says. "I looked at my member. If only it could have spoken! Enough about that. It was my night of love" (p. 31).

If it's not a satisfactory night, that's because—however we come, like Barthes, to the love of an idea—we love in the idea of love, loving ourselves loving. Moreover, as we see in Barthes and Beckett, there is something wanting in love, which we think of as a thing of silence, if it is not entirely spoken. If not for the words of love, failing as they do, there might not be not only a lover's discourse—but even in silence—anything like love at all.

Yet: no metalanguage, Barthes insists, in explaining how *A Lover's Discourse* is constructed. He wants to speak, as close as rhetoric permits, to a primary language. But that's an aspiration of the discourse which always frustrates its end, as in *The Unnamable,* where "the search for the means to put an end to things, an end to speech, is what enables the discourse to continue." In Barthes, the continuation eventually annuls the object of desire, so desire may desire itself. In Beckett, the discourse wants to serve another purpose than desire, "In the frenzy of utterance the concern for truth"—and a certain nostalgia for its profundity. "But not so fast," he says, like Lucky about his own autistic frenzy. "First dirty, then make clean" (*Unnamable*, p. 15). But even when the language is clean, transparent, as it can be in Beckett, it still shifts and confounds, like the thought of love itself, intractable, unreal, the speech of one addressing another who, in order to be there *as* other, *never speaks*. This makes of the amorous subject and the unnamable not a psychological but a structural portrait, which is not quite what Barthes wanted for his mother.

The discourse in each case has no case history. Nor is there anything like the specificity of History in the Winter Garden Photograph. It is a discourse which "exists only in outbursts of language, which occur at the whim of the trivial, of aleatory circumstances" (*Lover's Discourse*, p. 3). It's as if, for the unmooring moment, all other categories were abolished and there were, in the play of amorous feeling or its other, *desperation,* nothing but the Imaginary from which to speak, out of the momentum of *"an extreme solitude . . ."* (p. 1). It is this solitude from which the unnamable thing is generated, the other becoming the site of love where love embraces desperation. For Barthes, the other is, for all the power of his love, what occurs *without* him. That is why for all his love he feels annulled by the *other's* suffering. It is this realization which, in the movement of desire, calls for its finest tuning, a certain distancing by means of which the *disappearance* of the other is made endurable.

As for Beckett, the excruciating pathos which remains virtually un-relieved, despite all the measures taken, is the insufficiency of any distance, which can never be enough, *not distance,* for he is not convinced that the other occurs without him: "he did not like to feel against his skin the skin of another," says the figure of *Enough.* "Mucous membrane is a different matter. . . . If the question were put to me I would say that odd hands are ill-fitted for intimacy. Mine never felt at home in his. Some-times they let each other go. The clasp loosened and they fell apart. Whole minutes passed before they clasped again. Before his clasped mine again" (*First Love*, p. 54). At night, before they disappear in the dawn, they walked in a half sleep and the other touched "where he wished. Up to a certain point. The other was twined in my hair" (p. 60). The amorous distance, says Barthes, can be given a certain name: *delicacy*

(*Lover's Discourse,* p. 58). Even such delicacy exists for Beckett only in the propriety of an impeccable distance in the intimacy which always fails. From things about to disappear, he says delicately elsewhere, he turns away in time, but to watch them out of sight, no, no, he can't do it—even if the pathos returns.

Whether desperate or enough, the amorous subject shares with the Unnamable the desire "to slip," as Barthes says, "between the two members of the alternative: . . . *I have no hope, but all the same . . .*" (*Lover's Discourse,* p. 62). They drift, slip, slide, perish with anything but imprecision, choose not to choose; between to be and not to be (in love, in life): *to be continued . . .* If, however, the lover—the lunar child, off in the moon—" 'offers' nothing in the play of the signifier," as Barthes once proposed it with more or less gratuitousness for the postmodern text, that's because the lover is "under the ascendancy of the Image-repertoire" where, as "forms of coalescence" (imitation, representation, or the dodge of anamorphosis), the analogical demon presides (p. 96). The *bête noire* of the autobiography of Barthes—which starts with photographs which *"will never be anything but . . . imaginary"* (*Barthes by Barthes,* p. 3)—*is* analogy, which adds to its curse its irrepressible attachment to the Nature which seems to have forgotten Hamm, though Hamm, that fractured and irrepressible actor, has never forgotten Nature. Barthes says about the demon of analogy, shifting from third to first person, "it is actually the imaginary I am resisting: which is to say: the coalescence of the sign, the similitude of signifer and signified, the homeomorphism of images, the Mirror, the captivating bait" (p. 44). But for the lover, there is no resisting analogy, since the lover suffused with amorous feeling embraces the play of figuration in the Image-repertoire. "The art of combining is not my fault," says the aging and ever-desiring subject of Beckett's *Enough,* breasted, with Aquarius hands. "It's a curse from above. For the rest I would suggest not guilty" (*First Love,* p. 54).

Barthes is not quite not guilty, however, in *Barthes by Barthes,* as he confesses to being "troubled by an *image* of himself," suffering when he is named. But as the lover in *A Lover's Discourse,* he wants to be named, spoken, at least upon the loved one's lips, repeated to satiety. He looks in the Mirror, takes the bait, has a craving to be engulfed—a far cry, poetic as it was, from the semioclastic mission and style of the earlier Brechtian Barthes. The one who speaks in *Barthes by Barthes,* as if a character in a novel, conceives of the perfect human relationship in a vacancy of the image, which is always on the side of domination and death (p. 43). The one who speaks as lover to the other who does not speak is always already dispersed, ungathered, suffering a loss of structure, the gentle hemorrhage from the body. The one who melts, thaws, resolves into a dew, is drawn to the "dream creature *who does not speak*" and who, in dreams, is the silence of death—which causes the lover to feel, with death silent, there, already beside him, that there is no place for him anywhere, even in death.

By contrast, the subject of *Barthes by Barthes* is attracted, as in Morocco, to a dryer climate and another plenitude, undreamed, unglossed, free of assigned image, interpretation. It is exhausting, true, this *matte* quality of relationships, but "a triumph of civilization or the truly dialectical form of human discourse" (p. 43). The lover's discourse is, as we've seen, not dialectical. There is no order to the figures except the arbitrariness of nomination and the alphabet. They erupt, twist, writhe, flail, sweat into each other, collide, subside, explode again, no first or last figure, *no love story,* and with no more system than a "flight of mosquitoes. . . ." Yet they have a vibratory cohesion, the mythic stamina of the Erinyes (*Lover's Discourse,* p. 7), who exhausted themselves as Furies before they turned into goddesses of love, still vigilant on behalf of the Mother.

The strange "exercises" of the mother in the window of *From an Abandoned Work* are like the figures of the amorous discourse, which are not figures in the rhetorical sense but, as Barthes describes them, gymnastic or choreographic. The fragments of discourse are in their figuration like the statuary of ancient athletes, "what in the straining body can be immobilized" or arrested (*Lover's Discourse,* p. 4). But it is, as Beckett knows, a kind of "lunatic sport," these exercises, for "underneath each figure lies a sentence, frequently an unknown (unconscious?) one, which has its use in the signifying economy of the amorous subject" (*Lover's Discourse,* pp. 5–6). Dubious use, dubious subject. This, for Beckett, is the *pensum,* the onerous task which may, for all he knows, proceed from what-she-was, the mother "waving, waving, waving me back or on I don't know, or just waving, my sad helpless love, and I heard faintly her cries." The cries mingle with the cries with which the universe of discourse is suffused, so that perception also seems to be made helpless by the mother who, though so "white and so thin I could see past her" (*First Love,* p. 40), was never sufficiently *still* to allow perception at all. So it is that in Beckett the figure which is, in Barthes, the lover at work is the figure of an abandoned work.

Waved back or on, he doesn't know, his sad helpless love—the lover's

discourse in Beckett is a broken monologue of one who if he couldn't
love well loved only too much, and still loves, first love, always, always
in vain, thus the straining outbursts of the frustrated body of love,
the trivial, the aleatory, which in Beckett is also anal. For him, as for
the aging Yeats, love has pitched his mansion in the place of excrement,
as in that straining figure that Lucky makes when they order him to
dance—the Scapegoat's Agony? the Hard Stool? Pozzo says, "The Net.
He thinks he's entangled in a net" (*Godot,* p. 27). And indeed, when he
begins to speak it's in the onrushing momentum of love, quaquaquaqua, the lunatic sport, as if the entire lover's discourse were uttered
at once; in the apparent gibberish, the entire network: an intellectual
history of the phallogocentric tradition, its breakdown, Fartov and Be-
lcher etc., like the death of the God of Love. All of what rushes through
the mind in Lucky's speech is, as Barthes says, "*marked,* like the printout
of a code" (*Lover's Discourse,* p. 4) or—in that other, scatological tradition—the contents of a cloaca. The words have specific uses, but underneath each figure lies a sentence, one long almost unendurable
sentence.

This sentence, or rather "syntactical aria," is the *pensum,* the substance
of a judgment, the *burden* of the aria, or song, for there is always in the
lover's discourse the plaint, the unfulfillable words of love, as if in the
absence of the Word there are only words, words, words. It is no mere
coincidence that when Barthes writes of the sentence-aria running
through the head, it constitutes the figure of *Waiting,* since the sentences
are matrices of suspended figures which utter an affect which is forever
breaking off. As with the waiting in Beckett's play, if the other doesn't
come, the other is hallucinated, for waiting is a delirium. "The words are
never crazed," says Barthes, "(at most perverse) but [as in Lucky's
speech] the syntax is: is it not on the level of the sentence," he asks, "that
the subject seeks his place—and fails to find it or finds a place imposed
upon him by language?" (p. 6). The thing which runs beneath the
figures of love is a verbal hallucination, "a mutilated sentence"—*the
pensum.*

It spawns itself in Beckett as the obsessional love lyric of self-corrosive
thought in love with the thought of loving. To love love, to be in love
with loving is—as we also see in Barthes—to abrade with apprehension
the object of love, *to annul it,* as if the death of love were pronounced in
the marriage of true minds. The lover's anxiety, says Barthes, is "the fear
of mourning which has already occurred at the very origin of love. . . ."
When Barthes then describes the mourning at the loss of love, he

realizes that what he is lamenting is the demise of "a beloved structure, and I weep for the loss of love," he says, "not of him or her" (p. 30). So, the lamentations of Beckett are the mourning *of* the Image-repertoire itself, the beloved structure. There is a sort of perverse pleasure in the broken images of love, as well as the unbearable ambiguity in the remembrance of the thing annulled. "As to whether it was beautiful, the face, or had once been beautiful, I confess I could form no opinion." The narrator of *First Love* had also looked at photographs, with faces that he "might have found beautiful had [he] known even vaguely in what beauty was supposed to consist." His father's face on a death-bolster had suggested a possible aesthetic, but "the faces of the living, all grimace and flush, can they be described as objects?" (*First Love*, p. 27). Anything like objects of love? There is a certain advantage, Barthes suggests, in the annulment of the other by love, since it may be absorbed with a certain eloquence into the abstraction of amorous sentiment. One may be soothed by desiring what, being absent, can no longer threaten or harm. But then there is a turnabout and the absence is desired. It is disannulled in the amorous sentiment which is the suffrance of desire, as if the delicate awakening of love occurred in a kind of libidinal reversal, at the dew point, the pathos of a seminal flow: "I admired in spite of the dark," says the figure of *First Love*, "in spite of my fluster, the way still or scarcely flowing water reaches up, as though athirst, to that falling from the sky" (p. 27).

But what begins (again) with such delicacy becomes monstrous in love, the waters never quite meeting in the consummation of desire. Nor is it really, in Beckett, as in *A Lover's Discourse*, that the waters merely recede and the other departs, turns away, fails to show, withdraws. Rather, and more oppressive yet, the other approaches. Even in recession the other approaches, "the other advances full upon me. He emerges as from heavy hangings, advances a few steps, looks at me, then backs away. He is stopping and seems to be dragging invisible burdens. . . . He raises his eyes and I feel the long imploring gaze, as if I could do something for him" (*Unnamable*, p. 14). If Barthes rehearses what it is to be *in* love, Beckett conveys the terror of *being-loved*, the one who is loved gratuitously and asked to love *in return* without ever knowing what it is that we call love, for which one invents the obscurities which supply its rhetoric which always fails, like the very idea of love. It's as if the approach of love incapacitates the very thing that loves. As for the mother who loves, can one learn to love like that? From innate knowledge? asks the voice of *The Unnamable*, "is that conceivable? Not for me" (p. 12). The dysfunction seems to be in the knowledge of love itself, what cannot be known without love so that love itself might be known.

"But I seem to have retained certain descriptions, in spite of myself," the Unnamable goes on: "They gave me courses on love, on intelligence," the curriculum of the *pensum,* "most precious, most precious." But what has that to do with love? "I use it still, to scratch my arse with" (p. 13). And yet there's a point in Beckett when the arse is sufficiently scratched to become the *punctum* in the *pensum* "once known, long neglected, finally forgotten, to perform," before there's an end, "gaining ground, losing ground" in the labyrinthine torment that can't be grasped, or limited, or felt, or suffered, "no, not ever suffered" (p. 36)—and yet, when the very possibility of love is foreclosed, there is the "luminous none the less" (p. 16), the pathos in the *punctum* which comes from the heart in the head.

Among the stars and constellations, the protagonist of *First Love* can only make out the Wains, first shown him by his father. He has also discovered the tenderness of the earth for those with no other prospect but her "and how many graves in her giving, for the living"—including the newborn child whose cries he plays with as he once played with song, "on, back, on, back, if that may be called playing" (p. 35). Freud called it so in the child's *fort/da,* the reclamation of the mother by the throwing out and drawing back of the grandson's spool, like Krapp's spool, *spoool,* a way of averting the cries—weeping is not crying—"cry is cry, all that matters is that it should cease. For years I thought they would cease. Now I don't think so anymore. I could have done with other loves perhaps. But there it is, either you love or you don't" (p. 36). In this sense, but I won't presume, I'm not sure that Barthes did. It seems like good plain sense, this remembrance of first love, at the tortuous end of a lover's discourse, but it is torn with an alien strength, on, back, on, back, from the curse of a bleeding heart.

NOTES

1. Roland Barthes, *A Lover's Discourse: Fragments,* trans. Richard Howard (New York: Hill and Wang, 1978), p. 12. Subsequent references will appear in the text.

2. Samuel Beckett, *Endgame* (New York: Grove, 1958), p. 18. Subsequent references will appear in the text.

3. *Roland Barthes by Roland Barthes,* trans. Richard Howard (New York: Hill and Wang, 1977), pp. 51–52. Subsequent references will appear in the text.

4. *Camera Lucida: Reflections on Photography,* trans. Richard Howard (New York: Hill and Wang, 1981), p. 75. Subsequent references will appear in the text.

5. *Waiting for Godot* (New York: Grove, 1954), p. 58. Subsequent references to *Godot* will appear in the text.

6. Sigmund Freud, *The Interpretation of Dreams,* trans. James Strachey (New York: Avon, 1965), p. 617.

7. *From An Abandoned Work,* in *First Love and Other Shorts* (New York: Grove, 1974), pp. 47–48. Subsequent references to the pieces in *First Love* will appear in the text.

8. Antonin Artaud, *The Theater and Its Double,* trans. Mary Caroline Richards (New York: Grove, 1958), p. 52.

9. *Beyond the Pleasure Principle,* trans. James Strachey (New York: Norton, 1961), p. 33.

10. *The Unnamable* (New York: Grove, 1958), p. 31. Subsequent references will appear in the text.

11. *Proust* (New York: Grove, n.d.), p. 29.

DISSEMINATING SODOM

At the drab end of an all-night in the winter before the sixties I was making my way through the London tube. I was exhausted, parched under the eyes, and the light in the long passageway burned like chlorox. I was alone and the corridor vacant when there began as if from the ascending womb of the deepest Underground a far breath-clotted breaking wail ("Think now," said Eliot, "History has many cunning passages, contrived corridors / And issues"), and there soon came pullulating toward me at high prancing amphetamined pitch something like the end of Empire or like the screaming remains of the return of the repressed—pearl-white, vinyl, in polo pants and scarf—an englistered and giggling outburst of resplendent queer. *He was sensational!* Soon after, equally sensational, was the Profumo scandal. It was preceded a year or so before by the Wolfenden Report.

Between the two events, homosexual reform and prostituted politics, there was surely no movement of cause and effect, yet there was something more than proximity and, with that semiotic break coming up the tube, an imminent overturning of social codes. On the hard-mod circuit of weed and rock, in the clamorous youth culture also coming out, they were singing the revelations and celebrating the inversions. Nearby, above the station, there was the tie-dyed dominion of Carnaby Street, which in the scrambling of sexuality at higher decibels gave a stylistic impetus to the new mutations, that increasing confusion of gender seen lovingly for a while among the hippies and now more virulently in punk. "We're into chaos," says Johnny Rotten, "not music." The Wolfenden Report was into order not libidinal anarchy, but the problem with the libido (whether wholly male or other) is that it is equally troublesome when you restrain it too much or when, having legal jurisdiction, you presume to give it a partial chance. There is a tricky econometrics of repression; there is a slippery dialectics of desire. Let "perversion" feel an access of pleasure and there is for that insatiate moment not only a confusion of genders but nothing like erogenous zones.

That is something desire never seems to forget. Zoning was obviously important to those who prepared the Wolfenden Report, which wanted to regulate the flow of perversion between the private and public spheres. It seemed a reasonably civilized thing to do, the legitimation of homosexual relations between consenting adults (male). But what was there to consent to and who could possibly legitimate that galloping specter I had seen, pure ideolect, whose plunging and lungless soundings were a full-throttled forecast of much weirder things to come? "The lung, a stupid organ . . ., swells," wrote Roland Barthes in an early essay on vocal music, tipping off a sexuality he was later to confess, "but gets no erection; it is in the throat, place where the phonic metal hardens and is segmented, in the mask that *signifiance* explodes, bringing not the soul but *jouissance*"[1]—that lubricious momentariness of the polysemous body that is in the Kama Sutra of recent literary theory (and because our language has no word for it) utterly unstatable and something more than bliss. In "the grain of the voice" of that figure in the tube there was "an absolute flow of becoming," beyond Good and Evil, outside the Law, as unencompassable as it was unappeasable. Deep Throat was tame in comparison and, so far as we know, heterosexual, both politically and sexually straight. This warped energy was another matter. It could hardly be fitted into a statute, no more than certain varieties of B&D and S&M or child sex or the loosening of the incest taboo or what may seem not at all unnatural for an animal remembering to be gay, erotic ministrations of beasts. Fine word, legitimate. There are things now out of the closet at which the gods who stand up for bastards would blush.

And while these things are not all homosexual, it is through homosexual discourse, and the more radical feminisms, that we are asked to confront them and see what they are, "no gods but their lubricity," as Sade declared somewhere in the *120 Days of Sodom*. We still can't be sure after the quick ruin of Profumo, shaking up the cabinet, led to the emergence of Christine Keeler or, in this country, after the mysteries of Chappaquidick or the exposure of Wilbur Mills or after fucking on the steps of the Lincoln Memorial led to the salable notoriety of Rita Jenrette, how much illicit or audacious sex there is in the background of parliamentary or congressional politics; but it is hard to overestimate the seductive foregrounding of the formerly forbidden in the postoedipal discourse on sexuality and power. Not to mention the effusions of sex into every orifice and vesicle of the voluptuous thinking body. The sex which used to be, according to D. H. Lawrence, too much on the brain is being theorized, after the desublimating activism of the sixties, all over a self-reflexive body of desire in a kind of ecological distribution of "phallogocentric" power. And so far as we can tell not only from the fantasy sex of Plato's Retreat and the community sucks of the gay baths, but from the classified ads in the *Village Voice* or *Screw* or the Los Angeles *Advocate* (the major gay newspaper), or even from an occasional hint in the *New York Review of Books,* it is not all wishful theory.*

"They're fucking in the open," says Warda, the hieratic whore of Genet's *The Screens,* shocked, wanting to preserve the rigor and mystery of her ancient rites. And they're fucking everywhere and any which way the body allows, rubbing, sucking, 69, clitorally and anally, even more Roman than Greek, and it appears they think a good deal more about it, more subtly, if they're fucking similar bodies, and far more labyrinthinely if the similar bodies are women.

Confronted, then, with the widening dispensation of sodomous practice and the new crossbreeding of homosexual and feminist thought— with its deflationary critique of the phallocratic structures of power—I am very conscious of speaking of homosexuality in an equivocal voice as

---

*August, 1986: If the gay baths have recently been subject to closure, the theory which I am discussing is also threatened by AIDS. That was not at all in the news at the time I wrote this essay, nor when it was first published. AIDS is *not* a homosexual disease. Gays have been victimized by a virus and not the wages of sin. There are, of course, those only too ready to think that perversion is getting what it deserves. There are also those who further victimize the victims, out of ignorance, fear, bigotry, or some not unreasonable approximation of justifiable concern. While AIDS now looms as a major epidemic, crossing sexual preference, it remains—given the percentage of those already infected with the virus—an especially dreadful situation for all homosexual men, whether or not they had engaged in the more experimental or promiscuous lifestyles which made some of them particularly vulnerable. As for the disturbing ideas under discussion, I don't want to add to the multitudinous sins transmissible by heterosexuals in seizing upon disaster to reinforce my reservations. What was, for me, provocative to begin with, remains so, because it raised in its audacity the most threatening question of all, which is always a question of limits.

It was a question, however, largely ignored or overruled in the libidinal flow of theory, or left to those who were being left behind, as if it were their disease. What should be apparent now is that the question is contagious and nobody is immune. If the discourse still believes what it says, that would amount to encouraging gays to remain in double jeopardy which, as a matter of personal choice, even among consenting adults, jeopardizes others whether they've consented or not. I want to emphasize again, however, that some of the extreme or questionable forms of behavior which I've already mentioned in the essay are not—as we should know of AIDS—confined to gays. And while various sexual practices are more or less exclusive to gays, there are others which belong only to the nonrestrictive community of desire. That, as reflected and endorsed in homosexual and radical feminist discourse, was at least sufficiently attractive in thought to induce me to write this essay.

a heterosexual male with a reasonably accessible body but a maybe irredeemable genital fix. While some or even most male homosexuals are similarly fixed, with a shift of orifice for the orgasm or in dual masturbation, it is the increasing *feminization* of homosexuality, in behavior and theory, that is altering our conceptions of sexual possibility, causing us to rethink the nature of masculinity and femininity (or our resistance to the rethinking), every lymph node and sensuous capillary of the labyrinth of gender, raising the alluring and threatening prospect of a polysexuality irrespective of gender (sometimes of persons) and other classifications as well, age, criminality, neurosis, cruelty, madness, family (nest of incest), biological species: not only "becoming-woman" but "becoming-plant," man as vegetable, man as mineral, man and beast.[2]

There is in this becoming a suggestion of archaic correspondences and an older plenitude of being, as well as Artaud's dream of a body without organs and one streaming sexuality, the naked sonorous realization of an ultimate body flow. In the body politic of the becoming body, with its single sexuality, the encompassing term is feminine because alienated woman is assumed to be closer to the not-yet-specified and transformative situation of *desire*. ("Is me her was you dreamed before?" says the winnowing Fan in the transvestic revels of Joyce's Nighttown. "Was then she him you us since knew? Am all them and the same now we?") What is being sought in the new surrealist revisionism of Marx and Freud is a political reconstruction of the unconscious by all possible semiotic means. The emphasis in the discourse is on the subject speaking its own nature. The discovery of that nature—rejecting the hierarchical legacy of names and substance—must move, however, through the dominant systems of thought by passing through the phases of homosexuality and femininity in becoming-what-one-is[3] outside the coordinates of the heterosexual scheme or, as in new German film or Violent painting, in a discontinuous elsewhere within the existing scheme. The gay coming out is, then, only the beginning of a process in which the one male libido of Freud—both a by-product and instrument of a destructive and usurious power—is converted and recycled in the transsexual operations of a different breeder reactor, the tissues and membranes of the becoming-woman in whose sumptuously signifying body, a passive and pacifying nonpower, the savage cost of the old libidinal organization is defrayed.

The fondest fancies of desire are so myriad and persuasive in their new wondrous eroticism, releasing the old sexual taboos into life and thought and "writing," that we have not only the salubrious savor of a polymorphous sex, oral drive, anal drive, labile and duodenal, an unencumbered, unlocalized body without end, an immeasurable mantic space of unimpaired pleasure, but we also have fantasies of desire without fantasies, that is, *nonrepresentational desire,* imageless, pure vertiginous flow without zones or boundaries or mimetic blockages, the organless body without ego, no destiny, no closure, always-becoming selectively what it never was. In the no longer lewd but ludic body of libidinal exchange, what is being imagined is a sort of supply-side economics that is really staying the course, with ceaseless expenditure, rising income, and no withholding tax.

This post-Marxist romanticism is not, however, as ingenuous or utopian as it seems. It has already ingested a lot of history, and it understands that homosexuality, once defined by civil and canonical codes, has stopped being a juridical subject and has become a case, an autobiography, a life history which is now mixed up, as Michel Foucault has shown, with the production of truth. It is discourse which arises from what Ricoeur has called an ethos of suspicion, including Nietzsche as well as Marx and Freud, and it more or less assumes that nothing spoken by the voices of history, even when speaking of freedom, almost especially then, can be trusted to set us free.

It also knows quite well that in the vision of *one* sexuality remains, nonetheless, the spawning question of *sexuality.* We are still wondering whether it is inherent or a historical category, or where sexuality if it exists begins—that question disrupting the ethos of an infantile sexuality—and whether or not an asexuality (not celibacy) is possible, and where sexuality stops if it starts. If I reach out and touch somebody in friendship is that sexual or not? And what about the old trinitarian liaison of sex and killing and dying? Our conflicted attitudes toward homosexuality can no longer, as the erotic is caught up in theory like Leda in the beating wings of the swan, be assuaged merely by protecting the rights, say, of the amiable gay couple of our acquaintance who have a marriage as sweetly domestic as anything we have seen between man and woman (maybe more so). Nor is our potential revulsion narrowed down to the thought—as it was for Joseph Epstein some years ago in *The Atlantic Monthly*—that this domestic couple means one man's cock up another's ass, though I shall return to that revulsion later as something more than a rhetorical question in the tropics of discourse.

What we are being asked to respond to now is the fullest possible redemption in *more than thought* of the memory of gratification which, as we learned from Freud, is in the linguistic economy of the unconscious the metonymic ground of thought. It is not merely an amorous and tautological shift in the signifying chain, or a "vatic bisexuality,"[4] which is being urged upon us. What we are also being confronted with, in more than theory, are the kinkier pleasures of the homosexual fringe as an experimental index of self-chosen identity. As the subject speaks its own nature and, what's more, is about to act upon it, something sticks in the grain of the voice, resisting but still desiring, and is tempted to ask: How far are you willing to go in the pursuit (or defense) of *jouissance?* Sometimes it's hard to know who is asking whom. But the question is the carnalizing basis of a new metaphysics of sex with its transfigurations of pleasure in a thoroughly eroticized body and its desire to break permanently with all the subterfuges of bourgeois power, including the institution of marriage, reproduction, and the fatal couple of a dualistic sex. In the eye of desire, that copula of destiny is a living death, the mortal enemy of desire which, at whatever death-defying limit, insists not merely upon its civil rights but the unconditional extension of pleasure.

It is the insatiability of desire—and the ubiquity of the word—which is the germinating principle of the homosexual/feminist discourse, with its subversive reconnoitering of the body of desire, desire spilling over, onanistically, listening to itself, desiring, replicating but never the Same, deliberately playing with the quasi–etymological kinship of semantics and semen (passing it around from mouth to mouth), a cybernetic sex *seminating,* blurring the old party line of sexual ideology and refusing the Freudian categories, especially sexuality, insofar as it claims to be an irreducible life energy when it is no more than a historical formation or production of language that may have seen its day.

It was, ironically, a fatal couple who had also seen their day who anticipated the infinity, if not the infirmity, of this desire. "There's not a minute of our lives should stretch/Without some pleasure now," says Antony to Cleopatra (*Ant.* I.i. 46–47). In the seduction of eroticism by theory, it's as if the discourse were expelling or excreting Antony, that denatured figure of aggressive power, and enacting Cleopatra, "her soft hours" and "strong toil of grace," looking like sleep, "As sweet as balm, as soft as air, as gentle," the lost dream of libidinal glory; but in the membranous meridian of that (interpreted) dream, "an aspic trail" of infinite pleasure, the "slime" on the fig leaves of her "Immortal long-ings" (V.ii. 279–351).

"It is one of the obvious injustices of social life," wrote Freud in his essay "Civilized Sexual Morality and Modern Nervousness" (1908), "that the standard of culture should demand the same behaviour in sexual life from everyone—a course of conduct which, thanks to his nature, one person can attain without effort, whereas it imposes on another the severest mental sacrifices; though, indeed, the injustice is ordinarily nullified by disregard of the commands of morality."[5] Even in his most far-reaching premonitions of civilization's discontents, Freud possibly never anticipated the venereal currency of nullifying disregard. By emphasizing, so far, the extremes of homosexual practice and the privi-leged consciousness of homosexual theory, I do not mean to ignore the unpurged quotient of plain mental sacrifice or, as with the blacks, the simpler inequities which persist or the homosexuals who are still in hiding. Thus, in and around the conceptual intricacies of the discourse on desire, I want to talk of its social content, the current status of homosexuals, and the psychological reasons for the concentration on language in the politics of gay activism, after its earlier social gains. In recent years homosexuality has been thought of, as it appropriated the themes and strategies of radical politics, by analogy with racial prejudice, as a form of consciousness-raising, as a rejection of bourgeois models of mental health, as a refusal of psychological and behavioral servitude, as well as a liberation movement that plays out a new repertoire of ex-perimental sexuality as part of the ongoing theatricalization of everyday life. Within the homosexual subculture there is, moreover, a whole series of minority genres and crossovers with other subcultures: transvestites and sado-masochists, for instance, are not exclusively homosexual, and there are affinities in dispossession with other halfway beings, drug addicts, winos, prostitutes, convicts, punk rockers, rappers, children, and women who are coming out of the kitchen as the gays are coming out of the closet. While some of the gays are now militantly politicized—including "normal" women who have rejected the oppression of mar-riage and chosen lesbianism—there are still gays leading the same old double lives with a coded language that introjects a heterosexual norm.

The irreducible pain of the homosexual, whatever claims are made for present happiness, is the history of secrecy and past disgrace. And within the homosexual community, with its parodistic élan and sometimes

devastating critique of the spurious values and repressive sensual same-
ness of the heterosexual world, there is an aversion to its own
homogeneous sex and value distortions, possibly more perverse for all
the support given by gay organizations and Gay Pride, possibly the more
intense because of the apparent liberation. So, in Robert Patrick's play
T-Shirts, we have an older homosexual assailing a younger homosexual
with the harshest truth of the tormented matter, about young people so
screwed up in fact that they can't hold a job for a week, though they may
be in their third smash year as the "fist-fuckee" in the backroom of the
Anvil. "Why should you tell a kid like that he's systematically eroding his
ability to function as anything but a punchboard and an active element
in the exciting, expanding gay market?" which is "plugged into a con-
glomerate as heartless as Con Ed. . . ." The play's witty assaults and
self-abuse are conducted on a high alcoholic content, as in the blurring
conviviality of the Mafia-run gay bars. Why is it, however, that even the
"heavy leather isn't enough to stop [the] fits of shaking? Well, hell, what
would there be for an American to *do* if he did grow up?"[6] But then this
seemingly reactionary critique from within is canceled out somewhat
when the older gay, a well-known writer, says to the younger gay that if
he had a chance of getting any of the action he wouldn't have said a
negative word.

The pathos of the aging gay who has not managed to settle into a
long-term relationship is part of the folklore of the homosexual scene.
Many gays have of course found such relationships, and if there was
regression before, many have grown up impressively after the decision
to come out. Some have also written without any self-corroding wit about
their unashamed public life, as compared to the unintelligible hypocri-
sies of the straighter world which the gay, with a new openness and
honesty, has no trouble whatever rejecting. Or so it appears. "Some gays
begin to see heterosexuals," writes Peter Fisher in *The Gay Mystique,* "in
much the same light that heterosexuals have viewed homosexuals for
years. A new 'straight mystique' is arising in which the stereotypical
heterosexual appears as a tragic, self-defeating, sexually inhibited individual, hiding his sexuality in the closet, while the media exploit his
fascination with sex and his need to live up to society's roles."[7] And then
the question straights have traditionally asked gays who, as Fisher says,
have similar emotions, highs and lows, but with perhaps more current
satisfaction about the way they are living their lives: "Can heterosexuals
ever really be happy?"

I suppose the real question is, can any of us—heterosexual or homosexual or all the discomfited variations between—ever *really* be happy? And is happiness, whatever it is, really compatible with sexuality, whatever it is? Which is the question Freud finally came to, as well as one of the reasons why the homosexual/feminist discourse wants either to change the categories of sexuality or get rid of the concept altogether.

For Freud, it is a vain project. He believed it was also a vain project for psychoanalysis—presupposing an original bisexuality channeled into the biological conventions of masculine or feminine—to think it can solve the problem of homosexuality. In his essay on "The Psychogenesis of a Case of Homosexuality in a Woman," Freud concluded that psychoanalysis can do no more than disclose "the psychical mechanisms that resulted in determination of the object-choice, and [trace] the paths leading from them to the instinctual basis of the disposition."[8] In 1920, Freud wasn't ready to see—following the negative transference of a system that accounts for the woman acting like a man—that there might be the (chosen) alternative of a female homosexuality. But he did give us the cues for reading the psychical mechanisms as linguistic structures, whereupon we were led down a circuitous path of substitutions, displacements, and secondary revisions, none of which could be taken at their word, to the dialysis of recent theory with its relentless questioning of "the instinctual basis of the disposition." If what we're tracing is a construction of language, then why should we be treating it as a moral and social problem to begin with? It is that scandal which outrages both homosexuals and women—suffering the adduced history of a disposition to hysteria—who then summon up the original bisexuality in freer-flowing avatars of sensual difference and play down or around with the conventions of biology, with its binary assumption of an originary division.

But that hardly disposes of the problem, which in the discourse is converted to a "problematic." That there is need, however, for such wordplay around the thing called homosexuality cannot merely be ascribed to the conceptual mystifications of logocentric power unless, as does happen in the Derridean strain of the discourse, we see the "instituting trace" of such power in the very incipience of history, almost already there before the beginning of time. The symptoms of such power are also seen in psychoanalysis which is, unless lifted off the couch and opened into history, likely to be not history's speaking cure but its heuristic dead end. When we are reminded, however, that Freud's view of sexuality in the etiology of neurosis was derived from a system of thought that was paternal and hierarchical, a male-dominated structure of power seen through the proscenium arch(e) of the old oedipal drama in a nineteenth-century Viennese theater, we should also remember that Freud was very much aware of the evolutionary quality of his thought, the speculative contingency and temporal placement, "bearing in mind [what he put in a parenthesis of an early essay] that all men conceal the truth in these matters."[9] He certainly didn't exclude himself and was always prepared to see, so far as he could see, the incidence of sexual irregularities "in view of the pressure of present-day social conditions," which made it impossible to determine absolutely "what degree of deviation from normal sexual functioning was to be regarded as pathogenic."[10] If part of the problem was the notion of irregularities and another part to determine the normative, Freud eventually found it impossible to envisage an alteration of social conditions that would eliminate the pathogenic, making it all the more necessary to understand the dynamics of sexuality and, for him, its biological and perhaps chemical basis.

If desire is preeminent in the homosexual discourse, Freud always distrusted the nature of that desire, which he sees as an onanistic fixation to incestuous fantasies which may result in total impotence or, if sensual feeling remains active, "seeks only objects evoking no reminder of the incestuous persons forbidden to it." Erotic life is thus dissociated even when there are genuinely tender feelings for the substitute object. "Where such men love they have no desire and where they desire they cannot love. In order to keep their sensuality out of contact with the objects they love, they seek out objects whom they need not love. . . ." Or if (seemingly) loved, in the displacement of the forbidden object, degraded. There is no way in Freud's view—still observing the incest prohibition and, in 1912, shying away from homosexuality in women— that the object of homosexual love could be esteemed like the original sexual object. "As soon as the sexual object fulfills the condition of being degraded, sensual feeling can have free play, considerable sexual capacity and a high degree of pleasure can be developed."[11] As revocation of the incest barrier is approached and the terms of degradation rescinded, it would appear that the sexual capacities might widen and the degrees of pleasure soar. Freud doubts it. For him there is a threshold. While the homosexual/feminist discourse is either revising the threshold upward or vociferously denying that it is anything more than a discredited reflection of a self-debasing system of power, the post-Marxist historicism with which that is argued remains an open historical question. So does the justification of homosexuality in the historical deconstructions of power.

What does seem to be true—even after revisionist histories such as John Boswell's *Christianity, Social Tolerance, and Homosexuality*—is that homosexuality has in all periods been sufficiently disturbing as to make it the subject of discourse in more onerous ways than heterosexuality, for all the animus and savage detestation that arises in Western thought—from before St. Augustine to after Strindberg—against the division of the sexes and heterosexual love. There is no doubt that the correction of history and the invocation of precedent helps to constitute a desirable argument for greater social tolerance; but it is hardly true, as Boswell asserts, that only societies which are anxious and intolerant about homosexuality are likely to ask how homosexuality is caused.[12] Or if the anxiety persists through greater tolerance, as it does today, it may be that the questions being asked by those most (if not entirely) liberated from bias are being asked at an ideological level that has been escalated, as in homosexual discourse, by the failure of history to provide an unbiased answer to a question it has never silenced, and possibly never will.

As we assess, in this perspective, our deepest feelings about homosexuality, the issue would not seem to be whether it was approved in this period or that, or in other cultures. We know it was and still is, but the question remains whether such precedent is a certification of value. It might seem a barbarous question in ascertaining individual rights, but it is far from that in an ideological context where homosexuality is being advanced as a behavioral model and as a subversive proposition of corrective value. As for its presence in history, what we still do not know with any clarity, despite the proliferation of books and journals on the subject, is why homosexuality is tolerated in certain places and certain times and then loses favor and respect and is venomously persecuted. There is, according to the historian Keith Thomas, no sociology of homosexuality that explains the fluctuations of tolerance and why it is that until the bourgeois dominance of the modern era there has been "no Western society (not even ancient Greece) which has taken a very tolerant view of passive homosexuality by adult males." While we know from history and legend that active homosexuality has been acceptable among philosophers and warriors, the attribution to a man of the passive role "has always been an insult."[13]

   The sacerdotalizing of this insult has been the peculiar mission of Jean Genet, who has swallowed the insult like a wafer and made of it a form of unalterable destiny. One of the most deviously marginal figures of the feminized homosexual tradition, a cerebral preying mantis of desire, Genet has served as a model for subcultural styles and for a radical activism that he simultaneously subverts. He also eludes the theory which, in rationalizing sexual practices verging on crime, inevitably takes his name in vain. I will say more about that in a moment. Meanwhile, there is a kind of Genetic glee in the less saintly subversions of the insult that we see in any issue of a gay newspaper where sodomy is advertised with no deception as if—after revisionary Freud and the ascension of Genet—there were no longer any reason for a false bottom, so long as it has a suitable homeopathic price. What may otherwise be read as degradation may be construed as something else: the gay reversal of the act of passivity into a manifestation of the freest enterprise, a recapitalization of the libido for other purposes, like Marx turning Hegel on his head. And it would perhaps be less troubling to straights if they knew on what grounds they might object to it, if at all, instead of being asked, in the theoretical upending of their repression, what it is that should make them want to object.

   To repeat: what is most disturbing about the increasingly licensed excesses of homosexual behavior is not so much that it is taking place—because it is still somewhat cordoned off—but that it is being consciously enunciated as an ideological critique. For we are talking today not only about how particular individuals are choosing to live their own lives, or selling them short, but of *becoming-homosexual* as a political style and a body of thought, an ontological genealogy of revisionist morals.

   Sodomy has become a paradigm of sexual innovation and a methodology for the deconstruction of power. The homosexual underworld has had long intercourse with the avant-garde, and the most futuristic reach of its surfacing thought shares something of the reactionary tendency of any avant-garde. After a period of denunciation of history, or seeming indifference, the thing not accepted for its own sake is, in a reconstruction of history, then defended as a resumption of primal energies that were suppressed or aborted in the past. However true that may be, history like the heart seems to have its own reasons that are not, Foucault acknowledged, merely epistemic. And while both heart and history are sorely vulnerable to an infrastructure of thought that might over-determine the answers, these additional questions must be asked: What does becoming-homosexual have to offer not to the individual person who is, for whatever reason or in whatever way, deserving of the name, but to the social and political reality whose resistance may be weakening? And what does the emergence of homosexuality as an unproscribed spectrum of behaviors, a repertoire of emulable styles, each demanding more and more territory for their imperative desires, have to tell us about our collective lives and, for those who don't go by that name, the uncertain measures of our own desires? Whatever it does for those who are, by genesis or choice or proclamation, homosexuals.

Whatever must still be said on behalf of the rights of these individuals, including their right to act collectively, other imperatives and aversions arise as larger theoretical claims are made for the political wisdom of former perversions. As a nonreproductive model of social as well as psychic process, becoming-homosexual is part of the paraphilia of the postmodern, not only a new sexual politics but the reification of all politics, supersubtilized beyond the unnegotiable demands of the sixties, from which it is derived, into a more persuasive rhetoric of unsublimated desire. If anything like it is realizable in some unforeseeable future, it doesn't appear to have any supportable precedent in history, however revised. *Which is insufficient reason to ignore it.* For we have also learned from Freud that we remember most deeply what we are trying to forget, and there is a critical difference that nobody seems to understand between the thing that exists somehow within the living memory of history and our ability to verify that it was ever really there.

Still, just as there have been no documented matriarchies in history, the only societies in which homosexuality may have been encouraged as a matter of civic virtue were warrior societies, not the pacifying ones we are remembering or imagining. It is not at all certain even in warrior societies whether homosexuality was thought to be the cause of virtue, say courage in battle, or a coexisting phenomenon that still needed public justification, as it does in the widening dominion of our more indecisive balance of terror and invisible garrison state. As for the biological issue of reproduction, thwarted by homosexuality, one certainly doesn't have to picket for the Right to Life in order to see that there's at least one gross undersight in the otherwise discerning exposure of the repressive sexual cycle of the bourgeois family romance. Speaking of scandal, as they do in both homosexual and feminist discourse, it is in those cultures, aboriginal and modern, often cited as evidence of the propriety of other erotic practices, that we see reproduction controlled sometimes arbitrarily and often brutally, if at all; and at the far Eastern end of the French Connection—where the polysemous illusion is god—there is a tradition of amorous pleasure writ large not only on the multiply copulating figures of ancient temples but, to the political illumination of Indira Ghandi, on the uncontrollable postmodern enormity of a starving population.

Among the values being debated, true, is what you're willing to starve for. Or, in the discourse of the human sciences, what you consider to be human and whether it will survive at all, in the images by which it is known. But despite the critical eloquence of the discourse and the relaxation of taboos, those images are stubborn and remain the agencies of power. That the image of homosexuality has improved does not mean it has achieved, even in the gay power bloc of San Francisco, any determining status in our public life—unless one takes into account another inversion, an ingenious argument in the discourse.

This argument reconstitutes homosexuality not as deviant and marginal to the established order, but rather as its endogamous basis. Thus, Luce Irigaray reminds us that because trade in Western culture takes place mainly or even exclusively among men—women, like signs and money, being exchange—*"the very possibility of the socio-cultural order would necessitate homosexuality. . . .* Heterosexuality amounts to the assignment of roles in the economy. . . ." In this exchange mechanism, the red blood of sexuality is squeezed dry and what is sovereign is a pretense that *"does not yet recognize its endogamies."* Intead of being the exception to the rule of the bourgeois economy, homosexuality is, according to this theorization, the rule itself, disguised, probably "because the 'incest' at work in homosexuality must be kept in the realm of pretense."[14] The genealogy of the patriarchal order, with its Abrahams and Isaacs, the pederastic love between father and son, cannot be openly avowed. It can only be secreted in language, displaced into the symbolic. But it is homosexuality which is the regulating law of social functioning, trade among males with women as currency. When males, however, openly practice homosexuality they short-circuit the regulation of commerce and thus devalue the standard of value itself. If the penis is used for pleasure only, with no reproductive purpose, the phallus yields up its power.

In the patriarchal order, pleasure is the woman's game. Because of the system of trade, however, when a woman makes love to another woman she must naturally be a male homosexual, acquiring the virility that such commerce requires. So Freud's question about what a woman wants is, within this system, the wrong question. How can somebody who doesn't

really exist except as exchange want anything? "The only thing really
expected of her is that she *maintain, without fail, the circulation of pretense by
enveloping herself in femininity.*"[15] Here is where the feminist psychoanalysis corrects Freud's blindness about female homosexuality.
About the entire condition of the pretending woman, Irigaray asks:
What if the goods refuse to go to market? What if they develop another
kind of trade, for pleasure's sake, for pure libidinal enjoyment, without
appropriation, possession, capitalization? This would entail, to be sure,
the embarrassing radical necessity of liberating incest from "the realm
of pure pretense" which "has forbidden a certain economy of
abundance."[16]

Frankly, it is easier to imagine the liberation of incest than a cessation
of pretense, but until that happy day we will unfortunately have to
accommodate ourselves, after the earlier illusions of an economy of
abundance, to an economy of scarcity. That is made all the more difficult
here, despite the victory of French socialism, by the persistence of tight
money and the presumptive mandate of the Moral Majority. None of
this lessens by any means the number of homosexuals coming out in
those places at some safe distance from the new vigilance, nor does it
prevent many women, despite the frustration of the ERA, from reducing in small orbit the realm of pure pretense, whether as lesbians or
bisexuals or in the heterosexual world. But it would be naive to think
that the sovereignty of that world has been appreciably diminished by
the structural anthropology of Irigaray's argument. Nor does such argument relieve the daily pains and insult which the less theoretical discourse of gay activism is still trying to alleviate, with varying degrees of
militancy, in a rather civil way. For all the sanity and pretended superiority of the gay mystique, there is no way to minimize the affront that
heterosexuality still represents, and must necessarily represent, to the
homosexual ethos. To the extent that the dominant culture still defines
the homosexual role in it, however permissively, constructing that role as
a permutation of difference, however nuanced, the homosexual culture
must feel the imposed restriction of an estranging Law, even if that Law
is relabeled with its own name.

Homosexual oppression is historically specific. It depends not only on
current legal status, but where the self-defining homosexual subject
lives, does his work, carries on his affairs—in short, it also determines
the degree to which he is out of the closet or what, when he came out, he
decided to wear. You can do what you want in Soho, but you can't yet go

in drag to Time/Life or wear leather at the Citibank, even if there were a branch in Soho. (*She* will meanwhile notice, having less trouble with drag, that when I am not speaking in the second person I am using the double-purpose pronoun of the heterosexual grammar.) If the legal structures which first constrained the gays, causing them to play things in private or close to the vest, have now opened sufficiently as to encourage the self-focused pleasure-seeking of the gay community, and its polysexual extremisms, it has had trouble determining, as it was politicized, just how much unorthodoxy it could sustain without divesting itself of its legal gains. It was important, for instance, to let everybody know that gays do not go around seducing children, but the homosexual problematic becomes a problem when it speculates, as it does, upon the rights of those who *are* interested in child sex. Among the indeterminacies of *jouissance* and the found eloquence of the speaking subject is the question of who, when a child *is* violated, is speaking for the child? If we can't, they can't, but can the child?

It is a difficult problem, as they say in Court, for all parties concerned. I am not entirely sure that the Reverend Jerry Falwell wouldn't speak better on this subject than the homosexual discourse. As for the practical politics in the sexual politics of becoming-homosexual, there are times when the speaking subject does better not to speak for himself. The necessary presence of straights in any political alliance makes eventually, however, for a dilemma of identity that for all the common rhetoric does not similarly exist for blacks or other minority groups. If more gays than blacks continue to pass, it is because they are more vulnerable, and were to begin with, and are likely to remain so longer. Whatever the identity now being claimed or seized, no homosexual is raised *as* a homosexual, so that it is fallacious to think of the politicization of homosexuals as equivalent to that of blacks or Hispanics or women (who are not a minority and who disagree widely on sexual rights). If gays are not sexually unnatural, they are an unnatural constituency, without the cohesion of caste or class or the training from birth, within the knowing structure of the experienced family, that has permitted other oppressed groups to perfect their defense mechanisms in public and feel otherwise supported at home. The worst to be said, perhaps, for the homosexual appropriation of the word *gay* is not that it has deprived us of a spritely word for a lively experience, but that it has become part of the vanguard sexual illusion of a superior experience which remains severely dubious as the mere radical inversion, or parody, of the old charge of homosexual corruption. Instead of being pitiful, obscene, or depraved, the homosexual subject would be revealed by Gay Pride as vital and celebratory—not at all (or not all) limp-wristed, even macho, and if once in a while effeminate, *why not?*—rather than pinched into the self-defeating categories of heterosexual behavior and thought.

Genital heterosexuality has its troubles, but for the gay—aside from the stamina required in keeping it up to comply with the label—there is another sort of double bind, precisely because of the honorific reappropriation of sexual *difference.* To the extent that gays still pretend to be a challenge to the superstructure of bourgeois capitalism, they can't avoid the accentuation of the difference, and with it a more than theoretical deference to the old illicit energies of the homosexual underworld, and its canonical rhetoric of abominations. Thus returns the notion that there *is* something unique, arcane, encoded, queer that is subversive *by nature,* as if being gay were instinctively revolutionary, and by another kind of homeopathic magic, contagiously so. The result is that while theorists are trying to emancipate the discourse from the abstractions of Freudian sexuality, and the implication of an instinctual basis for the disposition—a homosexual *essence* that was a bad historical rap—the forlorn gay finds himself in the old binaries, up to the nines in the sexual category that he may have once wanted to disown because it had shamelessly totaled his entire being into that single determinant, as if sodomy, consubstantial, had entered his soul.

The reality is that the homosexual has undergone acculturation in a social order which invalidates what he has come to choose for himself. There is a potential strengthening of personal will, but as a social group homosexuals are no more than an aggregate of such wills, still disparate if not desperate, brothers and sisters under the skin maybe, but not out there where it can, as with most blacks, be seen, and still not as sure as blacks these days that they *want* it to be seen. If they do they have to *create a surface* which is a sign of choosing *against* since, whatever injuries they share with other minority groups, these other groups are also dominantly heterosexual, on the whole more puritanically so than bourgeois intellectuals. Thus, for the majority of homosexuals there is very small political comfort in the spreading of sodomous practice or in our growing consciousness that more or less everything is being permitted.

That most homosexuals can pass and have been passing for most of their lives means that when they decide to come out they are first choosing a subcultural identity which the blacks, say, may not have defined until recently but have at least shared from birth. Depending on where they come out, they must still be more or less clandestine. The problem of a double identity is hardly resolved. And for the individual gay, the homosexual community is a fragile fiction. There is still equivocation as to whether, except for sexual preference, he (or she) should present himself as just like everybody else or whether the parameters of that choice have other dimensions. Does he want to make an ideological case of it or, now that the confession is made, does he just want to be let alone? Whatever he wants, he is more likely than not to be drawn into an identity that comes only with approval of what he does. With rather indelibly mixed feelings about deviance, the rest of us will accept him as just like everybody else if he tempers the homosexual signs and, despite all theory, perpetuates the social order which politically denies his reality and secretly, despite all tolerance, scorns his values. The homosexual subject remains always to be believed, or tested, however tolerant we may be. The tolerance is bound to have a deposit of unavoidable condescension, as belated tolerance always does, and the psychic reality of that tolerance may even be subverted in *our* fantasies about *his* behavior in private. If he wants to be assimilated he has almost no alternative except to initate the social forms which reject what he represents. And what he *represents* is not by any means, and all the more because of the discourse, entirely clear to him.

To *become* a homosexual is first of all to overcome the stigma. The becoming subject must suppress within any personal sense of disorder or disease and convince himself that, whatever the charge, it cannot be true—unless he wants to take the path of the hard-core queer who, like Genet, makes it truer than true. There is, in any case, the subsequent necessity to become another who is precisely what one has learned previously to despise. The reality of the homosexual is irreparably, I think, a struggle with that history. The worst part of that struggle, only to be surmised, would seem to be the incrimination within rather than the openly declared enemy without. We are all scarred, but for the homosexual the scars were the results of wounds that had once to be tended in solitary, and for which there was no emergency ward. There must also be, with whatever healing or acquired defenses, however sophisticated now, the tremor of unrelieved frustration, maybe rage, at the clear knowledge that there are still—beyond all the insensitivity which you can easily dismiss and to which you are undeniably superior— those whom you know and respect but who, at some inexpressible level of sheer antipathy, still despise you, for which reason you may still be despising yourself.

If that is made more bearable by special achievement, as with the homosexual artist, or by the sustenance of a homosexual community, it is nevertheless a problem to be conducting a good part of your life, despite the compensating argot of a homosexual style, in the binary language of the straight world where you earn your daily bread. As for the bourgeois homosexual trying to split that class identification apart and break away from heterosexual thought, he reads our newspapers, sees our plays (whose all-dominating image-system, televised, is hardly undermined when appropriated by Pop and camp), signs the same checks, collects dividends from the same bank, invests as we do in the same money markets and common stock, and is if anything—because of the cycling of surplus value through the fashionable mores of the homosexual ghetto—more vulnerable to consumerism as well. And if he thinks at all about these contradictions, of which he is very well aware, he may have been spurred to not-forgetting by the recent column of a gay dissident in the formerly radical tabloid now owned by Rupert Murdoch, who made his fortune after Wolfenden in British newspapers where sodomy is still the chiefest scandal of a meretricious sex.

It is these living contradictions of a written world which have caused gay activists to shift attention from the civil rights of homosexuality to the language which established the category, the production of signs and their dissemination. Whatever the transgression of nature by culture—that genetic question set aside—homosexuals are made of language. They are also trying to remake themselves by language. So we are not only aware of gays who, while cruising, display signs to advertise for a specific kind of encounter, a typology of perversion, but also of gays, often the same, who are trying to disburden themselves of the stain of perversion from the maybe indelible inscriptions of the heterosexual world which still determine their habits of mind.

While gay socialists are struggling with these impediments and trying to reconstruct their political strategies, the fact that gays do cross over and pass disrupts the logic of a class analysis and makes inevitably for the continuance of alienation. Meanwhile, in America, the idea of a dominant class is less indeterminate, showing its truer colors in these days of welfare cuts and higher-income tax reprieve. The value of the dollar may go up and down on the international market, but it is the language of the dominant class that remains our major currency. The business of life, including the task of extracting an identity from domination, or choosing the bondage and domination you prefer, is carried on in borrowed words. It is a debt that is, as Derrida and Foucault have impressively shown, almost impossible to pay off because of the long enunciation of history through the metaphysical tradition of logocentric power.

Only someone like Genet, who seems to have been born outside of language or on its most unremembered margin, approaches the debt as if it were indelible, never apparently wanting to pay it off, increasing guilt by aggravating the liability. He moves among us (or did) like the thief he is, stealing language like he steals objects, not laundering the stolen goods but caressing the stains and converting the soiled words into iconic gestures as if he were speaking in the grievous doubleness of a glyphic foreign tongue. It is the strategy of alienation so intricately conceived we can hardly identify it as strategy, and we're not entirely sure it is. Genet has suffered the solitary confinement of a displacement so severe it causes him to *see* words, as Sartre has pointed out, as irreparably separated from what they name. It is a faculty or opposing power not picked up from theory or the history of poetry but from some engrailed and divinatory separateness in himself. Even within the French tradition of the accursed homosexual attached, like Vautrin and Charlus, to the demonisms of the criminal underworld, Genet's discourse, for all its baroque purple passion, is a thing unto itself. Since it is a thing which has had, nevertheless, its insidious influence on subcultural activism, homosexual style, polysexual practice, and the insurgence of radical feminisms, I want to pursue it through some last distinctions about the discourse to some quasi conclusions about becoming-being and the homosexual problematic.

If respectable homosexuals back off from the demonisms, and sometimes discount Genet, that's certainly to be expected. While they are trying to make reasonable adjustments to a divided world, reducing guilt or living with it as best they can, Genet is rabidly compounding it, accepting the reprobation, owning up to it all, the worst that can be thought of him, and more, with or without proof always ready to smell a fault. As Sartre has shown in his sanctification of Genet, he wants to discover within himself, by an ascetic discipline of vice, more than enough reasons for accepting the names by which he is reviled: coward, traitor, liar, thief, pervert, scum of the earth. Genet's rigor is to receive from the bottom of his heart and from the past, *from behind*, the charges that are made against him. He defines himself in the most obsequious of all gestures, an utter negativity, *bending over*, helping the other, the image of Authority, to cancel him and turn *him* into an object, since he was to *begin with* stolen goods. Genet's discovery that he was a homosexual cannot, according to Sartre, be separated from his will to become one in order to endow his past with a meaning and a name and to insure the performance of a future.

But the future is a performance, and a tortuous one at that. "Sexually," says Sartre, "Genet is first of all a raped child. This first rape [being caught as a thief from behind] was the gaze of the other, who took him by surprise, penetrated him, transformed him into an object."[17] For Genet, the rape was a condemnation. He thought himself deflowered and assumed the passivity of the woman's role. He has been admired for this in some feminist theory; but sometimes, in the lore of buggery, one gets the impression, as with Sade's Bressac, that the catamite, by letting himself be penetrated, reclaims the pleasure from the woman which causes her to declare a sexuality that, whatever her oppression, possibly because of the oppression, a man shall never know. (Other feminists distrust Genet, and for good reason.) It is a way of repossessing from the woman even her absence and even more—in a crafty displacement of incestuous desire—protecting the mother by *becoming the mother*, in all the powerless passivity of an obliging power.

The bending over is, then, the emblematic assumption of a submissive force, the heraldic sign of a libidinal stance which presupposes no first person, no ego, no *face* of power, but rather a strengthening negativity that wants nothing more than to be open and accessible, *used without conditions*, dis-abused. The softened sphincter, like a hymeneal veil, presents another economy of desire, rejecting the exploitation and capitalization of the libido in the service of reproduction which, in the politics of heterosexuality, creates a surplus value that is inevitably brutalized, raped, or stolen away. There is an egolessness in the diplomacy of the anus. It is the fecundity of the swarming hole, the void, the place of darkness, entry to the *not-yet*, as with the puerperal in-capacity of the woman. *It is the place of imitation's end.* If the rupture of the hymen is, for certain feminists and Derrida, a metaphor of/for *undecidability*, shifting the origins of signification from its castrating gesture to the breaking of the veil, the desire is for the end of pretense, *dis*-semination without dissembling, the seed sowing the seed sowing, the plenitude of a pregnancy without birth. In Sade, however, this circuitous path around the incest barrier is exposed as a fantasy, and Bressac must kill his mother because the mimicry to end all mimicry can never succeed.

Genet never wants it to succeed. He needs the image of the unattainable mother (the *hysterica passio* which, in order to keep his phallic identity from succumbing to madness, Lear must push down, the "swelling sorrow") for the purposes of an eternal mimicry, a transumption of mimesis, *transuranic,* the decantation of an enveloping absence, like the missing Queen at her embroidery in the Brothel reflectively disappearing in the threaded pool. In the reflected play of nature-making consciousness, becoming-being, Genet went through a reversal in which consciousness itself becomes objectified, "and the imperceptible object of consciousness assumes the rank of an absolute subject which watches him. Of course," writes Sartre, "this is achieved at the cost of further effort: it involves becoming a *consciousness watched from behind.* Before the transpiercing gazes of the just, he must feel himself fleeing toward himself from behind himself; he must play, must mime, until he feels a kind of inner flowing" (p. 145). It is the flowing which is also sought by Roland Barthes in *A Lover's Discourse,* but with a sort of old-maidish brilliance in the playful *écriture* trying to subtract the reprobation and attenuate the guilt. (There is, in Barthes, always a certain charm that passes beyond judgment, succeeding there. As for the mother, she is most powerfully present in her final absence, in the book on photography written just before his death.) Sometimes, in the flowing consciousness of a flaccid theory, there is not only a disavowal of guilt but a wishfulfilling dismissal of otherness as well, no object no subject, only the unashamed pleasuring of desire, its own *one one one one etc.,* in the solipsistic turnings of desire.

For Genet, that is a hopeless prospect. He could never be the beloved one in any case, but only the unappeased lover, the *wanting being* essential to his project, which is a preemptive modernist consummation of the unfulfillable postmodern project of infinite deferral in the labyrinthine teasing out of thought. "All that is left for him," says Sartre, "is to put up with *being*," which is always seen as stolen or otherwise gazed upon, as it was for Shakespeare in his sonnets and as it was for Artaud, a mere ghost of a specular identity, which makes it no wonder we see Genet opposed to Hegel in the self-mirroring Derridean *Glas.* While Genet is still one of the gospels of homosexual discourse, there is for him, then, not-gratification, gratuitous, the penance of putting up with the absence. "One man feels his transcendence in his penis; another his passivity. . . . The raw fact is ambiguous; the meaning depends on the individual" (p. 80). That's the existential Sartre appropriating Genet, but very close to the signifying mark. For the one who becomes an object the penis is not, as for the sexual hunter, a weapon, but rather "a still life, a *thing*" (p. 80), despite its tumescence which only signifies what the phallus signifies in Lacanian thought, the dominance of the Name of the Father, the future of the illusion by which identities are made. It is the illusory future which Genet, that imperceptible being, absolutely requires. His power is in the magical operation of an absolute obeisance to the pure appearance of a missing power. His being is a supersaturated theatricality. As a homosexual lover, it is this pure appearance that he worships, *as* appearance. "Not that he resigns himself to the mirage," adds Sartre, defining the existential limit of a hallucinatory desire, "he *loves* it as the thin film which separates being from nothingness" (p. 104).

What Genet adores in his brutalizing thugs and pimps is not the insufficiency whose name is love but *deficiency* itself, an indifference which is something far less exalted than Artaud's Cruelty, since they are seen as pure destructive forces, "first and foremost," as Sartre puts it, "the *non:* nonlife, nonlove, nonpresence, nongood" (p. 104). That is a far silencing cry from that unexamined life on the other side of representation—all the life that is *not* theater—which Artaud and Derrida desire. In Genet, the self-canceling attributes of a sodomizing absence resemble the categorical erasures of the homosexual discourse for which, with more or less demonism, they became an exemplary model. But the subversion of categories in the new homosexualities and feminisms— indebted to Artaud through Derrida and extended in "schizo-analysis"[18]—was meant to uncathect arrested energies and release the libidinal flow without sanctions, whereas in Genet there is always the *prohibition,* as well as the more appalling desire for *immobility,* the immanence of a stasis, a last-ditch metaphysics of the unmoved mover.

The fierce and galvanic cock that impales him from behind, all that raw phallic energy, is the reversed image of Genet's own fierce desire for petrifaction. In the unsensual severity of the perverse ceremony, the orgasm of the "beloved," the male orgasm, is absolute. All pain, severance, solitude, and denial is serving that. All sacrifice by the lover is made, in a consummation of shame, so that the absolute may, ejaculating, come into being.

While other homosexuals try to throw off the socialized burden of the unnatural, Genet has made of it a doxology, accepting the unnatural as his nature. He is subject to the gaze directed at a monstrosity, and if there has been an appropriation of the feminine it is the Medusa complex, not as it is seen, however, by Hélène Cixous in a deliberate misprision of Genet, uncastrated woman, beautiful and laughing, a "spacious, singing flesh" of constant transformation which "derives pleasure from this gift of alterability."[19] Whatever the insinuating amplitude of Genet's emotions, they are no such desiring pleasure, drawn as they are to those pimps and mugs, the impervious stoniness of indifferent matter. In its most brilliant transformation, the Medusa in Genet is a giant phallus made of diamond and, like the totem of the Police Chief in *The Balcony*, reflected to infinity. For Genet, there is something awe-inspiring and beautiful in this image of Authority as endlessly reflected appearance, the Evil which is absence, an absolute being utterly mirrored, the image of an imageless death.

It is this death-into-being which is for Genet the true and only homosexual identity. It is the perverse (what other word?) conception of one who has learned to receive the emission of what he is, like the lover who wants to become the loved one only so that he might experience the seminal reception of his own unreproduceable beauty. In *The Balcony*, which I directed some years ago, I always had the feeling that in the Andromeda network of preoedipal power—woven into the play as invisibly as the Logos, speaking (so far as we could tell) with the same voice—the figure Genet most identified with was the Envoy who comes into the Funeral Studio with the long-waited Word from the absent Queen, whom he weaves into her embroidery in a ravel of evasive words that only extends the network. He rather looks forward, it seems, to homosexual necrophilia and turns out to be, in one surprising moment, something of a thug. In this mortuary of desire, we are light years, of course, from the commonsense pragmatism of a satisfying homosexual relationship, either the friendliness of a casual affair or the domestication of a gay marriage, and even some distance from the sado-masochistic becomings of leather, spikes, and bikes. In this metaphysics of homosexual identity, identity is strict, a stricture like a scripture, where the homosexual act is a cerebral expenditure in a waste of shame, *freely chosen, wasting shame, laying it waste,* in the inversion of purified subject to degraded object, its stubborn plenitude to be seen, snared, stolen away, like thought—which is why Derrida, after thinking about Artaud in *"La parole soufflée,"*[20] later turned to Genet, whose project is also a project of language.

For even while he is prepared to accept the names which are branding him with shame, there is an identity in words which is forever escaping, the ontological fissure which is Evil for Genet, the currency of a nonbeing which makes of his life—at least as seen by Sartre—an unceasing prospect of self-causation. He is caught up in Plato's "bastard dream" of that something other than good which is other than being and therefore other than cause or consciousness, and yet nothing other than itself, an impossible nullity. The project of self-cause catches him up, too, breathless, in an unthinkable subjectivity, a phantasmagoria of conscious nonbeing which would be pure consciousness and the perfect completion of a willful passivity, the dematerialization of all that might have encumbered it: the bourgeois stolen property, all the surplus value—stolen back, fenced, liquidated.

Genet's homosexuality cannot therefore be a condition of permanence but only an obsessive quest. "Why *you?*" The question asked by the burglar and picked up by Sartre as to why *he*, Genet, in particular should steal, is the same question to be asked of his sexuality. True: homosexuality is not a given. True: homosexuality is something chosen. But nevertheless: "Why *you?*" Sartre explains with equally labyrinthine ingenuity the uses of homosexuality in the self-mortifying project which is a seizure of being in its steady cancellations. But the burglar's question is Hegelian, querying a different self. It wants to *place* Genet's decision to steal, but his thievery refuses like his homosexuality to be anything but pure contingency, never giving itself over to the Hegelian particular which is itself given over to the remorseless project of a universalizing spirit.

Genet's unthinkable subjectivity tries to be just that, unthinkable. It is a noncategorical nondialectical individuality, "which has no common measure with the universal and particular, which cannot be fixed in concepts but can only take risks and live its life. Genet does not resolve the contradiction; he lives it. If it transcended itself within him toward any synthesis, *Jean Genet* would disappear. The terms must be kept together *by means of speed*" (p. 185), like Leila and Saïd racing through the indeterminacies of *The Screens,* that drawn and quartered landscape of revolutionary desire which in a near-miracle of *trompe l'oeil* seems not only to achieve a transsexual union but a union of the living and the dead. Genet can no more imagine, however, joining the *community* of the dead than he can, despite his consorting with pimps and burglars and traitors and worse, imagine himself as part of a community of thieves. What would be queerer than queer is to imagine Genet, despite his activist detour with the Black Panthers, as an honored resident of Christopher Street.

In Genet, erotic humiliation of the homosexual exists within the pattern of anointed perversion. There is nothing so degrading that is not tortured into something with an aura of the sacred. Whether the same can be said—using the tone of their own self-derision—for any belt-whipped or scum-swallowing fairy in the West Village or on Castro Street is quite another matter. It may be, as they argue in the poststructuralist schizoanalysis of Deleuze and Guattari, that each of the nuances of the seemingly obscene is an incremental break with the repressive codes of prescriptive power. (For Genet, the power always returns.) Looking, however, at the ecstasies of bondage and domination from a safe heterosexual distance, it does seem as if the brutality, transcended somehow by the artistry and ascesis of Genet, is unredeemed by theory or semiotics or vaseline.

"The course of the world will not be changed by a few faked states of soul, a few operations performed on language" (p. 202). Maybe so, maybe not. What Sartre said about Genet in an almost perverse sequence of his martyrizing book arose with unexpected revulsion of feeling, during the anointing, from the persuasive force of his own stunning commentary. Caught up in a dazzle of contradictions that might justify any criminal expedience (as he later did in his preface to Fanon, possibly the most reprehensible thing he ever wrote), Sartre withdraws from the destructive logic and alluring sophisms not on moral grounds but because the contradictions would change nothing in the order of the world and, for all their cunning, be pleasing to conservatives. For the truth is, according to Sartre (at that moment), they are rhetoric only, and the behavioral strategies, the dervish dance of appearances, pure theater.

I have already suggested how the rhetoric has infiltrated the homosexual discourse at the intersection with radical feminisms, with their "desire to live self from within, a desire for the swollen belly, for language, for blood."[21] As for the actual dramaturgy of Genet, if it went through a sluggish theater with the unlasting brevity of an electric shock, there are still repercussions in more outcast forms of theater and the borderline kinds of performance, including autoperformance; and the empurpled sexual fantasies are still coloring not only the campy spectacles of the Theater of the Ridiculous, but the more dispossessed yet public body of desire, and the even more outlandish performances of subcultural identity. There is not only the bizarre violence now commercialized in punk, the fracturing resonance of a plasmatic music with its strange alliance of skinheads, teddy boys, and reggae blacks who obviously have never heard of Genet's sainthood but who, in a politics of gratuitous rage, might have been pleasing to Sartre by surprising Mrs. Thatcher.

But the revulsion of Sartre sometimes takes place on the simplest of all possible grounds, not on any obscurely epistemological field, but in terms of his personal experience with Genet. The most poignant moment in Sartre's long book occurs when he says—after admiring some brilliant convolution of impersonal thought—that he understands Genet far better than Genet understands him. I think that's probably true, but then I'd like to believe sometimes, when I am confronted with the homosexual discourse and its corrosive deconstructions of what I may represent, that I understand homosexuals far better than they understand me. Of course, that's a meager vanity and may be no more than a defense against the seductions of the discourse and encroaching sodom. A withdrawal from either is not to be construed, it should by now be clear, as a premature ejaculation of old moral reproach. I admire the discourse as the most suggestive thought we have among us today. So far as sodomy is concerned, the issue seems to come down to what another Antony, the historical one, speaking of things Roman, conveys as the general attitude of Roman males. In a letter to Augustus (they were both married at the time), cited by Boswell in a footnote to his history of homosexuality and social tolerance, Antony asks the (maybe too cynical) question: "Can it matter where or in whom you put it?"[22]

I must confess I think it does. I think it does ideologically. So do those who think it doesn't. If we are not merely talking metaphors, then anyone who approaches not only male buggery but the even more lurid aspects of the new experimental sex may as well, without false tolerance, stake out his aversions and limits. Back in the early sixties I wrote about an actress (as it happens, my former wife) who, during rehearsals of *The Balcony* in San Francisco, was as open to the deidentifying whirl of Genet's fantasies as any woman could be, whatever her sexual preferences, but who at one vertiginous moment cried out fiercely against the imminence of becoming-otherness she felt imposing itself on her. It was like a pure seizure of rematerializing ego, unashamed. In a world of undecidability, that has also to be reckoned with, *that* choice, refusing the slippage of ego, however constrained by heterosexual categories, however illusory it might be. For myself, the really determining factor in what—allowing for all possible stress on self-accusation—you choose for yourself sexually is *disgust*. That, too, is ideological. We are learning from recent psychoanalytical theory that there is a politics of the unconscious. It is not necessarily an irrational politics. As a linguistic structure the unconscious is not merely a place of dislocations but our oldest mental faculty, where we do our deepest thinking. I think there is no more arguing with disgust than with the undeniable force of perversion. They are both no doubt determined by an agglomerate of causes, genetic, familial, symbolic, unknown. But ultimately, *in the moment*, outside of cause, there is just disgust, making what is impossible for me reprehensible in you, though liberal principle, which has helped make it legally possible for you, may prevent me from saying or showing what I think. That's pretty much what happened when, thinking I would enjoy it, I walked up Christopher Street last summer at the fag end of the depleted carnival of Gay Pride Day, with a disgust unexpected and almost uncontained by principle. It was all the more important then to have a sense of reasonably unchanging identity to bring reinstated conviction to indeterminate feelings, even if—in the ideological dispersions of the discourse and the disseminating spirit of the carnival—the identity is a bourgeois illusion and mere liberal principle scorned.

In over thirty years in the theater—and not only in plays by Genet—I have explored as an occupational hazard every sordid emotion or seeming perversion or enticing deflection of gender, and have done exercises that have involved not only discreet couplings by members of the same sex or transvestite versions of the self, but some as free-flowing and polymorphous as Love's Body or as garish as anything bargained for in a leather-and-buckle bar. Nevertheless, though I'll usually fight for the right of each of us to his own perversions, I may not want, under the pressure of theory and despite the itchiness of my art, to try on yours and, what's worse, rather wish you wouldn't. Nor am I convinced that what you are doing isn't perverse in the most pejorative sense, or what Freud called "an otiose diversion. . . ."[23] There is, when I have that embarrassing, arrogant, or reprehensible feeling, a shadow of principle which warns that your perversion is going to make it impossible for me, at some warped upped ante of desire, to defend you. I realize that assumes that power will continue to be structured—inadequate as it is to this newly eminent domain—so that I find myself on the side of the Law. It's not something of which I'm especially proud, no more than I was at feeling disgust. The peculiar thing is that I was almost ashamed.

But it isn't wholly a matter of Law, rather a kind of social security in the libidinal economy of desire. It is obviously not going to do any of us any good to pretend that we can tell other reasonable, and especially unreasonable, people how to live their lives. We all know that others are doing things at which we'll simply have to wince. Besides, we are all sufficiently infringed upon by established vigilance that those whose feelings are more versatile should never be relenting in distrusting their own aversions. There are times, in responding to any kind of innovation, in art, in sex, where what would seem to be required is a temporary vow of silence. But we do need to think out the consequences of what, without our saying anything, followed the free-flowing insistence of self-authorizing liberty in previously suppressed groups, as well as the festive play of appearances around long-canceled certainties. At the outer limit of the disappearance of the old scandal, homosexuality becomes like incest according to Lévi-Strauss, the answer to which there is no question; that is, not a deviation to be explained but the explanation of a deviation. That is, at least, the demystifying claim of the homosexual style, refusing ideology. But: is the style the man or something more than the man, also ideological, urging us in the path of the deviation? That is the problem of homosexual identity, the questioning of the answer to which there is no question.

The critical moment in any discourse is when, beyond what it asks of itself, it suggests how others ought to live. Whether sexuality is given or chosen, there is a deceit of coherence at the surface of being—especially so when one creates a double surface. Which is to say no more of appearing homosexuals than one says of the invisible other, whoever he happens to be, that it's possible to live with nothing but appearances so long as you don't take appearances for granted and make of them a way of life, as the discourse sometimes does. Nor, as we have seen in the political economy, can social security be taken for granted. It is as good and durable as the system of order, political or libidinal—*they are not finally the same*—which surrounds it. In the uncertain and centerless order that commonly surrounds us all—which may return us other than blissfully to atoms and the void—identity may be up for grabs, and some of us apparently want to grab all we can before it goes, abandoning all pretense in presumptions of the other. But there is a qualification of otherness which along with the becomings—the uninterrupted present-ness of a desiring body—remembers what Derrida, in his essay on "Violence and Metaphysics," attributes to Levinas, "that desire is respect and knowledge of the other as other, the ethico-metaphysical moment whose transgression consciousness *must* forbid itself."[24] If there is such a thing as homosexual consciousness, it will have to determine where and how, at what threshold of assent, that transgression occurs. But it can hardly be left to the indeterminate autonomy of the body of desire, since there is the vast evidentiality of history (not to mention the greatest poetry) which reminds us, however exalted we may be by the becomings of desire, that it is desire which also exhausts us and violates us and may undo our being.

NOTES

1. Roland Barthes, *Image-Music-Text,* trans. Stephen Heath (New York: Hill and Wang, 1977), p. 183.

2. See, e.g., George Stambolian and Elaine Marks (eds.), *Homosexualities and French Literature: Cultural Contexts/Critical Texts* (Ithaca: Cornell University Press, 1979), and the *Semiotext(e)* issue (vol. 4, no. 1 [1981]) on *Polysexuality.* While both of these reflect, like the newer literary criticism, the impact of French Freud, the homosexual underworld hardly needed such theoretical guidance, for it was there in the avant-garde and, as we can see from the literature, served as a theoretical model. As for the critique of phallocratic power and the overthrow of the oedipal patriarchy, apocalyptic visions are not confined to the French, as we can see in the last chapter of Juliet Mitchell's otherwise faithful Freudianism in *Psychoanalysis and Feminism: Freud, Reich, Laing and Women* (New York: Vintage, 1975).

3. Félix Guattari, "The Liberation of Desire," trans. George Stambolian, in *Homosexualities,* p. 58.

4. Hélène Cixous, "The Laugh of the Medusa," trans. Keith Cohen and Paula Cohen, in *New French Feminisms,* ed. Elaine Marks and Isabelle de Courtivron (Amherst: University of Massachusetts Press, 1980), p. 254.

5. Sigmund Freud, in *Sexuality and the Psychology of Love,* ed. Philip Rieff (New York: Collier, 1978), p. 29. The page numbers in later citations from Freud's essays will be from this volume.

6. In *Gay Plays: The First Collection,* ed. William M. Hoffman (New York: Avon, 1979), pp. 34–35.

7. Peter Fisher, *The Gay Mystique: The Myth and Reality of Male Homosexuality* (New York: Day Books, 1978), p. 227.

8. Freud, p. 158.

9. Freud, "My Views on the Part Played by Sexuality in the Aetiology of Neuroses" (1905), p. 11.

10. Ibid., p. 12.

11. Freud, "The Most Prevalent Form of Degradation in Erotic Life" (1912), p. 62.

12. John Boswell, *Christianity, Social Tolerance, and Homosexuality: Gay People in Western Europe from the Beginning of the Christian Era to the Fourteenth Century* (Chicago: University of Chicago Press, 1980), pp. 48–49, 55–59.

13. Keith Thomas, *The New York Review of Books* (December 4, 1980), p. 29.

14. Luce Irigaray, "When the Goods Get Together," trans. Claudia Reeder, in *New French Feminisms,* p. 107.

15. Ibid., p. 108.

16. Ibid., p. 110.

17. Jean-Paul Sartre, *Saint Genet: Actor and Martyr* (New York: Braziller, 1963), p. 79. Subsequent references will appear in the text.

18. See Gilles Deleuze and Félix Guattari, *Anti-Oedipus: Capitalism and Schizophrenia,* trans. Robert Hurley, Mark Seem, and Helen R. Lane (New York: Viking, 1977).

19. *New French Feminisms,* p. 260.

20. Jacques Derrida, in *Writing and Difference,* trans. Alan Bass (Chicago: University of Chicago Press, 1978), pp. 169–95.

21. Cixous, in *New French Feminisms,* p. 261.

22. Boswell, p. 62, n. 4.

23. Freud, " 'Civilized' Sexual Morality and Modern Nervousness" (1908), p. 37.

24. Derrida, p. 92.

THE MAKEUP OF MEMORY IN THE WINTER OF OUR DISCONTENT

> Fifteen apparitions have I seen;
> The worst a coat upon a coat-hanger.
>
> —W. B. Yeats, "The Apparitions"

> . . . no doubt the discovery that they
> have grown old causes less sadness to
> many people than it did to me. But in the
> first place old age, in this respect, is like
> death. Some men confront them both with
> indifference, not because they have more
> courage than others but because they have
> less imagination.
>
> —Marcel Proust, *Time Regained*

> Enough my old breasts feel his old hand.
>
> —Samuel Beckett, *Enough*

My mother wore lipstick until the day she died. She also wore it into the grave. That last fetish of an appearance was not quite her own, but she would certainly have approved the cosmetic ministrations of the undertaker, which corresponded to her vanity and a taste for excess. There was always too much lipstick, and nothing any of us could say about it would dissuade her. She was simply unembarrassed. By decorum, by our taste, by time. The lipstick was the insignia of a self-enamored presence which everybody adored. It had nothing to do, I think, with refusing to age. My mother, though born in Brooklyn, was not sufficiently American to be fixated on youth. If that were so, the makeup might have been applied more subtly, with more restraint. Instead, there was a bright penumbra of crimson on her lips and a lurid swath of rouge upon her cheeks. There was nothing surreptitious about it, as with the aging

Gilberte in *Time Regained,* who even blew her nose with caution lest her makeup show its colors, as Marcel observed one day amidst his disenchantments, the "sumptuous palette" in her handkerchief.[1] So far as aging was on my mother's mind—as she brushed incessantly her thinning black hair before the mirror like a triptych in her bedroom—it was as if she adorned it with a sort of bedizened satisfaction on her face.

The triple image in the mirror did not signify, moreover, any division in the self, no splitting of identity. It would never have occurred to my mother that anybody could be more than one. The overlaid and successive selves which constitute a life in the solipsistic mirrors of the postmodern would have seemed too burdensome a luxury for a woman whose abundance and major pleasure were in admiring what she was. Or if, to my surprise, she were thinking in those sessions of self-reflection through multiple facets of a past, the variousness of cast-off roles, what was being repeated in the mirror was the role she really preferred. She seemed to treasure the image and gazed at it through the long afternoon, humming or murmuring, until she almost seemed asleep.

She also liked to have her picture taken. She was not at all like the mother of Roland Barthes, who would place herself in front of the camera's lens *"with discretion,"* for there was always a touch of theatricalism in the painted propriety of my mother, a primping into a posture before the click. Writing of his mother in those delicately confessional passages of *Camera Lucida* which seem retrospectively like a premonition of his death, Barthes says: "She did not struggle with her image, as I do mine: she did not *suppose* herself."[2] Nor, I suppose, *ex*pose herself either, the desire for which—*full* exposure, the inexhaustible *manifestation* of the singularity of our being—we struggle for and against all our lives. The struggle continues even when, resigned to age, we think we're merely giving up the ghost. Whatever it is that we may be withholding, now or then, it is naturally a losing cause. "He that has eyes to see and ears to hear," wrote Freud in an early study of hysteria, "may convince himself that no mortal can keep a secret. If his lips are silent, he chatters with his fingertips; betrayal oozes out of him at every pore."[3]

So, who are you fooling? my mother might say, no hysteric. There was nothing like a supposition in her face. No *struggle* with an image either. The makeup was never applied evenly or ever the same, just a blur and not a line around the mouth. Proust speaks of "the inaccurate language of our own vanity" (*Time Regained,* p. 976), but I wonder, for there was something impeccable in the overdoing. If Proust is right, maybe not vanity at all. So, what are you hiding? she'd say as if, even painted an inch thick, concealment were in vain, as it is without makeup in the pretense of unconcealment. Despite the makeup and because of it—like the undisguised specificity of the illusoriness of theater—the import of the image was always there, legible, laughable, emblematic, mortifyingly bare. She seemed, through the inexpungeable red gaudiness of the cover-up that made me blush, totally and infectiously exposed. Whatever my mother may have been when younger—and some early pictures show her as lovely and unguarded with no makeup at all—she seemed perfectly masked by what she had become, and all the more beguiling for that.

Barthes speaks of "the figure of sovereign *innocence*" which he perceived in a faded sepia print of his mother as a little girl. What she seemed to have inherited from no one, not the parents who loved her badly, sustained itself as an "assertion of gentleness" (*Camera Lucida*, p. 69) which distinguished her with age. When she gave herself to a photograph like an elemental goodness it seemed to him to "replace a moral value with a higher one—a civil value" (p. 67). My mother was too narcissistic for that. Freud wrote of neurotics who fetishize the body as a sexual object, "limiting their susceptibility to influence." As I've already indicated, my mother was similarly unsusceptible. But when she caressed and fondled her body—even as she grew heavier and the skin slackened with age—it was, as Freud suggested, a systemic persistence of that primary narcissism, not at all abnormal, and not easily surrendered with age, which is "the libidinal complement of the egoism of the instinct of self-preservation,"[4] of which the lipstick seemed a literal inscription. It is this narcissism which, as Lacan restates Freud, stands between the subject and the desire for death, although there was something in the ablutions that seemed like a preparation for death. My mother was surely exploitative, but with no loss of an alluring motherliness in her auto-affection, maybe all the more motherly, or nurturing, as a result. I am seeing her now, obviously, through the leniency of the years, still struggling with an aversion in my everlasting delight over the memory of this patently self-indulgent and imperturbably funny woman. If there was no civil value in what she offered to a lens, there was something older there, sovereign but far from innocent, maybe a mythic value—though I, like Barthes, also have an aversion to myth.

It has been said—and Barthes reminds us—that Jews have renounced the Image in order to protect themselves in the diaspora of illusion from worshiping the primacy of the Mother. But my mother was not *that* Mother, nor a mere Jewish mother either. Like the kindness of Barthes's mother which, he says, "belonged to no system" and, at the limit of morality, was "specifically *out-of-play*" (*Camera Lucida*, p. 69), my mother's self-engendering was a thing unto itself, immodest, inimitable, heterodox, and—as I grew older, the image of her image, its *remembrance*, becoming mine—retrospectively unique. She could cook an entire meal without rising from her chair because everybody, seduced, quite willingly did the work. "Would you mind taking the milk out of the ice box. Could you get me a little salt. Sit, peel the potatoes." Neighbors would do her shopping for her. Or my father would drive her around. Why were we glad to do her bidding, though it often seemed absurd? In Freudian terms, she seemed to occupy as she aged "an unassailable libido-position which we ourselves [had] abandoned."[5] Perhaps it was because she spared us the good example, had no mere opinions, made no claims—even when she was overtaken by sickness—about gracefully growing old.

I realize as I say this that my mother was at most a year or two older when she died than I am now, but she would never have supposed—as I prolong the expectancy of a youthful middle age—that she was anything other than old and, even before her hair whitened (how white, when she lay dead, its thinning blackness was!), she merely took for granted that death was near at hand. Whatever the motives in her makeup, she was not surprised by time. "I had not a single grey hair, my moustache was black," says the narrator of Proust's novel, as he questions the revelation of "the terrible fact"—that he had grown old, everybody having laughed when he referred to himself as young:

> And now I began to understand what old age was—old age, which perhaps of all the realities is the one which we preserve for longest in our life as a purely abstract conception, looking at calendars, dating our letters, seeing our friends marry and then in their turn the children of our friends, and yet, either from fear or from sloth, not understanding what all this means, until the day when we behold an unknown silhouette, like that of M. d'Argencourt, which teaches us that we are living in a new world. . . . (*Time Regained*, pp. 973–74)

Within her narrow compass, my mother knew her world. She was decidedly afraid of death and, as with the makeup, uninhibited in pain. Through her rimless red lips would come a boundless cry, not quite archetypal because so distinctly hers. "Gas, gas," she'd say, as if squeezing it from her breast, and then the cry ascending, "*it's kill-ing meee!*" But as the gas subsided, if it was ever really gas, her shameless humor revived. "What'd you want I should do, dance?" she'd say to my father when he said she almost scared us all to death. It made no difference how painful the gas, the makeup was indelibly there.

My mother did not so much, as she grew older, want to be approved or wanted, like others her age. She never reproached anybody, as the elderly sometimes do, with not giving her enough love. As for giving love herself, none of us felt denied, but she was one of those whose aging endowed her—if it wasn't there before—with the gift of being loved. But if that was insufficient she could always love herself. That was not at all true of my father who, when he suffered a double stroke which left him in a wheelchair and blind in one eye, took it as a sign of weakness, almost a personal fault and, in the excess of pride with which he had lived, refused any solace or therapy and virtually inflicted upon himself the lonely humiliation of death. When I flew across the country to visit him, the television would be on. He'd stare intently at the screen no matter what was there, never looking at me with his single eye, as if canceling the oedipal contract and asking, among all the hopeless desires, that we forget his crippled being, as if he'd never been at all. Not so my mother, in sickness or in health. She was not an accomplished woman, far from that, but she wanted to be remembered, remembered there and then, and remembered for what *she* remembered in the festivity on her face.

Proust speaks of those for whom our love "has been so nearly continuous that the image we retain of them is no more than a sort of vague average between an infinity of imperceptibly different images . . ." (p. 878). By some aboriginal inspiration my mother had averted that, or almost, as she also thwarted time, arranging in the mirror to her personal satisfaction the englistered gaze she'd present to death. Her hair thinned and grayed for all the brushing, but as I look at her image now it's only the photographs that age.

Amidst the *clichés* of old photographs, the redoubled quick of memory—which to Proust seemed less reliable than its involuntary return—this view of my mother may be no more than a trick of imagination, which doesn't necessarily improve with age. If I were, to be truthful, and I am trying to be, making up this portrait of my mother, adorning it here and there, overdoing it a little bit, that would itself be a prospectus of age, the correlative of her makeup, the autobiography of the auto-affection, a semblance of a self-assumption, which is what autobiography is, the conversion of all otherness into the bodily legend of a self, the necessary fiction of age. "In the people whom we love," Proust observes, "there is, immanent, a certain dream which we cannot always discern but which we pursue." If we stumble in the pursuit it's because, as he adds, there cannot help but be something like error and aberration in all our loves (pp. 869–70). As the loves accumulate and fail, the dream recedes. Which may be why we mostly think the imagination is more active in youth which is, besides, thought to be closer to the other Mother who is, as mistress of illusion, sovereign in the aging dream.

"Hear him," writes Wallace Stevens of the child whose "Questions Are Remarks," before whom objects arise without history or rhetoric and whose question, even about the mother, seems complete. "He does not say," not yet, as the aged Stevens says in the poem, " 'Mother, my mother, who are you,'/The way the drowsy, infant, old men do."[6] I have not been saying that either, not yet, the remark as question, "Mother, my mother, who are you?" which awaits a further time, though I am edging toward it now. But as I recall the memorial makeup on my mother's face, that testamentary lifemask in the funeral home, it occurs to me that it is only by virtue of the imagination that, coming of age, all the remembered promises narrowed down, the prospects may seem more limitless than they were before. That's because the bottomless source of the future is the inexhaustible past, as it is in Proust when Marcel discovers, through an irruption of repercussive memory on the uneven paving stones, that the only real paradise is the paradise that is lost.

In the famous passage on involuntary memory, Proust speaks of how "the simplest act or gesture [of the past] remains immured as within a thousand sealed vessels" (*Time Regained,* p. 903), the breaking open of which releases anxiety about the future into an appetite for life that is immense. In Proust, as in Stevens, this anamnesis comes through a kind of seasoned amnesia, or parapraxis, the grace of drowsiness, like my mother's before the mirror, an unsubsiding attentiveness to the dimming rhetoric of age. Memory, for Proust, is not only a mental category. There is, as well, an involuntary memory of the limbs to accompany that other memory set off by the madeleine dipped in tea. This corporeal memory, torpid as it is, a sterile imitation of the other, nevertheless outlasts it and may be awakened by the will of chance through a kind of nurtured desperation. As Stevens says in a late poem, "Need names on its breath/Categories of bleak necessity" which, "just to name," attains by "right of knowing, another plane" ("Sail of Ulysses," p. 393). He writes of that categorical imperative elsewhere as a poverty in the space of life, familiar to age, where we come upon a feminine figure, "the sibyl of the self,/The self as sibyl, whose diamond" *is* poverty, a sort of bejeweled exhaustion whose earthly ground is need. The sibyl's shape seems, in "The Sail of Ulysses," an avatar of the imagination whose object, as in Proust, is absence and whose energy is depletion:

> . . . a blind thing fumbling for its form,
> A form that is lame, a hand, a back
> To be remembered, the old shape
> Worn and leaning to nothingness,
> A woman looking down the road,
> A child asleep in its own life. (p. 393).

Which is the unnamed old man, in the poem entitled "A Child Asleep in Its Own Life," whose mother is not complete, the unnamed old man who broods on all the rest of the old men, those we shall become, "Distant, yet close enough to wake/The chords above your bed to-night" (p. 393).

Speaking of distance, it is certainly a long way from the uneducated egocentricity or the nurtured narcissism of my mother to the elegant solipsism of Stevens and Proust. But I want to move from the remembrance of her image to some further thoughts about memory and the imagination and—what is more typical of the rest of us—aging and its discontents, or the uneasiness of aging as the span of life increases and the time for it recedes.

I said of my mother that she seemed to reflect a mythic value, but that I have an aversion to myth. That's because "we never lived in a time/When mythology was possible," as Stevens says in a last poem, like Freud in his final work. What we recover from time, then, if we recover it at all, is an image which "must be of the nature of its creator," as this remembrance of my mother is consubstantial with my self, *fictive* because remembered, its substance out of mind. "That," says Stevens, "raises the question of the image's truth" ("A Mythology Reflects Its Region," p. 398). I don't deny it: what is mirrored in memory is the mirror. Imagination is a function of memory whose expanse is a great divide. It is a division which seems to widen with age, like the aggravation of a grievous fault. That fault is mirrored, as Lacan suggests, in the motor incapacity of the child fumbling for its form, as if born through something forgotten, "an original organic disarray" in the "*specific prematurity of birth*. . . ."[7] It is as if our failures of memory are archaic but propitious, arising "in the dimension of a vital dehiscence [or . . .] negative libido" which is constitutive of what we are (*Écrits*, p. 21), and which seems to return in the specific maturity of age, when we are really old, like the old man asleep in the child's life. Or was it the other way around?

That question is a remark. As we fear a loss of being with age, there is also, with so much more to remember, an anxiety about forgetting. It's like the compounding of the amnesia in our normal psychic life, which may be the trace of that original fault. When I say amnesia now, I mean our tendency to forget, just that, the *necessity* of it. For the truth is we're always forgetting. We think we're putting things aside—out of caution, fear, tact, dismay—only to discover they're no longer there. There is in the selective inattention, screening, slips, oversight, and censorship through which we mature inevitably a point of diminishing returns—or the unexpected virulence of the return of the repressed.

Henry James advised the novelist to be one upon whom nothing is lost. He was speaking of a kind of absolute pitch of remembrance that you're unlikely to be born with and must attain, not only with the experience of age but, by right of knowing, with the rigor of art. "Rigor of beauty is the quest," said William Carlos Williams in *Paterson,* that palimpsest of upwelling age which seems a renewal of life. "But how will you know beauty when it is locked in the mind past all remonstrance?" Locked as the mind is, things escape us, even when memory is as active as it is in Williams, who is forced to roll up the sum "by defective means."[8] Even when the means, though defective, are subtle beyond thought, as they are in Proust and James, there is something in the mind which, as James says of the American scene, puts out interrogative feelers, the questions which aren't remarks but only endless questions. Like: where is our life in memory when it is not being remembered—or remembered *as being?* It is a response to that question which led in Freud to the concept of the unconscious in psychoanalysis, where we have grown familiar with the child asleep in the old man's life, awakened as he is by the vicissitudes of the instincts in the rolling up of age.

Freud restates the problem of what escapes us at the opening of a note on what the unconscious has come to mean about a dozen years after *The Interpretation of Dreams:*

> A conception—or any other mental element—which is now *present* to my consciousness may become *absent* the next moment, and may become *present again,* after an interval, unchanged, and, as we say, from memory, not as a result of a fresh perception by our senses. It is this fact which we are accustomed to account for by the supposition that during the interval the conception has been present in our mind, although *latent* in conscious-

ness. In what shape it may have existed while present in the mind and latent in consciousness we have no means of guessing.[9]

It is, however, the imagination which presumes, guessing at the shape of an absence—a sibyl's shape?—and bringing it back alive, through some affinity with the unconscious in which the latency abides.

The unconscious doesn't seem, at first, like the most natural setting for the aged, so far as we expect them to be wise, restrained, and stabilizing agencies in our lives without the license of the still-unruly libidinal desires. "O sir, you are old," they say to King Lear. "Nature in you stands on the very verge / Of his confine" (II.iv.1414–43). There are multiple connotations of nature in *King Lear,* but here it suggests the life which has not only reached its limit but needs to be controlled. "You should be ruled," says Regan (II.iv.143), as if addressing the unconscious itself, which we normally think of as the domain of the irrational. But it is not quite that. In the unconscious system, as Freud describes it, there is "no negation, no dubiety, no varying degree of certainty"—all of which, as anxiety, are liabilities of age, when the natural functions weaken and the somatic vitality declines. The processes of the unconscious are, moreover, timeless, neither ordered temporally nor altered by the passage of time, all of what we have known and done and still to be imagined enabled there, bearing "in fact . . . no relation to time at all."[10]

Unconsciousness is a regular, vital, and inevitable phase in the activity of our thought. As Freud taught us in perhaps his greatest teaching, the unconscious—what we think of as irrational—is our oldest *mental* faculty, as dreams are the deepest registers of thought. It is, however, a deprivation in the processes of the unconscious that we are liable to suffer with age, injury to its civilizing virtue by encroachment on its civil rights. For the social ordinances continue, through all the relaxing of taboos, to see that the unaging libido is ruled so that the elderly act their age, letting the troublesome child sleep. Of course, it is those still shaken by the specific prematurity of birth, the unreconciled children who—as the aged breed past all expectations, not always with an aging grace—grow impatient with their almost obscene ubiquity. So we consign them with mixed feelings to a sort of exiled behavior which, as the children themselves join the multitudes of age, they may later come to regret. It is this pressure upon the old, often unspoken and solicitous, to *be* old, to act their age and at the same time contain the incontinence endemic to age—not only the loose bowels of the insufferable body but the unseemly persistence of regressive desire—which causes the elderly to be wounded in their narcissism,[11] egregiously injured where the ego was and, unfortunately, unsufferably, where the id still is.

It was that—being wounded in her narcissism—which Proust's Aunt Léonie, hypochondriac as she was, never let happen to her, and which my mother, admiring her image, seemed to refuse through all the appeals, jokes, and even insults about her makeup. For all their self-indulgences, they were fortunate that their obsessions seemed to have a natural charm, witty in its way and invulnerable, which kept them from being resented and left them independent in their dependencies and undeterred by age. While they were both quite conscious of approaching death, they wanted—as Stevens says of the aging Penelope waiting for her lover-husband in "The World as Meditation"—"nothing [it] could not bring her by coming alone" (p. 381). "If I live to be a hundred . . .," my mother would often say, only to indicate that there was nothing she wanted from life that had to rely on that. Nor would the promise of such longevity cause either of those women to abandon her idiosyncrasies, which were a mark of self-possession, in order to accommodate pleasures neglected before and made possible by age. They would both have been indifferent to the overcompensations of some of our senior citizens who, in a culture sending mixed signals about age, find themselves dancing to the media-sponsored tune of recovered youth which is inevitably the delusive diminuendo not of the sibyl's shape but of the siren's song.

Much has been said and done, true, with the most benevolent of intentions, to guide those who are aging in making the best of the years that are left, instead of relinquishing them to a feeling of uselessness and another period of self-denial. But as with everything else in American life which emerges from neglect in persuasive numbers, the elderly have become sellable prospects in the marketplace of amelioration. There is that other poverty in the space of life which, pensioned off, also makes the aged better consumers and tourists, as well as a voting bloc. For every Gray Panther there are thousands at Disney World. There's surely no reason whatever why the aged shouldn't enjoy their belated measure of material blessings, and I'm uncomfortable deriding the pleasures that others have been waiting for. Yet some of the aged themselves are looking askance at the newly abounding solicitations to the diversions from the more unspeakable needs, like my seventy-five-year-old aunt who returned from Florida because she was tired of pretending she still liked to dance, flirt with octogenarians, and play shuffleboard.

When the opposing pressure is off, *not* to act their age, my guess is that the elderly, more likely than not, want to acknowledge age as it is, meeting it as equals, as the man meets the Echo in Yeats's poem, shouting "a secret to the stone," which consists of a question made, now that he is old and ill, of all he has said and done: "I lie awake night after night," he says, "And never get the answers right." The poem suggests that our narcissism can also be wounded by being diverted from the question, which is asked in various ways until it culminates in this:

> O Rocky Voice,
> Shall we in that great night rejoice?
> What do we know but that we face
> One another in this place?[12]

But when, confronted with the question, the others look away, what we can see in the community of the aged are the newer signs of rejuvenation masking the older disguises and avoidance. What is powerful in the later poems of Yeats is not only the spectacle of the intrepid old man, still horny, letting himself be shameless and mad, but that he never forgives the ignominy of age, its bodily decrepitude, which threatens the sexual drive. Remembering, however, that love has pitched its mansion in the place of excrement, he turns over like a bagman the smelly detritus of life, the "mound of refuse" which constitutes a past, and from which—if there is any life and poetry left—they will have to be made: "Old kettles, old bottles, and a broken can,/Old iron, old bones, old rags, that raving slut/Who keeps the till" ("Circus Animals' Desertion," p. 336) and who, even through my mother's mask, inevitably disfigures life.

There are some newer literary theorists for whom age is no excuse and who might raise more than an eyebrow over the hysterical feminine figure at the till picking up the libidinal cost. It is perhaps worth remarking, however, that Yeats anticipates in this passage not only the plays of Beckett, with their exhaustive enumeration of the grotesque comedy of age, with its amputated paternity and ashbins of being, but the postmodern strategy of *bricolage,* starting from the littered ground up. If he borrows, as Derrida says of the *bricoleur,* from the scattered text of a heritage that is more or less coherent and more or less in ruins,[13] he does so not with the callow parapraxis of postoedipal desire but with an older passion from the depths of age. Yeats's own critique of the solutions of humanism can be devastating, but what is clear beyond cavil is that there is for him no adequate response to the problem of aging in the ceaseless play of signifiers through an infinitely deferrable end. "Those images that yet/Fresh images beget" come from the "fury and the mire of human veins" and not from language alone, though the language is charged with the complexities of blood and age, as it tries to imagine a place where "blood-begotten spirits come," beyond language, beyond life ("Byzantium," pp. 243–44).

"I am old, I belong to mythology," says the Old Man who introduces Yeats's last play, *The Death of Cuchulain*. But we recognize it as a desperate wish-fulfillment as he goes on to assault "that old maid history"[14] which makes the assertion a tenuous proposition—what caused Stevens to say that we live in a time when mythology is impossible. "I spit! I spit! I spit!" the Old Man repeats as the stage darkens on his rage and the curtain falls. "Myths are anonymous," says Lévi-Strauss,[15] but the voice behind the Old Man is surely not, and even Cuchulain, who fought the waves, receives six mortal wounds in his perfect narcissism. The "flesh my flesh has gripped/I both adore and loath," says the Singer at the end of the play, as he sees the image of Cuchulain in the bloodbath of the Post Office, as the muscular body of myth gives way to the illusions of history and the insoluble questions of age.[16] While Yeats is able to imagine the Chinaman of *Lapis Lazuli* whose ancient, glittering eyes are gay, the attritions of history are such, its depredations upon love's body, that—while soul may clap its hands and sing, like the severed head of Cuchulain, for every tatter in its mortal dress—there's nothing like a starry *jouissance* making any the less onerous the awful debilities of age.

"I do not myself find it agreeable to be 90," wrote Rebecca West just before she died, "and I cannot imagine why it would seem so to other people. It is not that you have fears [though you do] about your own death, it is that your upholstery is already dead around you."[17] As Proust remarks, however, speaking of fragments of existence and fugitive things, there are those capable of living with the delusion that they *can* talk to the furniture because, while uncertain of themselves, they believe it is really alive (*Time Regained*, p. 909). And sometimes, too, the memories arise, furtive, out of focus, alien, like fantasies of a past, and those who are talking to the furniture can talk to no one else. "[E]very fixation at a so-called instinctual stage," writes Lacan, "is above all a historical scar: a page of shame that is forgotten or undone, or a page of glory that compels" (*Ecrits*, p. 52). Speaking of certain almost incommunicable "prodigies" of experience, Henry James despairs of dealing with them directly or objectively. "We want it clear, goodness knows," he writes, "but we also want it thick, and *we get the thickness in the human consciousness that entertains and records, that amplifies and interprets* it." The more elusive the memory or blurred with age, the more necessary it is, as James says of these prodigies, for the fragility of the memory to preserve itself, imperiled as it is, by "*looming through some other history*—the indispensable history of somebody's *normal* relation to something."[18] It is, then, through the loomings and laminations of the remembered—the thickness of a doubled consciousness—that, facing one another in this place, we may restore ourselves to the future, which is history unfolding in the indispensable other. "*You speak. You say.*" says Stevens in "As You Leave the Room," as he recapitulates, sparely, his poetic career. Has it been merely what skeletons think about? Is he no more than "A countryman of all the bones of the world?" (p. 396).

There is something in the disposition of the major modernists—Stevens, James, Proust, Mann, Woolf, Joyce, Eliot, Marx, and Freud—that has an affinity with age and aging, as we do not encounter it among the offspring of the dead fathers of the postmodern which, to the extent that it disclaims history in favor of an uninterrupted present without the impediment of remembrance, lacks the thickness. It is a disadvantaged history, of course, the history of the modern, because it is a history dominated and written by men. But we are, at the moment, thinking of aging in that history which, even when made and written by women, is the only history I can imagine in which we come to age. You'll have to forgive me—it may be a fault of age—that I am not good at imagining, even as we move through outer space and science fiction or marginal cultures with no conception of history, the outside or the end of history. Such as it is, the deepest experience of the modern seems to occur not as it occurs but through an aura of time as reversal and repetition, the reaching back through a kind of belatedness to the memory reconceived. "Now, here, the snow I had forgotten," says Stevens, or the other, the one who speaks, who *says*, certifying in the evanescence of remembered snow the reality disbelieved. "And yet nothing has been changed except what is/Unreal, as if nothing had been changed at all" (p. 396).

The reaching back is, according to Proust, the distinctive work of the artist whose struggle is "to discern beneath matter, beneath experience, beneath words, something that is different from them," although it is possible, like Stevens, to speak of poetry as words about things which wouldn't exist without the words. A literature which thinks, however, of history as coded by words and words by history will distrust such talk as further mystification, there being—according to recent literary thought—nothing beneath words but more words, the only or major difference. Yet Proust is concerned with another difference brought on, perhaps, by the failing names for things which *do* exist in a world made out of words: "exactly the reverse of that which, in those everyday lives which we live with our gaze averted from ourself, is at every moment being accomplished" by all that "which we falsely call life." What one hopes for, then, is not only the capacity to live a life, but to *have* lived it, to have the experience *of* our experience, the secondariness, so that we can make "visible to ourselves that life of ours which cannot effectually observe itself and of which the observable manifestations need to be translated and, often, to be read backwards and laboriously deciphered" (*Time Regained,* p. 932). In this reading backward, in the *literariness* of the idea of translation itself, there is—as in the talking cure of psychoanalysis—the suggestive power of repetition, bringing into consciousness the life which without being *said,* that is, *repeated,* would not in a sense have been lived at all—as if the origin of the experience we think the cause of it, *the one beneath,* is the capacity to think it the cause. In this respect, it is well to remember, as Lacan points out, that the amnesia of repression is one of the most lively forms of memory, which may be invoked by psychoanalytic process to the extent that it *is* a literary process. There is a sense, too, in which the voids of memory with age are an opening into imagination, so long as the aged are not made to feel that a failing memory is a felony of sorts. "Incomplete and dim memories of the past," writes Freud, are the substance of tradition and "a great incentive to the artist," as they might be to the person grown old, "for he is free to fill in the gaps according to the behests of his imagination. . . ."[19]

But what about the forgotten aged without, perhaps, this poetic instinct for repossession, so damaged by history, the scars so thick, not the consciousness, that the memories, receding, are not only fragile but so deeply lodged and distorted in the unconscious that—even in the presence of the other with a "normal relation to something"—they are almost inaccessible?

I suspect that is the more general condition of aging in our time when history, accumulating in the self-consciousness of history, still looms as Marx described it, as the nightmare from which we are trying to awaken. There is, moreover, the liability with age that, along with the recurrencies and coming attractions of memory, we accumulate the reruns of repression, the social masks, the powers of imagination weakened by the character armor, a myriad of defenses, baffles, screenings, evasions—those supersaturated symptoms of the civil order displaced into the psyche from whence, recycled, they show up in the performance of everyday life as nothing but a repertoire of stage fright. Our vanity and our passions, says Proust, "our spirit of imitation," intensify the anxiety of the performance, along with abstract intelligence and habit, especially habit, the great deadener, according to Beckett. For Proust and Beckett, as for Freud, undoing the work of repression means traveling "back in the direction from which we have come to the depths where what has really existed lies unknown within us." (*Time Regained*, p. 932). If art is a discipline of *de*conditioning, erasing habit, it may occur in age by accident, as senescence strips us of vanity. But there is just as likely to be in the process of growing old a compounding of those same habits and passions through long-formed reflexes of self-imitation, encouraged by the weakness of others, which is a pass of safe conduct through the perils of change.

What we see in Proust as in Beckett, who studied Proust and Freud, is a powerful drive to bring into consciousness all of what belongs to it. So long as it remains in a primary or inaccessible state it constitutes part of our life which, in its essence, remains unlived. Unfortunately, the censorship is resourceful not only in the civil order but at every level of the psychic systems, and "what belongs to consciousness," as Freud remarks, "is not always in consciousness. . . . The truth is that it is not only what is repressed that remains alien to consciousness, but also some of the impulses which dominate our ego and which therefore form the strongest functional antithesis to what is repressed."[20] As we age in this condition we are doubly impaired, self-deprived, twice distanced. There's no reason at all to believe that age will necessarily release inhibition by reducing the temporal claims of life, as we might expect. We are more likely as we age to go on preferring what Proust, and Eliot, considers that death-in-life which we elaborate for ourselves with gaze averted from the interior of being that is being-denied. "When we have arrived at reality," said Proust, "we must, to express and preserve it, prevent the intrusion of all those extraneous elements which at every moment the gathered speed of habit lays at our feet" (*Time Regained*, p. 934).

But for those who, even when they've grown old, have not arrived at such reality—unless age itself, the raw fact of age, felt, is unequivocally that—the gathered speed of habit is itself an habituated momentum. There is also the possibility that, as Freud points out, the materials of primary repression are likely to have developed over the years in "unchecked and luxuriant fashion," ramifying "like a fungus, so to speak, in the dark" and taking on those extreme forms of expression which, when translated by analysis and revealed to the neurotic, seem alien and frightening.[21] As for the aged, such expression may look like habit when, to alleviate the terror, the damming of the eventually damaged and illusory strength of instinct is diverted into something akin to obsessional neurosis. Once again, it is the undoing of habit, so far as habit is not a comfort but a deterrent to desire, which is, I would think, the deepest wish of age.

The inability to reduce the symptoms below a certain level without destroying the civil value Barthes saw in his mother caused Freud to speak forlornly at the end of a long clinical career of civilization and its discontents. It's as though he were in mourning for the irreversible aging of a world which doesn't know what to make of its history, like so many of the elderly who feel that time has invalidated all they have seen and known, and much of what they've believed—never more than in our own time, when the abrasive momentum of history, swifter than ever before, has left still-remembered values almost geologically behind. So it is that in the graying of time they involuntarily assume another role, which seems somehow like a congestion of history, a cardiac arrest, which maybe needs a triple bypass. Unlike my mother, who seemed to design the role on her face in the image of a desire with an unembarrassed past, like a refusal to forget its promise, we find ourselves playing roles that seem intolerably miscast, and like most obedient actors—in the economy of a theater which reflects the economy of death—we don't say anything about it because we're thankful to have a part, however diminshed, particularly as we age. And as we speak then the lines that have been written for us or, like aging actors doing walk-ons watching dolefully from the wings, what might be better remembered has been substantially lost. It's as though something in our history has deprived us of age in the winter of our discontent.

Thus we may become old, as it were, unseasoned, bereft, caught up in a process in which biological destiny, played out in the *mise-en-scène* of the unconscious, is either over before we know it or happening to someone else, while we wonder where it began. Where, indeed, does it begin, although we think we know where it ends? "If I am no longer young," writes Jules Renard, "I should like to know at what hour of what day my youth left me," as we feel it leave the dashing Vronsky in Tolstoy's *Anna Karenina* at the moment when, in a catastrophe of self-perception, he discovers the fatal bald spot on his head. In *The Death of Ivan Ilych,* a worse calamity befalls when Ilych, hanging the drapes in his affluent new home, bruises his side against the knob of the window frame. It's as if there's an acceleration of age through the illusions of normality and the residues of benighted youth. The terrible pain subsides, but what returns, with a sense of pressure in the side and a queer taste in the mouth, is a general irritability that mars an enviable life, as if something pernicious and ungraspable had been there all along, "and nothing he could do would deliver him from *It.* And what was worst of all was that *It* drew his attention to itself not in order to make him take some action but only that he should look at *It,* look it straight in the face: look at it and without doing anything, suffer inexpressibly."[22]

Ilych wants to attribute his illness to the bruise in the side which is, however, but the memory-trace of an unlocalized horror which causes him to scream for three days before it falls away "from two sides, from ten sides, and from all sides."[23] It has a long tradition of impossible representation. In the medieval play *Everyman,* the coming of death is impressively proclaimed to the last unbelieving vanities of life. Today, one of the troubling vanities is longevity itself, and the prospect of an indefinite extension of life in whatever indeterminable forms, through the mutations of genetic engineering and the marvels of intensive care. Here the problems of aging run into the ethics of an intolerable dying, as well as the ghostlier demarcations of the origins of growing old. As Ronald Blythe puts it in *The View in Winter,* "In hospitals up and down the land lie finished lives that have been cut dead by death." Instead of death announcing itself to us—whether as the antic in the hollow crown or the insidious bruise in the side—"we may have to announce ourselves to death."[24] As we anticipate meanwhile, with exercise and better diets, an older age for us all, I am inclined to feel, as they apparently did in other shorter-living generations, that no matter where we are in life— whether nubile, lucent, lucky, or senescent—we live our lives in death which, like the unconscious, has no beginning or end, but is rather the medium of the illusion which is the eventuality of life.

Aging, I think, has no established period in our lives. But I am now making the necessary distinction between aging and merely being old.

Proust gives us in *Time Regained*, like a natural historian, a scrupulous and often ruthlessly stunning taxonomy of old age. With the question of aging, however, there is the question of perception: who is doing the perceiving? and from what bias or coign of vantage? Some of the specimens in Proust's museum, or rather *Kunst* or *Wunderkammer*—those late Renaissance collections of the marvelous and the strange—seemed older or younger, repulsive or attractive, depending on perceptual distance: "It was dependent upon the spectator, who to see them as young had to place himself correctly and to view them only with that distant inspection which diminishes its object like the lens selected by an oculist for a long-sighted elderly person; old age here, like the presence of infusoria in a drop of water, was made apparent not so much by the advance of years as by a greater degree of accuracy in the scale of the observer's vision" (p. 989). Beckett, in his essay on Proust, speaks about the infection of the object by the subjectivity of perception, the disease of perception itself where, when the object is human, we are dealing with differing systems of synchronization that are, as in the perception of age from within or without, more than likely to be hopelessly out of phase.

There are those, besides, who are hopelessly out of phase within themselves. I have known some, officially young or looking unaged, colleagues, even students, re-encountered friends, who seem to me unfathomably old, as if born with an overdose of entropy. Or you can see the curded promise in the complexions of verdigris. It is often the outward projection of depressing self-contempt. Marcel remarks too, amidst the geriatric figures of the Guermantes party where the past came rushing back, some who were "not old men, they were very young men in an advanced stage of withering" (p. 979). They hadn't ripened with age because, with specific prematurity—"the marks of life . . . not deeply scored" (p. 929)—they were absolute for death which, as Proust conjectured, seemed indifferent to them, as if there were not enough life to be bothered with in the end. "Ripeness is all," says the dispossessed Edgar in *King Lear* (V.ii.11), after he meets *his* blinded father and learns more of what it is to be desperate and old. In a world where the gods seem to be killing us for their sport, one may *want* to die, as Gloucester does, though in a kind of talking cure Edgar constructs the necessary suicide and recovers his father miraculously to life. He helps him to see with younger eyes sharpened by betrayal, madness, and degradation, which still have to look on death. In the last scene, when age seems stretched so far "upon the rack of this tough world" (V.iii.315) that it seems to suffuse the living with the dead, it is Edgar who says before the dead march to the promised end: "The oldest hath borne most; we that are young/Shall never see so much, nor live so long" (V.ii.326–27). It is strange how moving and accurate these strange lines feel, even now, when we're likely to live longer.

There is, however, a deference to the endurance of age which seems to belong to a forgotten world. Yet the atrocities inflicted upon age in *King Lear* should be chastening in still another way: aging and dying are universal, true, but aside from the fact that some, like Cordelia, die wantonly before their time, there is a scandal of aging, too, in which age is hastened unnaturally by the viciousness of history and the pollution of politics, so that while life expectancy stretches here, in the same old tough world there multitudes are wracked, old, terribly old, even the children are old, with the age that comes of misery in an uncommiserable time. Here, as we try to adjust our attitudes about aging as the aged wax and increase, we can be sentimental about the respect for the elders of other cultures where the price of such respect—as with the astonishing magnitudes of their mortuary art—is that people are being starved if not tortured to death. "World, world, O world!" exclaimed Edgar when, as if at the beginning of historical time, he first saw the bleeding eyeballs of his mutilated father. "But that thy strange mutations make us hate thee,/Life would not yield to age" (IV.1.10–12).

Death defeats all, they used to say, including wealth and power. But there is an acrid disease of age, an odor of age, that is an excretion of power, not only the seepage of the body's organic failing but of caste and class, something sullen in the economic disposition of things, an expense of spirit in the historical waste of shame. "The train smelled like the inside of an old man's hat—smelled of darkness, hair, tobacco," writes John Hawkes in *The Lime Twig*. "There were smells coming off the woman too, smells that lived in her despite the odor of coke and burning rails. Smells of shoe black and rotting lace, smells that were never killed by cleaning nor destroyed by the rain. The woman's strong body, her clothing, her hairpins and hair—all were greased with the smells of age."[25] So far as some come to age, it is not, as we see in Hawkes, by living for life but *against* life, or as if there were no more to living than oblivion on the brain, yielding not so much to age but to a sort of breathing extinction in the disgrace of history. At the same time there are those, like certain characters in Dostoyevsky, who even when young seem to be untellably old, as if they've lived several lives over and would continue to live, however hideously, through the last fell inch of life, and who—in the wild fringe benefits of that inch exultant!—seem to live more life than our social security or scientists ever dreamed. That fervor to live comes from a resistance to death almost deranged which is not quite the poetic rage, rage, so moving in Dylan Thomas against the dying of the light.

We die, we know it, what is there to know? except that it can't be known. And if you have a certain kind of temperament this will drive you crazy, as our greatest literature knows. I must admit, though we have been looking elsewhere for better attitudes toward dying, that my imagination has been enduringly stirred by such literature, almost to the point of joy, all the more so because it's unbearable, like the final suffering of the heroic Freud. The irony of such suffering, like his labors, is that it seems outside the scope of any conceivable model of aging. For most of us the tragic burden is too great, as it always is with tragedy. We don't have the gift, we're not prepared to pay the cost. And besides, we weren't chosen. Which is why, today, in the absence of tragedy, we're rather relieved with other forms. As for the illusions of other cultures which serve to reappropriate the suffering of age and the brute fact of dying into the ceaseless continuum of something unnamable and maybe other than being, I don't pretend to understand them. When, however, I think of aging and the imagination, there is an elegance of cold certitude which seems to me enviable if not emulable, utterly moving and irreducibly right. Few minds will come to this because it is a condition of mind which understands that the imagination's deity, if one must have a myth, is an unswerving and implacable goddess, "Maiden of icy stone/With no anatomy," whose service is unsparing of the ego that refuses to be dissolved, as it is of the language which falsifies itself in the vicinity of death, to which you can only bring a life—if you have enough of it to offer:

> What brings me here? Old age.
> Here is the written page.
> What is your pleasure now?[26]

I am quoting from a beloved teacher, a poet, a critic, an implacably stubborn and controversial man whose wisdom exceeded the faults of his age, which he knew only too well.

When the marks of life *are* scored, you can only hope you know the score. "I became my own obituary," said Sartre in his autobiography, sometime before he died.[27] Which is not to say his life *is* his death, but rather an accounting of it, a reckoning, which can only occur at the inception of age by living it retrospectively. Which inevitably means the assumption of a solitude that can only be realized in the being-for-death. Freud speaks of it as the death instinct in *Beyond the Pleasure Principle*, the urge to restore some earlier state of things where the organism was at rest. Thus, the amazing proposition of Freud that, whatever course it takes, the aim of life is death. Or, as Lacan approaches it through the poetics of the Freudian discourse, the death instinct is associated with the repetition compulsion as the essential expression of "the limit of the historical function of the subject" (*Écrits*, p. 103), the subject being the one who, splitting off from the ego and passing into language, "brings back into the present time the origins of his own person" (p. 47), becoming the one who *has been*. Lacan borrows from Heidegger the possibility in death of something which is "ownmost, unconditional, unsupersedable, certain and as such indeterminable. . . ." The possibility as a limit "is at every instant present" in what the subject-as-history "possesses as achieved. This limit represents the past in its real form, that is to say, . . . the past which reveals itself reversed in repetition" (p. 103).

One of the sources of anxiety about the new omnipresence of the aged, particularly in America, is still our delinquent sense of history, the correlative of which is the sequestering of the aged in historyless communities, the timewarped parceling out of memory in condominiums and nursing homes. "Today people live in rooms that have never been touched by death," wrote Walter Benjamin in his essay on the storyteller Leskov, "dry dwellers of eternity. . . ." If he anticipated almost half a century ago the current critique of the ghettoizing of the aged, Benjamin also sees in death the source of narrativity, the tale that must be told. It is in the imminence of death that the "unforgettable emerges" and "man's knowledge or wisdom, but above all his real life—and this is the stuff that stories are made of—first assumes transmissible form. . . ."[28] (As we shall see, however, there is something of a problem in the enunciation of the subject in the system of transmission.) We may deduce from Freud and Lacan that the life which comes rushing back in death—say, in the stereotype of drowning—arises from the desire for death through which we affirm ourselves in life. The onrush of a return is long prefigured in the circling back of instinctual life. In the memory-trace of desire, there is a movement toward otherness which, more than the instincts of self-preservation or self-assertion, moves the subject to its own proper death.

If Freud qualifies the disturbing notion of the death instinct by speaking of the sexual instincts, conservative as they are, as the true life instincts—"Eros, the preserver of all things"—that's because he also sees the life of the organism moving in a "vacillating rhythm" through "ever more complicated *detours* before reaching its aim of death." Freud's thought, and the retrogressive path he is describing, is not unlike the circuitousness of storytelling itself, from Borges back to the *Arabian Nights*. Much has been made of this in new literary theory, and I'm not going to labor it now. "What we are left with," says Freud, for all the detours, is what has been posited early in the work, "that the organism wishes to die in its own fashion."[29]

But there's the problem, since dying in one's own fashion may no longer be, for that subject, self-fashioning. "We obey," said Stevens, "the coaxings of our end" ("Ulysses," p. 392). Without misprizing, or minimizing, the less abstractly teasing simple pains and fears, the chills and fevers of the elderly abreast of death, I also sometimes think there is no such thing as aging even when people *are* old, because they miss the coaxings, through too long obedience, perhaps, to something other than the end. So, while everybody has a story to tell as the unforgettable emerges, it appears to be forgotten and the story isn't being told because it *hasn't* achieved transmissible form. While it may be moving at times to see old people suspended in themselves like Yeats's long-legged fly upon the stream, their minds moving upon silence, the silence may not be much sustenance, or substance. And for such—as for any of us for whom the bleak necessity remains silent when it would be categorically better spoken—there is only further pain. "What I seek in speech," says Lacan, "is the response of the other. What constitutes me as subject is my question." Remarks are insufficient. What is the question of the person growing old? I suspect the question is: *Why me?* "In order to be recognized by the other," says Lacan, "I utter what was only in view of what will be." So, too, with the memories of age, which are not merely part of one's personal history but a rhetoric, a petition as well, seeking the one who *can* respond: "In order to find him, I call him by a name that he must assume or refuse in order to reply to me" (*Écrits*, p. 86). But the deepest pathos of age may be when nobody responds because, for whatever reasons, the name has been forgotten.

If there were such a thing as the poetics of aging, we might say it is a failure of the imagination to have imagined, as one nears the exhaustion of life, "the absence of imagination" which is "[it]self to be imagined," as Stevens observes as if thinking of Proust, Swann's Way, the Other Way, the depleted circling of the essential solitude, "the great pond and its waste of lilies, all this/Had to be imagined as inevitable knowledge,/ Required, as necessity requires" ("Ulysses," p. 383), after the leaves have fallen in "The Plain Sense of Things." Plain as it is (for Stevens), a poem of winter and its discontents, it has something of the bereft beatitude of the "yellow leaves, or none, or few" of Shakespeare's sonnet where, in a kind of double take on the falling leaves—the few were none, *there,* then fallen—we come with age to the "Bare ruined choirs where late the sweet birds sang" (Son. 73.1–4). But whether they sing or not depends, I suppose, on the presence of the imagination in the imagining of its absence, "imagination dead imagine," as Beckett said, beyond his seventieth year, in the ironically elegiac voice which brings to age the nothingness which is a little less, *lessness,* words doing their best in the metonymic incapacity of words and age, their Negative Capability, what Stevens calls elsewhere figures of capable imagination, reflecting the nothing that is not there and the nothing that is.

The life so short, the craft so long to learn, we learn from poetry which learns from age, as in *Lear,* how nothing will come of nothing with more than nothing seems. "Now that I'm entering night," writes Beckett in *Enough,* who is intimate with nothing, "I have kinds of gleams in my skull."[30] "The sedge has withered from the lake/And no birds sing," writes Keats, who never lived to be old, about another sibyl's shape, in "La Belle Dame Sans Merci," and I hear instead of the absence of the song the negative of the absence, the no-birds *sing,* as in "the palm at the end of the mind" the birds also sing, in the sumptuous bleakness at the end of Stevens's poems, as they do on the golden bough of Yeats's Byzantium, another creation of age which arises, out of the consciousness of being old, from the foul rag and bone shop of the heart. It is a richness in the categories of need, like "the cry of the leaves [in Stevens] which do not transcend themselves" but, like Shakespeare's leaves not quivering but shaking *against* the cold, give one the feeling, through "an exertion that declines," of "the life of that which gives life as it is" ("Course of a Particular," p. 367).

Without that feeling—and its achievement is a lifetime's exertion which accident may impair—what can there be in old age but even in the garrulousness of the old an unspoken confusion, not "the chatter that is then true legend" ("Ulysses," p. 391), as the early momentum subsides, and then the loss of anticipation, sclerotic time, the shamed agitations of uncertain desire, lamed eros, panic, the dying fall, not to mention the specific and unfigured incapacities, the accretions of disease, dry mouth, sore knuckles, brittle skin, weak knees, dim eyes, running sores, varicose veins, longer healing, palsy, arthritis, short and repellent breath, odors, gas, gas, unsubsiding, angina, cancer, senility itself, unsphinctered helplessness and shamed dependence, the litany of unaccountable somatic disasters and unnamable agonies that testify in the lamentations to something that was, when it was here, never entirely known, and only the emptiness tangible now, that absence, babbling, dread, now, when the last failed apprehension of it is gone, in "the stale grandeur of annihilation" ("Lebensweisheitspielerei," p. 384).

For the real impediment to an aging which is other than mere attrition is, for all we've appeared to live, the mere appearance of living, which is not quite the same as what I've tried to recall in the hyperbolic figure of my madeup mother, the commemorative living of an appearance. Nor have I been, in remembering her, recommending that inheritance as anything like a paradigm of age, for I have no illusion through all its remembered charm about the boundaries of her triple mirror nor, after having spent so much of my life aging in the theater, the mirrored limits of any appearance.

"How swift life runs from January to December!" writes Virginia Woolf in *The Waves*. "We are all swept on by the torrent of things grown so familiar that they cast no shade."[31] It is never enough to have made the most of our time or to live out an impalpable future, for we always desire, in the virility of the present moment, the thing which went before, and our fear about the future is, even before it comes, that it was never meant to last. Among the torrent of things grown so familiar that they cast no shadow are the things we meant to do that we've never done for want of time, opportunity, or courage, and few of us will be able to avoid that. Most of those who say they do, lie, which is perhaps another form of commemoration. Among the things that are disappointing in age is the inability to be any wiser or more courageous, or to meet principle any more squarely than you did when you were young, though you are older and you know the time is running out when, with some last scruple of integrity, you can keep the promise to yourself. I would like to say a good deal more about the best of our desires and the embarrassment of knowing that they will never be fulfilled, not because desire is endless and always desiring desire, but because for one good reason or another we've grown comfortable failing ourselves. I suppose, however, that to know these things of oneself is part of the meaning of aging and of having been, at the limit of the historical function of the subject, one who has been as much as he can be after all, and more because one knows it.

But there is also a perturbation of aging that comes, just over the threshold of consciousness from want of consciousness, a last sad intimation of the life we've never lived because essentially unremembered, so that there is a sense of having suffered somehow an irreparable loss that, because not known, we cannot even mourn. "It is poverty's speech which seeks us out the most," writes Stevens in old age about the older philosopher dying in Rome. "And you—it is you that speak it without speech. . . ." There is a sensory plenitude in the grace of this remembrance, "Your dozing in the depths of wakefulness/In the warmth of your bed, at the edge of your chair, alive/Yet living in two worlds . . ." (pp. 272–73). But when, in the declensions of an ending, there is a solitude without sense, the mere poverty of the unremembered, it adds to the last depreciations of age another discontent, and what was once, if memory serves, a rite of passage out of time is only, now, without then, more time to be endured.

NOTES

1. *Time Regained*, in vol. 3 of Marcel Proust, *Remembrance of Things Past*, trans. C. K. Scott Moncrieff, Terence Kilmartin, Andreas Mayor (New York: Random House, 1981), p. 721. Subsequent references will appear in the text.

2. Roland Barthes, *Camera Lucida: Reflections on Photography*, trans. Richard Howard (New York: Hill and Wang, 1981), p. 67. Subsequent references will appear in the text.

3. Sigmund Freud, *Dora: An Analysis of a Case of Hysteria*, intro. Philip Rieff (New York: Collier, 1963), p. 96.

4. "On Narcissism: An Introduction," in *General Psychological Theory* intro. Philip Rieff (New York: Collier, 1963), p. 56.

5. Ibid., p. 70.

6. Wallace Stevens, "Questions Are Remarks," in *The Palm at the End of the Mind*, ed. Holly Stevens (New York: Vintage, 1972), p. 353. Subsequent references to poems in this volume will appear in the text.

7. Jacques Lacan, *Écrits: A Selection*, trans. Alan Sheridan (New York: Norton, 1977), p. 4. Subsequent references will appear in the text.

8. William Carlos Williams, *Paterson* (New York: New Directions, 1963), p. 11.

9. "A Note on the Unconscious in Psychoanalysis," in *General Psychological Theory*, p. 49.

10. "The Unconscious," in ibid., pp. 134–35.

11. See Ronald Blythe, *The View in Winter* (New York: Harcourt Brace Jovanovich, 1979), p. 9.

12. "The Man and the Echo," in *The Collected Poems of W. B. Yeats* (New York: Macmillan, 1960), p. 338. Subsequent references to poems in this volume will appear in the text.

13. Jacques Derrida, "Structure, Sign, and Play in the Discourse of the Human Sciences," in *Writing and Difference*, trans. Alan Bass (Chicago: University of Chicago Press, 1978), p. 283.

14. "The Death of Cuchulain," in *The Collected Plays of W. B. Yeats* (New York: Macmillan, 1953), p. 439.

15. Claude Lévi-Strauss, *The Raw and the Cooked*, trans. John and Doreen Weightman (New York: Harper and Row, 1969), p. 18.

16. Yeats, *Collected Plays*, p. 445.

17. Rebecca West, quoted in *The New York Times*, 16 March 1983.

18. Henry James, preface to "The Altar of the Dead," in *The Art of the Novel: Critical Prefaces*, ed. R. P. Blackmur (New York: Scribner's, 1962), p. 256.

19. *Moses and Monotheism*, trans. Katherine Jones (New York: Vintage, 1955), p. 89.

20. "The Unconscious," in *General Psychological Theory*, p. 139.

21. "Repression," in ibid., p. 107.

22. Leo Tolstoy, *The Death of Ivan Ilych and Other Stories* (New York: Signet, 1960), p. 133.

23. Ibid., p. 155.

24. Blythe, *The View in Winter*, p. 4.

25. John Hawkes, *The Lime Twig* (New York: New Directions, 1961), p. 72.

26. Yvor Winters, "To the Moon," in *The Collected Poems of Yvor Winters*, intro. Donald Davie (Chicago: Swallow, 1978), p. 185.

27. Jean-Paul Sartre, *Les Mots* (Paris: Gallimard, 1968), p. 171.

28. Walter Benjamin, *Illuminations*, ed. Hannah Arendt, trans. Harry Zohn (New York: Schocken, 1968), p. 94.

29. *Beyond the Pleasure Principle*, trans. and ed. James Strachey, intro. Gregory Zilboorg (New York: Norton, 1961), p. 33.

30. *First Love*, p. 54.

31. Virginia Woolf, *The Waves* (New York: Harcourt, Brace, 1931), p. 216.

UNIVERSALS OF PERFORMANCE; OR, AMORTIZING PLAY

Henry James, whose struggle with the theater left performative traces in the consciousness of his prose, wrote succinctly in one of his prefaces of the drama as an *ado*. There is in the brevity of the word an almost molecular view of performance, like the Freudian *fort/da*, the child's game of disappearance and return, played with a spool, in which by the repetitive deferral of pleasure the reality principle is enjoyed. According to Freud, the disappearance which is being performed is the departure of the child's mother. The *fort/da* is an ado which pivots on an absence. We know from Shakespeare that it is possible to make, in theater, much ado about nothing; and we know from Beckett, and Zeami, that it is possible to perform the seeming absence of an ado as a precise nothing to be done.

Nothing may come of nothing, but it would also be precise to think of that replicated nothing as a substantive *ado*. For there is a crucial particle of difference—especially where nothing is concerned—between that and just doing, between just breathing eating sleeping loving and *performing* those functions of just living; that is, with more or less deliberation, doing the *act* of breathing, eating, sleeping, loving, like Didi/Gogo *do* the tree in *Godot*. It is a difference as distinct as the presence or absence of punctuation in the previous sentence. The most minimal performance is a differentiating act: *fort* (gone)/*da* (there). It is an act which introduces (or is introduced by) an element of consciousness in the function, like "the *economic* motive"—the yield of pleasure in the anxiety—of the apparently gratuitous play of Freud's grandson rehearsing the two-act drama of his wooden reel: the representation of a lack which is the recovery of a loss.[1]

What is universal in performance—aside from the ambiguity as to which comes first—are the marks of punctuation which are inflections (or economic indices) of *consciousness* even in performance which, like autistic play, speaking in tongues, or Sufi whirling, seems to occur without it. In those performances which seem more like a raga than a drama, where the "story" behind it is dispersed, attenuated, or "musicated," like the compositions of Steve Reich or Charlemagne Palestine, or extended over many years like a tribal cycle, you may have to wait longer to discern it. There seems to me, however, no point in talking about performance, no less universals of performance, unless you discern it, although *who* exactly is doing the discerning—and whether inside or outside—is so critical an issue *in performance* that the problem itself can be considered a universal. To what degree and when the members of a tribe are aware, in the absence of anthropologists, of the performative nature of the long space of living between the sacraments, is a case in point; but we can also see the problem in the most minimal performance. When, say, Chris Burden announced that he was going to disappear, and then disappeared, it would have been a quite different performance if, with no further ado, he simply disappeared without the announcement, whether or not he returned.

The difference between the ado and just doing would appear to be self-evident except for the current discourse on performance which, now refusing, now accepting, more or less obscures the ontological gap between the actuality of everyday life and the actuality of a performance, between the ongoing processes of a culture and—with symptoms of ergotropic behavior: quickened pulse, flaring nostrils, sweat secretion, eye dilation—the emergence of "dramatic time."[2] The discourse is inseparable from the praxis of recent performance which has widened its parameters to include the activities of everyday life, even while aware of an opposing tendency: a narrowing asepsis of performance which, by burning away the signs of ordinary life, seems to widen the ontological gap. Sometimes the two tendencies are encouraged simultaneously with no sense of contradiction. We have seen in the strategies of performance which aspire to Total Theater the desire for *more* theater and the desire for *less* theater, with more or less theatricalized permutations on the theme of less is more. There appears to be, for instance, in the new paratheatrical enterprise of Grotowski—what he calls a Theater of Sources—the somewhat utopian desire to replace the illusion of Total Theater with the promise of Total Life. Whatever the ontological status of that quest, we have become attentive in recent years to modes of performance which involve transformations and exchanges in the here-and-now, more or less ritualized, more or less participatory, more or less risky and irreversible, more or less "actuals,"[3] where the doings are ados. In the study of aboriginal cultures, we have been made aware of the accretions of everyday life which become, with inflexions of ceremony but no clear demarcation from just living, occasions of performance.

Conversely, there are accretions of everyday life which are still—in theater and other cultural practices—felt as impediments to performance. That accounts in part for the stagings of initiation in ritual process and, in the marriage of acting craft and spiritual exercises, the stress on *de*conditioning, getting rid of the habits, down to the most rudimentary basis of our actual living. I can hardly think of a technique of performance, even the most naturalistic, which doesn't reconceive of the breathing we take for granted as a bodily process to be explored or a spiritual discipline to be acquired. "Kill the breathing! Kill the rhythm!" repeats the dancing Master—whether Azuma or Merce Cunningham— trying to break the reflexive attachment of the rhythm of respiration, and thus the movement of the dance, to the measure of the music.[4] Whether synchronous or ruptured, the universal movement of performance is through an equivocating cadence of more or less performance. If movement, according to *The Secret of the Golden Flower*, "is only another name for mastery,"[5] there is nothing named performance which is not, at the last declension of a shadow's breath, concerned with the degree of mastery in the movement, and the degree of measure as well.

The Japanese Noh drama, the Tai Chi Ch'uan, the *Hevehe* cycle of the Elema in New Guinea, Richard Wagner's or Robert Wilson's operas, a voodoo ritual or a High Mass seem to require time as the condition for forgetting it. But how much time, O Lord, with timeliness? Take *time,* says the director to the actor in a realistic play being rehearsed under an Equity contract; *take* time, says the therapist to the patient in an analytical session which costs sixty dollars an hour. The protraction of time is in every case, real or illusory, a mode of deconditioning, bringing performance back to "life." The question always remains, however, as to how *much* performance and how *long* and, in performance as in life, how much *life*—and how much apparent or disguised agitation over the temporality. If you think for an instant about timing in acting, you will eventually be caught up in a metaphysic. Whether prescribed or felt out, the determining of time is a universal of performance. It determines in turn the relations between what seems then familiar and what strange, the artificial and the natural, the sense of just being or being some*one*, the presentation of a self, a service in time or time-serving, whether measured by a clock, hypocrisy (the actor's duplicity), or the scruple on the price of a ticket. That is not only true of theatrical performance. One may look, as I tend to do, upon a baseball game as the Japanese Noh drama of American culture. I remember the long summer afternoons with the Bushwicks and the House of David which, even before floodlights came into the ballpark, seemed hardly subject to time. But once the networks took over the game, there were two dimensions of time: one orchestrated with breaks for commercials and the other, when electronic scoreboards came into the ballpark, a collateral entertainment—with fireworks, waterfalls, more commercials, and instant replays on the scene—which is always filling up time.

Sometimes the accretions of time in everyday life are the accretions of technique. Aside from the natural tendency to breathe in time to the music, dancers who had been studying ballet since next to infancy need to be, when they come to modern dance, saved from the perils of the barre. Cunningham has always said that he didn't want "steps" in his technique; Stanislavski did, and didn't. Cunningham, for all his openness, always shows traces of ballet in his own movement; and Stanislavski, who was trained in opera at a time when singers were in peril if they moved, could not entirely have escaped certain reflexes which were, no doubt, compensated for in the emotional memories of his method. They were both seeking, through the exactions of technique, forms of *natural* movement. It is the distinction, however, between just doing and performing the doing that made it possible for Stanislavski to say that the hardest thing for an actor to do on stage, though he has been doing it all his life, is to walk. It took him time to teach his actors to walk but when they were deconditioned and started to walk again, he wanted it to seem as if they were doing it as they had always done.

Doing it as it has always been done seems to be, whether sacred or profane, a universal of performance, even when it appears to be done as if for the first time. There has been a serious effort over the last generation to eliminate the *as if*, to return performance to *unmediated* experience, as with The Living Theater, but with whatever measure of "truth" or "authenticity" it is at best only appearance. There is nothing more illusory in performance than the illusion of the unmediated. It can be a very powerful illusion in the theater, but it *is* theater, and it is *theater*, the truth of illusion, which haunts *all* performance whether or not it occurs in the theater, where it is more than doubled over. It is, actually, the unavoidable *doubling* in life, in a feedback circuit with theater, that has induced Richard Schechner, after much experiment with actuals which attempted (more or less) unmediated activity with an emphasis on the here-and-now, to accede to the "restoration of behavior" which he now distinguishes as "the main characteristic of performance," from shamanism and therapy to social drama and aesthetic theater.[6] What distinguishes the performative ethos of the postmodern—in a time of recuperation from the illusions of theater-as-life—is not only redoubled awareness of what is being restored, but an exponential play around the combinatory sets of stored or past experience which is, since there is utterly no assurance of an uninterrupted present, all we can make of a dubious future.

There has been, then, a chastening accession of belatedness in the dialectic of appearances. And it points to the almost undeniable remembrance of history that *there is something in the nature of theater which from the very beginning of theater has always resisted being theater.* Or "always already" resisted, as Jacques Derrida might say, if there were no beginning of theater, and thus no nature but a trace. It is, indeed, the inevitable *reappearance of history* in performance which corrects the illusion of performance that refuses the future of illusion—the reign of representation—and insists that the theater *is* life or, if not yet so, that it must be so. That this insistence can be a historical illusion of apocalyptic dimensions we have seen in Artaud and can still see in Derrida's essay on Artaud, "The Theater of Cruelty and the Closure of Representation."[7] If we can imagine, however, a state which is the becoming of theater or all theater or beyond theater, we can also imagine a state before theater which would appear to be something other than theater, what we have sometimes *named* life, which could not possibly *be* theater.

For like the sign in a hypothetical simple state, as idea or image or perception, the theatrical *gestus*, the signifying element *of* theater "can become a sign," as Foucault says, "only on condition that it manifests, in addition, the relation that links it to what it signifies. It must represent; but that representation, in turn, must also be represented within it. That is a condition indispensable to the binary organization of the sign. . . . The signifying idea becomes double, since superimposed upon the idea that is replacing another [the representation within] is also the idea of its representative power."[8] Derrida himself has elsewhere pointed out, in the denial of origins, the origin of doubling: "Representation mingles with what it represents, to the point where one speaks as one writes, one thinks as if the represented were nothing more than the shadow or reflection of the representer." Then, in the high melodrama of post-structuralist theory, which resembles the anxiety over perception in the Jacobean theater, he speaks of the "dangerous promiscuity and . . . nefarious complicity between the reflection and the reflected which lets itself be seduced narcissistically. In this play of representation, the point of origin becomes ungraspable. . . . For what is reflected is split *in itself* and not only as an addition to itself of its image. The reflection, the image, the double, splits what it doubles. The origin of the speculation becomes a difference. What can look at itself is not one; and the law of the addition of the origin to its representation, of the thing to its image, is that one plus one makes at least three."[9] Which is, at the logocentric impasse of the Western metaphysical tradition, like performing the Tai Chi or repeating the Tao which "begot one./One begot two. Two begot three"—out of which arises the created universe, the "ten thousand things" with their ceaseless play of difference in the exchanges of *yin* and *yang*,[10] as if reality were a performance.

The *substance* of the theatrical in the idea of performance is the critical question in the act of performance. Nor is it merely a question of the succession of theatrical forms or modes of performance within those forms. It has rather to do with the radical critique of representation and, in the animus of recent thought, an intense distrust of the almost lethal legacy of a savage god who never meant the theater to reveal itself as such, nor for representation to show its duplicitous face. The central figure in this critique, as in the most important theatrical experiment of the last generation, is Artaud, whose Theater of Cruelty is not a form of New Theater waiting to be born, but a primordial and juridical power whose urge, as Derrida shows, is the abolition of representation, which seals off the division between theater and life as it separates birth from death. "The void, the place that is empty and waiting for this theater which has not [as we say] 'begun to exist,' " writes Derrida, "thus measures only the strange distance which separates us from implacable necessity, from the *present* (or rather the contemporary, *active*) affirmation." Artaud's theater is not a representation. To the degree that life is unrepresentable, it is meant to be the *equal* of life, "the nonrepresentable origin of representation."[11]

In this mission, the enemy is mimesis, which breeds the lie of humanism, with its myth of individuation. What we see rather in the image of man is the grotesque offspring of the theater's self-perpetuating enormity: ego, self, personality, a mere reproductive subject, slave to the ideological apparatus of reproduction, who must learn to free himself from false acting by true performance (thus, too, the distinction between the actor and the performer which has turned up in recent years). So far as the *institution* of theater is concerned, if it is ever to be anything except a part of the apparatus, it must become the designated site of the extermination of the mimetic. In various zealous, adulterate, radically innocent, or depleted versions of this thought, innovation and renovation in the contemporary theater have proceeded. It can obviously be nothing less than a falling away of thought from the affirmation which, despite itself, lets itself be evacuated by the doubling and redoubling of a negation in performance, as if the neural force of representation were itself the indemnifying Plague. It is the problem that Artaud himself was never able to resolve, what drove him mad, though he seemed to come at the finest filament of his nerve-wracked thought as close as humanly possible to the nonrepresentable origin of performance where "the true theater . . . is born out of a kind of organized anarchy after philosophical battles which are the passionate aspect of . . . primitive unifications."[12]

As we become enamored of the unifications which we project upon "primitive" cultures, we tend to forget that even performances which are presumed to be outside representation exist within its enclosure. Without the enclosure, we would find ourselves, so to speak, within a performance that, whatever it may continue in an uninterrupted present, had never really begun, since it would only continue as *seeming*, like a dream. Denying the enclosure, the "stage edge" of the *mise-en-scène* of the unconscious, is to find yourself in Artaud's position, crying out in dreams, knowing you're dreaming and exerting the will to the point of madness, whipping your "innateness" so that it might prevail, as Artaud claimed for himself, on both sides of the dream. It is a noble if manic ambition. None of us, however, has ever seen a performance which, in the revulsion against the mimetic, the desire to banish seeming, has not (the more effective it is) radically increased the quotient of *pre*tense, the disruption of time by seeming—*especially if we have seen it.*

As we understand more acutely from the interpretation of dreams, with their decoys of displacement and secondary revision, it is of the nature of performance to *be seen.* (I remember a moment in the presentation of a Yaqui ritual by the tribal chief—*his* interpretation of the Christo Rey ceremony—when he was explaining the origin of the *tam-*

peleo, the ritual drum. It was part of the saga of his personal creation myth, and he was very conscious of being studied by those who were there [all of whom he took to be anthropologists] as he told the story: a tree was cut, the wood was soaked, and then bent, and soaked some more, the ends joined. When the drum was sealed, a hole was bored in the side so the sound could escape, and then another for the emission of a longer sound and—just as we were forgetting that this version *was* a performance—he lifted the drum and looked at us through one of the holes, demonstrating how the drum might be used as a fixating instrument of the cruel performing eye. In that look we passed from a reconstruction of the spirit-world of the *huya iniya* to the solipsistic world of post-Genetic performance, where the watchers are watching the watchers watch. . . .) The boundary of performance is a *specular* boundary, marked by speculation, the *idea* of a boundary. So, too, the boundary of a dream is the condition of the dreamer in the enclosure of sleep which, admittedly, may blur into the semblance of a waking dream, like the *huya iniya* of the Yaquis or like the somnambulistic ambition in the oneiric performances of Robert Wilson.

So long, however, as there is a performance to be referred to *as such* it occurs within a circumference of representation with its tangential, ecliptic, and encyclical lines of power. What blurs in the immanence of seeming are the features of that power, which needs to be taken into account in the current speculation on the state of performance in art and culture. It is not so much a matter of formalist experiment or behavioral innovation or ethnological renewal—all of which is taking place—but a breaking down of the structure of belonging which is, at the same time, inscribed in the becoming of representations which are, through the acceleration of cultural exchange, accumulating in a repertoire which is worldwide. If there is an infusion of energy as cultures cross, it is always competing with the universal extension of the apparatus of reproduction. Even as the imagery appears to change, the image-making systems appear to reflect the implacable and unchangeable image of an imageless and invisible power. This was a prospect which the theater always foresaw, from the hallucinations of Cassandra to the fantasies of Genet, since it was its own living, interminable, and recurring image.

As we think, then, about the future of performance, the questions are simultaneously technological and metaphysical. It makes no difference that some performance is far from conceptual and some of it, experimenting with the abolition of mimesis, next to brainless. The

metaphysics comes in, as Artaud and Nietzsche thought, but not always
as they wished, through the skin, into the muscles, epistemically. We
know that Artaud's critique of occidental theater was part of a grander
design for a Final Solution. He wanted to pulverize the contaminated
structure of Western understanding, a contamination which has unfortunately spread at an alarming rate as we exchange, with whatever
benefits, conceptual diseases with other parts of the world. Most ambi-
tions in the theater itself, or in other Performance Art, are neither so
rabid nor all-consuming, so venereal as Artaud's. But they are, if tenta-
tive or partial, responses to the same disturbance, at least those that have
any cultural weight. Another villain of the piece, a blood relation of
mimesis, is *speech,* mark of a theological space of performance where the
primacy of the Logos continues to prevail. It prevails, despite the antiverbal experiments of the sixties, not merely in the proliferation of
born-again Christians but in the ramified disguises of the Author-Text,
that overpowering absence which unceasingly "regulates the time or the
meaning of representation,"[13] not in the intrinsic purity of the actor's
desire but according to the wishes and authority of that anterior force.
The picture has been extensively painted in critical theory, perhaps
over-painted: the idea that we are all in servitude to an interpretation
which gives the illusion of an acting freedom but really comes from
elsewhere, so that what is being performed is, in Artaud's view, the
excrement of another mind.

Any way you look at it—which may be the price of looking—the
theater is the place where nothing is being transacted except what has
been imposed on the disfigured body of thought of an infinite chain of
representation. The missing links of this chain, its *structure of disappearance,* wind through the body politic and are strengthened, as
Genet suggested in *The Balcony,* by the delusions of revolution, which
maintains the chain of servitude intact. We felt something like that after
the sixties (when "the whole world" was "watching"), and it appears to be
no different after every insurrection around the globe. On the stage as
we normally know it, long after the prompter's box disappeared from
view, we still felt a suspect and filthy breath, a vitiating whisper in the
vomitorium. Or there was something in the cellarage or the wings or
muffled in the teasers and tormentors, prescribing the words to be
spoken or the figures of the dance or—even with the representation
musicated or masticated in a participatory theater where dinner is
served—still cooking the stew or calling the tune, like the rather de-

ranged figure in a theaterwork of my own, *The Donner Party, Its Crossing* (whose subject was cannibalism), where the square dance kept turning and turning in the exhaustive pursuit of a vanishing power. It is against this power that performance continues to struggle, always coming round, with no higher aspiration than another reversal of history in the play of appearances: the liberation of the performer as an *actor* who, laminated with appearance, struggles *to appear.*

By whatever means the actor achieves autonomy—whether through charisma or flagrancy or transgression of the Text or by sheer power of apparent understanding (the rarest presence)—the machinery of the theater quickly disables the appearance and marshals itself around a space of subversion, so long as there *is* a performance. No seeming self-denial on the part of an actor, no pretense of immediacy, however momentarily powerful or time-effacing, can amplify the privileged instant, for it is only for the instant timeless—and once again the theater suffuses the truth with its presence, the only *presence* which is there. It is then that we realize that approval has been, in our very assent to the transgression of performance, institutionalized, historicized, *on borrowed time.* The theater is a space of amortization. The interest is in the performance, and there is no performance without interest on a loan that can never be paid.

What is true of the actor is also true of the regenerative illusion of an *empty space* (Peter Brook's term) in which the actor has been seeking immediacy, usually missing its point. This is all the more true when the actor goes halfway across the world and rolls out a carpet in an aboriginal village, presumably to start from scratch, improvisationally, with elemental stories or something like pure play. No sooner is it looked at with anything like performance in mind, the empty space is a space of consciousness, also subject to time, and to the attritions of time, as if there were nothing but history in the nap. What is thought of as a space of risk or danger has a relapsable or collapsable edge. The collapse is, if first into the abyss of wonder (or the exotic), then into the trough of the commonplace. Even the astonishing quickly becomes—especially in the world of publicity, adjunct of the image-system (*is* there another world?)—a household word.

It is the momentary usurpation of "reality" by the truth of performance that, like the *(cliché)* photographic memory it soon becomes, validates the usurped system theoretically. And it is the system, with *its* sense of time (linear or synchronous) which is really the subject of play.

It determines the steps or their apparent absence in the dance. It allows for the propriety of the event, however disturbing or obscene (against the scene) it may appear to be. The more it appears so by unavoidable reproduction, the more tautologically assured is the validation. Common sense tells us that what we experience at a play or other performance is not so tortuously deceptive as all this, but it is the purpose of common sense to overcome the real insidiousness of epistemological deceits lest, in reproducing them mentally—as Hamlet did, or Artaud—we may go mad. It is the power of Derrida's critique of Foucault on madness that he demonstrates how even the performance of madness, and its valorizing discourse, can never move outside the system of speech because "madness is indeed, especially and generally, silence, stifled speech, within a caesura and a wound that *opens up* life as *historicity in general*,"[14] which prevents madness—the limit of the unmediated—from ever being mad enough, as we can also see persuasively in *King Lear*.

To recapitulate: what seems to be confirmed by the pursuit of unmediated experience through performance is that there is something in the very nature of performance which, like the repeating spool of the *fort/da* (Krapp's extrapolated sp*ooo*l), implies *no first time,* no origin, but only recurrence and reproduction, whether improvised or ritualized, rehearsed or aleatoric, whether the performance is meant to give the impression of an unviolated naturalness or the dutiful and hieratic obedience to a code. That is why a performance seems *written* even if there is no Text, for the writing seems imbedded in the conservatism of the instincts and the linguistic operations of the unconscious. It seems, moreover, corporeally inscribed, even when there's a performance without any body, nothing but an absence, like the graffiti on the once-smooth body of the only too palpable Ghost.

With all the actable and unactable intricacies of the play within the play—that palimpsest of performance which breaks down the text in the image of the Text—*Hamlet* seems to affirm more than any other play in the canon that *what is universal in performance is the consciousness of performance.* That is nowhere more palpable than at those moments of negative capability when, after all the rationalizing intemperateness of the performance, there appears to be a (re)*lapse* of consciousness and—as if there were a cultural transference, a metathesis, a genetic crossing of East and West—there is some respite from the splitting infinitives of representation (to be or not to be) and only the *letting be*. When I speak, therefore, of the consciousness of performance, I am stressing the consciousness in the grain of performance—no outside no inside—which in certain kinds of performance may appear not to be there but, as in a topological warp, is there in its appearance, appearing not-to-be.

Even in the resistance to appearance, as in the *Verfremdungseffekt* derived by Brecht from Chinese acting, appearance is universal to performance. What makes it so? Thinking makes it so. Which is to say: the consciousness *of* performance. A baby may be performing without consciousness, or so it appears (Marx insists that the whole history of the world is in the sensory expression of any moment, and Freud reminds us that the unconscious is our oldest mental faculty), but what would we know of performance if the world were full of babies. As with the disenchantments of the world, so with other states of elapsed consciousness. It's the falling away from trance, or its doubling in split consciousness, that makes us aware of trance as performance, as well as the possibility—engrained in the most skeptical thought of performance, in performance as a thinking body—that the world may be entranced.

"What, has this thing appeared again tonight?" (*Ham.*, I.i.21). Obviously, if it appears there's going to be trouble for the performance. But if it doesn't appear there will be no performance, or not much worth mentioning if there is a performance. And that's true I would suppose, East or West, or at whatever meridian of performance anywhere in the world. The thing seems to suggest the almost unnamable form of some ancestral figure, not only the Hamletic ghost, but the Japanese *shite,* the Balinese *patih,* the *shave* of the Shona in East-Central Africa, or the God of Abraham in the Oberammagau Passion Play. Coleridge spoke of the credibilizing power of the omnibus word *thing.* Whatever the power is behind that power—like the power which summons away the Ghost which came in the Name of the Father—the thing is sufficiently indeterminate that one feels it has to do with more than the mere physical presence of a probably improbable ghost, or from what terrestrial direction the appearance occurs (although in some cultures, true, it won't appear unless it comes from the right direction, like "The Older Father" entering the ramada of the Yaquis). What we are anticipating, rather, in the goings and comings of these ghosts is the *ghostliness* that moves the performance. That is universal. Over the long history of performance it has moved by many names: as Destiny, Providence, Eternal Return, Oedipus Complex or Viconian Gyre: or as an inspiriting force or *influence,* often associated with the breath, such as *pneuma, taksu, shakti, ki;* or as some dematerialization of the Text into a fusion of vapor and power, like the fiery white letters of the Kabbalah or the smoke from the *shabbath* candles that my grandmother, hooded by a napkin, wafted up her nose in one of the lovelier performances of my childhood; or as the "complete, sonorous, streaming naked realization"[15] which was, if Artaud's vision is true, the Orphic writing on the wall behind the Mysteries of Plato's Cave.

It is to the writing on the wall that, if there is an Eternal Return, the performance always returns. If it's never quite the same, that's because there is something mortifying in the mystery. Think again of the space of amortization. As with the economics of the psyche, it is half in love with death. Whatever the ghostly thing, there is an abrasion in performance (the "rub"), some interior resistance to the aboriginal romance of a pure libidinal flow. That is the real substance of the representational split which doubles over and over. The splitting occurs, as Freud discerned, not within the libido alone but, with a kind of activating *rigor mortis*, between the libido and death, which solicits and subverts and precludes representation. It is exactly what goes out of sight that we most desperately want to see. That's why we find ourselves, at the uttermost consummation of performance, in the uncanny position of *spectators*. It is uncanny because, in some inexplicable way (though Freud comes uncannily close to explaining it), *we are seeing what we saw before.* And that is true not only for those who attend upon the event, spectators at the start, but for those who become, through the event, participants, and for those who began as performers, in a kind of reversal of roles. It is as if, as Artaud says of the power of "true illusion," we are situated "magically, in *real terms* . . . between dream and events"[16]—his alternative to Aristotle's situation of tragedy between philosophy and history. If repetition is fundamental to performance, it is—after all or to begin with—death which rejects pure presence and dooms us to repetition. For Freud, the performance is always already scored in the irreducible dualism of the drives, although he also saw what Euripides foresaw in *The Bacchae,* that presence is not forbidden by some Apollonian power with whom Dionysus must make his peace; it is always already forbidden in the Dionysian power itself.

There are two realities meeting, then, at a single vanishing point, life and death, art and life, the thing itself and its double, which prepares the ground for performance. I don't want to rehearse all the reasons why we might think of it as sacred ground, except to say that it is inherent in the memory imbedded in the ground, like "the uncontrollable mystery on

the bestial floor" in Yeats's poem or the Funeral Studio in the brain cell
of Genet's Brothel. Once we think of death as already "at the origin of a
life which can defend itself against death only through an *economy* of
death, through deferment, repetition, reserve," we may realize how
powerful a force memory is in the life of performance with its intrinsic
secondariness, as it sustains the enigma of a *first time*. As Derrida explains
in his account of memory as the constituting principle of the psyche in
Freud, it is in the first time—which can only be *thought of* as a trace of
originary violence and pain, in the contact of life and death—that repetition has already begun. It was there in the beginning which is always
beginning again.

   Whatever course the history of the theater takes afterward, the condition of theater is an *initiatory breach* which remembers the primal violence. That is why Freud—like tragic drama and, so far as I can see,
every major form of theater, with more or less memory of the tragic—
"accords a privilege to pain."[17] What we once thought of as catharsis is
an equivocal aversion to an excess of pain which, lest it ruin the psychical
organization, must be deferred, like death, even by those cultures which
extend the deferral through stages (or stagings) of death. We may defer
it by laughter or meditation or random play or trance, or by the dream
of an actual which is a perpetual present, but "Life is already threatened
by the origin of the memory which constitutes it, and by the breaching
which it resists, the effraction which it can contain only be repeating
it."[18] What is being repeated in the tautological cycle of performance—
replay, reenactment, restoration, the play within the play within—is the
memory of the origin of the memory which is being solicited and resisted. It is in this recursive way that performance is a testament to a life
which seems to look like death because it is always being left behind.

   There are, of course, ceremonial occasions which are joyous, but if
there is in the disappearing space of performance something of a ceme-
tery too, the wonder is that this world of the dead can tell us as much as it
does about the living. The reason is that it is only in terms of the living
that we imagine the world of the dead. Yet there is a sense in which the
performer is always imagining his own death. He may project it into the
future as another deferral, but it seems to come like memory from
behind, as if it had already happened. That's why, too, there is always
the residue of a lie or a self-deception in the claim of the actor or shaman
or hungan that he is wholly (self)possessed and does not see himself
performing. Shakespeare dwells upon this evasion in the sonnets—a

virtual manual of performance which is sonorously intimate with possession. The self-observing voice of the sonnets speaks explicitly at one
point of the "unperfect actor on the stage,/Who with his fear is put *besides
his part*" (23.1–2, emphasis mine). There are glimpses of a perfect actor,
but he might as well be an effigy for, "moving others," he is himself "as
stone," pure influence, but subject of an invisible power (94.1–4). If the
actor does not see himself performing, he is nonetheless a spectator
because of this duplicity in the presence of the Other, the familiar, the
double, the formerly buried avatar of a constantly duplicating self. In a
culture which appears to have no such concept as the self, that (un)-
consecrated victim of the Word, the repressed appearance will be an
ancestral *figure* which, whatever case you want to make for the spirit
world, is just as likely to be a figure of speech.

It is, however, in the presence of the seemingly dead that we can
see—as we have come to see in recent years—that the archaic ceremonies
from which the theater was presumably born did not preclude theater;
that is, ritual has no priority. It might indeed have *followed* theater in the
instituting trace, although the institutions of ritual and theater are coextensive in time, mirroring and mirrored in the same mystery. If we were
rummaging, though, in the long history of anthropological guesses as to
which ritual form—year-gods, vegetation ceremonies, shamanism, etc.—
tells us most about the emergence of theater from whatever was not-
theater (assuming there was an emergence and it was not forever there),
my inclination would be to focus, as Genet so acutely did, on some death
rite or funeral ceremony as primal, a rite of *separation* rather than a rite
of incorporation (Van Gennep's terms), which would seem to come after
the more primordial fact—just as the cosmic marriage ceremony and the
hymeneal feast came rather arbitarily not only after the tragic drama but
after the disruptions of comedy as well, as in the betrothal of the old fart
Pisthetairos to the young beauty Basileia, Miss Universe, like some *deus-
ex* ingenuity to heal an irreparable breach.

The point is, again, that there is no performance without separation
or division, though the nature of performance may preserve, more or
less reverently or irreverently, the memory of a time—the now-famous
illud tempus—when there was *no* separation. That is another way of
describing the recurring aspiration of performance to efface itself or—
in the irresistible shading of performance into theater theater into performance—whatever it is that is *theatrical,* the substance of all divisions,
in performance, especially if the ritual is sacred. (I remember being

present at a Eucharist, as an observer, when the communicants went up to receive the wafer and the wine, and the priest reciting the liturgy reversed the order of the offering in the repetition of the words. I believe I was the only one who heard it, maybe not even the priest and the woman before him when it happened, who was going to be ordained and with whom, I had reason to suspect, he was having an affair. It is interesting to speculate about the nature of that performance if I hadn't been there and—in what appeared to be a "perfect ceremony of love's rite" (*Son.* 23.6)—nobody had heard it, though my separating presence might have induced it by already theatricalizing the event.) Even in shamanism, there is an *aftering* effect that comes of separation. The spirit-ancestor, at some indeterminate space of being or nonbeing, perhaps among the dead, teaches the shaman to dance and sing. Then there is a synapse where the shamanic soul is released by ancestral powers and, as if awaking from a dream, remembers what he has been taught. The dance and song are efforts to rehearse back the hereditary world from which the shaman is separated. Sometimes the shaman forgets and, as if some punitive expedition has been ordered from the underworld, spirits appear and in another separation tear his body apart so he may the better remember.

In the modern theater, the rites of separation came out of the ethos of suspicion as a heuristic strategy, as if separation were reflecting on separation. It is probably just as well, in the gullible order of things, that there is now and then an intelligence like Brecht's which tries to dispel the mystery in performance by looking at it from a distance, while not at all depreciating just how stubborn the mystery is. What is, I think, still incisive about Brecht's theory of Alienation is that it distrusts not only the illusions of performance that sponsor a repressive oedipal force in the infrastructure of our culture, but the antioedipal enchantment as well, fortified now by the impact of other cultures. If one reads carefully the essay on Chinese acting, it is clear that it is not the arcanities that attract him, no more than an unrestricted subconscious in the actor. And if we think through the charges of the "Short Organum" against the obfuscating agencies of bourgeois theater, we may also be reminded that the empowering forces or creative energies of non-Western cultures, those I've already named, as well as *shun toeng, prana, kokoro,* and the metamorphosing versions of *ki,* are not necessarily divine emanations but as much historical constructs as sexuality, gender, race, and class, with all the liabilities of such constructs in the social and political world.

If we furthermore think for a moment about history, we may recall just how empowering they can also be. Like the creative energies, they have been attached to spiritual disciplines, more or less efficacious (and more or less destructive), as performance must be, whatever the unnamable force that through the green fuse drives the appearance.

Brecht preferred to stress in performance not the intangible power but the *structure* of appearances and the historical *gestus: what*'s happening and *why* and who is paying for it at one end or the other of a scale of victimization, which is another measure of performance, including as it does the status of the performer and the social cost of a mystifying energy which pays tribute to other unmoved movers, maybe more crippling forms of absent power, like *dharma*. I am not trying to deflate the alluring and truly creative traditions behind such concepts, which I don't pretend to understand, though I've spent years studying certain spiritual techniques and ritual processes as an extension of the art of acting. What I am trying to do is suggest that there is in any performance the universal question, spoken or unspoken, of *what are we performing for?* (This became a serious issue in my own theaterwork with KRAKEN when, for instance, we decided to do, in the evolution of a technique [called *ghosting*], the Tai Chi Ch'uan rather than Yoga or Aikido or any other of the martial arts. Why one rather than another? Why a martial art? Why, in fact, among all the conceivable forms an actor might study, any particular choice in the definition of a method? Even among Western techniques of, say, modern dance or mime—whose dance? whose mime? in respect to what? what for? and what, even in the generation of a "universal" technique like Grotowski's, what does *it* preclude?)

We can see in the politics of older cultures that they are also dealing with the return of the repressed. If we've screened them out, they've screened us out. To younger people in those cultures, struggling to retain perhaps (some not) what is generic and life-giving in the long deformities of traditional order, that may also mean the recognition, as on the other side of a mutual dream, of creative energies which we are, in the postindustrial world, only too swiftly dismissing, like the life-giving power of another historical construct, quite visible in Brecht, the indignant brainpower of the rational mind. Which is not what they mean—in the cybernetic universe which seems to resemble those other, earlier, or remoter worlds—by software.

In any case, what Brecht asked us to do, confronted with any play of appearances, is to observe critically, with a reserve of consciousness

outside performance, though he was early on aware that both the instruments of perception and the ideological structure of perception alter
the appearance of what is seen. He would have been unpersuaded,
surely, by the new doxology of play which suggests, as I have done
myself, that it may be impossible to get outside performance in the
illusory structure of World-Play. Brecht readily knew, moreover, that
there was a necessary pretense in an apparently legible structure which
may certainly have, as in his stagings of his own plays, a misleading
enchantment. But what was always important in Brecht—who after all
started his career inspired by Rimbaud, worshipping Baal, going to
nontheatrical performance, and anticipating Genet—was the tireless
effort, not often conspicuous in the solipsism and domesticated shamanism of postmodern performance, to navigate the fine line between the
visible appearance and the invisible happening, the dream and the
event, the doing and the ado, keeping his eye on the actual in the most
empirical sense, as a distinct matter of historical perception.

On that empirical basis, all performance moves between expectancy
and observance, between attentiveness to what happens and astonishment at what appears. The performances of a given culture may stress
one more than the other, but no performance is either all happening or
all appearance. And there is no way of resolving which comes first, the
happening or the appearance, no more than there is of performing
some gesture of the Tai Chi and determining as it is performed whether
the *chi* flowed so that the sparrow's tail could be grasped or whether, in
grasping the sparrow's tail, and only then, illusory as it seems, the *chi*
flowed, like the *lightness* which Brecht wanted from his actors when they
left East Germany to play in London. I can't imagine a cultural form
which really has anything conclusive to say about the fugitive relationship between the premonitory act and the actualization, the incipience
and the immanence, whether you make the gesture in order to have the
vision or have the vision so the gesture may be made. And that applies to
other kinds of performance which seem, at first sight, to have little to do
with these subtleties of appearance with their patina of theatricality. I am
thinking, for example, of Lynn Swann running the patterns of a passing
route or Nadia Comaneci on a vaulting horse or Philippe Petit on a high
wire between the towers of the World Trade Center or, mixing virtuosity
and appearance in the most self-conscious of performances, Muham-
mad Ali in that once audacious ado, dancing like a butterfly and stinging
like a bee. I am not sure, all nuances considered, that there is any kind of

performance that is nonmimetic, since what is being performed is—the more perilous the performance, like Swann's patterns or Ali's shuffle—an image of perfection in the head.

But, returning from such marvels of performance to the theatricalizing of everyday life, not only the appearance of the actual but, nowadays, the supplement of reflexive consciousness about that appearance: if there is no performance without consciousness, there is also the exercise of consciousness in watching a performance in which those who seem to be performing are under the illusion that they are merely living. I say under the illusion because, were they to think about it at all, that first reflection, they would be susceptible to the vice of performative consciousness which theatricalizes everything it looks upon, seeing the living as nothing but performance. As for those who know they're performing, they may call attention to it, but we know there are also techniques of performance, not only the Method, designed to make them forget it. Whether or not the consciousness of performance is to be forgotten is perhaps the major issue of the history of performance, as it certainly is of postmodernism. It does not, however, appear to be the same problem for those cultures which are taken as models of performative consciousness without *self*-consciousness *about* performance, because they are still perhaps on the aboriginal margins of history.

But, as everybody knows, not for long. It is a curious thing, too, to be thinking about universals of performance at a time when performance itself seems to be universal. As we widened the scope of performance to include not only theater events in theaters or environments or other dispersed places, we have also had to consider a variety of hybrid happenings and conceptual events, as well as sports, games, circuses, rituals, politics, fashion, therapies, sexual practices, private fantasies and illicit ceremonies, informal gatherings or rehearsed stagings, with or without texts, virtuals or actuals, plays not only without plot or character but with or without people—not to mention those more or less elusive shadows of the performing self which by disappearing accretions of performance eventually refuse the concepts we associate with people: personality or presence or a self. We have come to admit within the field of performance not only behavior(s) in everyday life but what used to be the disciplines by means of which we approached an understanding of behavior, what the French call the Human Sciences: philosophy, linguistics, anthropology, and psychoanalysis, with conceptual crossovers into the biological domain of genetics, ethology, and brain science.

All this gestation of performance in nontheatrical disciplines has been summoned up and perhaps summarized in the performative virtuosity of our literature, particularly literary theory.

Along with the valorization of play in the postmodern, we have taken with considerable seriousness the theatrical notion that all the space of the world is a stage or, with varying magnitudes and commutations of illusion, a cosmic manifestation of a universe of play. The play within the play occurs—more or less "framed," as well as "written"—at every level of the great chain of being or, in the unchained signifiers of a polysemous discourse, some recursive or reptilian equivalent. The uroboric play includes forms of behavior and irruptions of play not dreamable in our philosophy or studied in the fieldwork of ethnographers or yet available for deconstruction in our theory. As our view of performance expands almost galactically through the infinite space of thought, we find it curving back like the linguistic and historical constructs of a performative consciousness, to embrace, tautologically, the interminable play or chamber drama of the *mise-en-scène* of the unconscious.

Granted, then, the bewildering plenitude of performance, if not its absoluteness, I have tried to pursue—in thinking about what is universal in performance—the thing which appears in that subjunctive moment when whatever was there before becomes a performance. Or, so far as it is imaginable, that which in performance is other than that which is *not* performance, the cipher which marks it off from, shall we say, life? or shall we say, death? There is, within the new dispensation of theatricalizing consciousness, a surfeit of performance that almost teases us out of thought. But what I've wanted to approach in this discourse on performance—and to perceive in the theaterwork I have done—is what in performance can almost *not be seen because it is thought.* "Is this not something more than fantasy?" (*Ham.,* I.i.54). We are not always sure. If it cannot be seen, it has nevertheless—like the flowers in Eliot's *Burnt Norton* or the Japanese *ikebena* (which makes flowers live)[19]—the look of something that is looked at. That is, as an aspect of thought, also universal in performance. There has always been—not only in Hamlet and Rousseau, but in other cultures—a dream of performance without theater, nothing to see and nothing to show, like the Taoist mirror. What I have been trying to evoke is as delicate and fragile, perhaps, as the imagined performance of that dream, or like the curtain between the greenroom and the *hashigakari* in the Noh theater, that intimation of a diaphanous membrane between the world of spirits and the diurnal world or, for that matter, gravely, the equally fragile difference between the Phantasmal Noh and the Present Noh or between the Dramatic Noh and the Refined Noh, or the state of being in which the actor was *before* he appeared (who was he?) on the *hashigakari* carrying, as it appears (who is he now?), his ghostly space with him.

I think we are very close then to the most elemental consciousness of performance which *precipitates* performance, whatever else it becomes. That thing is universal in performance, in the ideographic Noh and in the looser mimetic language of the most realistic of appearances. It has been said of Eleanora Duse that ther subtlety was a secrecy, the absence of all rhetoric. She seemed exempt from the Logos even when speaking words. If legend can be believed, she allowed herself in the very act of performance to be *overlooked*. It was not simply humility, rather like a refusal to appear or to be discovered in performance. She seemed to do her acting on that selvedge of performance where performance with anything less would cease to exist. Yet it was not that disguise of performance in psychological acting which pretends that it is not performing. Moving others, she was not as stone, but what she was, materially, it was hard to say. I have always retained (from I know not where) an image of her wholly alive in perfect stillness, then something passing over her face like the faintest show of thought, not the play of a nerve, *only thought,* and you would suddenly know she was dying. I mean dying right there, *actually,* articulating the dying, with a radiance of apprehension so breathtaking that, in the rhythm of your breathing, you could hardly escape your own death. Of course, you *are* dying too, actually, right there, in the play of thought, though it is overlooked, and it is likely to be missed if it is in the course of performance merely thought and not *shown*—unless you are a Duse, who seemed to show it by merely thought.

Someone is dying in front of your eyes. That is another universal of performance. There are, to be sure, a myriad of ways in which the history of performance has been able to disguise or displace that elemental fact. You can joke about it, you can laugh it off, you can perform great feats of physical skill, but the image of it is before your eyes all the more because you are looking, even if the space is empty. You can't escape that look even if you close your eyes. Every look is the Law, which kills, as Kafka knew, who wrote a doomsday book of performance.

Performance occurs in a middle region between the world of transparency and the world of opacity. There is an ideal vision, such as
Rousseau's, of a fête or carnival in which all the obscurities cease and all
of us are, because outside the realm of exchange and reproduction, no
more than what we appear to be, and no less. We see that world in the
wine harvest of *La Nouvelle Héloise,* the unperformed *claritas* of the open
air, rustic and convivial, without boundaries, classless (or with all classes
participating), a unison of reciprocity and shared being such as utopias
have imagined and probably no culture, even the most rustic and convivial, has ever approached. It is a *mise-en-scène* without a gaze, everything seen and nothing to show. There is nothing remotely like the edge
of a stage, as if repression had been lifted in the unconscious, where
there is always a stage. As we understand from the operations of the
unconscious, there is no way to eliminate the edge which is reconstituted
"elsewhere" in the expenditure of the desire to eliminate it. There may
be some approximation of a spectacle-without-looking in the case of an
aboriginal ceremony or in what we think of as high ritual process like a
Mass, where the spectator and the spectacle presumably merge. But then
the coalescence occurs below the gaze of a god or a totem or, trying to
determine the absence of a seeming in what only seems to be there, a
visiting anthropologist, wavering in the pathos of his own performance,
between presence and absence, visibility and invisibility, even with the
end of imperialism, the incorrigible representative of an occupying
power.

When the gaze returns to its source, from the invisible frontier of all
desire, we are back to that other vision of performance, essentially
theatrical, which is made of (dis)appearances and, with various illusions
of other purpose, deploys appearance to no further end but its ceaseless
reappearance. That process reflects a world which, so far as it can be
distinguished, is as endlessly interpretable as a dream—and which is
sometimes marvelously reinterpreted *by* appearance. All the varieties of
performative experience move between the two imaginings of its real
presence in whatever objective or symbolic forms. But even when
appearance is imagined as absent, it is appearance that dominates the
idea of performance, since it suggests what would not be there, in
performance, if it were merely lived or experienced without distinction.

The ulterior motive, I would suppose, of the desire to identify universals of performance has been stated by Victor Turner in his recent

book *From Ritual to Theater.** In concluding his introduction with "an appeal for global cultural understanding," he mentions the attempts "being made by a handful of anthropologists and theater scholars and practitioners to generate an anthropology and theater of experience" for the purpose of mutual understanding across cultures. "The ethnographies, literatures, ritual, and theatrical traditions of the world now lie open to us as the basis for a new transcultural communicative synthesis through performance. For the first time we may be moving towards a sharing of cultural experiences, the manifold 'forms of objectivated mind' restored through performance to something like their pristine effectual contouring."[20]

I hesitate to be a spoilsport in this admirable mission, but if we are seeking to perceive universals of performance aside from their outer show—bodies, space, light, sound, gesture, motion, dress or undress, more or less dramatic content, coherent or scattered narrative, song and dance, masking and mimicry, exhibition of skills, shamanic or mimetic, and an auditory more or less specular or participatory, itself either gathered or dispersed—then we will inevitably come back to that suspended moment of a Duse or on the *hashigakari*, when the ghostly thing appears, the latent substance of performance which is divisive, solitary, alien, and apart. Whatever the appearance or actuality of communitas, performance is a testament to what separates. In the empty space, an empty solitude. I may be reflecting no more than the escalation of estrangement in our time, the doubling of separation, when I say *that* remains the thing which is most moving in performance, and always was: its essential aloneness. You can see it in the effectual contours of the most pristine forms of acting, as on the high wire with Philippe Petit. For what we think of as stage presence is related to that aloneness, the nature of the performer who, in a primordial substitution or displacement, is born on the site of the Other. It is the one thing which, if there is no communicative synthesis at all, nothing but a breach, also crosses cultures.

We can see it in the resemblance of Zeami's *yugen*, whether as "trans-

---

*Victor Turner has died since this was written, the legacy of his manifold learning reminding us—though I take issue with him here—of at least a double loss, to anthropology and to performance theory. As he had drawn theater people to anthropology, he had by theory and force of example turned anthropologists onto performance, and even caused some of them to *do* anthropology by means of performance. Few of them, however, can be expected to have either his eloquent breadth of knowledge or his large-hearted exuberance.

cendental phantasm" or "subtle fascination,"[21] to Stanislavski's Public Solitude, which is the rudimentary estrangement of what he elsewhere calls "charm." It is a substantiating presence which is just about as elusive as the "naked charm" and "strangeness" of subatomic physics. (As for the psychological acting associated with Stanislavski, I want to make amends for what I said somewhat invidiously before. I should add in all cultural equity that, while it has had a bad press in our experimental theater, for its presumptions of ego, its techniques of concentration, focus, and centering are universal; and their generating sources— *emotional memory* and *sense memory*—are no more mystifying than and are equally evocative as their correlatives in the creative energies of other cultures. As for the ego, despite its bad press in the West, it is being widely adopted, or some self-reliant facsimile, by people in other cultures who have never had any social identity but dispossession. Psychological acting is of course also associated with the vices of the mimetic, but if there was something wanting in our experimental theater—aside from a theoretical critique of the valorization of performance to the detriment of acting—it was the enviable meticulousness of histrionic skill required for an acute psychological portrayal of what we once thought of as character.) In considering the principle of *yugen* recently, Eugenio Barba emphasized the property of fascination in the temperament of the performer, as a transition from his remarks on *prana* or *ki-hai* ("profound agreement" of the spirit with the body) to his discussion of *shakti,* the creative energy which is genderless but represented in the image of a woman.[22] It is the traditional dispossession of the woman which may account for this, her apartness which is encompassing, like the womb of the universe.

And indeed, if one traces it, *yugen* was originally a poetic term which suggested a pensiveness arising from estrangement and loneliness, as in the following twelfth-century *haiku* of Saigyo: "Insensible as I am, I share/the loneliness of the autumn dusk/at the Swamp of the Solitary-snipe."[23] By the close of the Kamakura period (1184–1335), *yugen* came to signify a delicate brightness, like a moon-ray on a passing cloud or the subtle fascination of the glitter of snow falling. But the acquired brightness is still permeated by loneliness and pensive motion, as in the exquisite lines of Thomas Nashe about queens dying young and fair and brightness falling from the air. I believe that here both traditions touch upon that quality of the performer which is universal, the sense of removal or distance, however possessed, whether a virtuoso on a trapeze in a circus or, with all the illusions of choral unity, whatever it was that caused the first actor to separate himself from the communitarian pathos, knowing perhaps that even surrounded he was essentially alone, in the Public Solitude which is the precondition of his charm, his fascination, his representativeness, and his power. It is also the precondition, like some genetic repercussion in the form, of the appearance of the second actor, in Aeschylus, and the third actor, in Sophocles, those incremental separations that led from the seeming harmony of the Chorus to the equivocal catechism of the dialogue which, even in its dispersions and lapses through many actors, as in the silences of Chekov's plays, eventually dominated the theater, along with the hermeneutical Text, which we have been trying to dissolve back, via Artaud, into the naked sonorous streaming realization out of which the Chorus seemed to be born.

Performance may transform the one performing. That it has the capacity to transform seems to be universal. But at the level of community, whatever the powers of performance once were, they no longer are. For one thing, the performative instinct has been so distributed in art and thought and everyday life that we find it harder to discern the special value of performance *as* transformation, when transformation seems, moreover, in a culture of signs—with the supersaturation of images in the media—a universal way of life. It is also hard to think, as Plato did, of performance as something perilous because of the intensity of its imagining power. We simply do not take the powers of art and imagination as seriously as Plato did, or as seriously as they take poetry, say, in the Soviet Union. I suppose it takes some authoritarian political order to make it seem important, a matter of life and death. When you go to jail for it, you will listen to it. The transformative threat of performance seems to require an agency of repression. That agency has certainly not disappeared, but its invisibility in a world of high visibility, that is, in a culture of signs, is a qualitatively different problem from that faced by performance before or elsewhere, say in the "empire of signs" (Barthes) that gives meaning to the Bunraku or the Japanese tea ceremony. I also suspect that's a threatened empire.

In any case, performance of that kind is not well served, it would seem, by the illusions of the democratic. We are still not sure that performance of any kind was really well served by the illusions of the sixties, which spread the desublimating gospel of performance and tried, more or less clumsily, to appropriate the media, the image-making apparatus, whose powers are vast and omniverous and inarguable. The outcome of all the subversion was a conspiracy with the invisible, all the more when the theater went underground with the radical politics. What it succeeded in doing by making everything theater was to thin the theater out, so that it has had to learn again how to *be* theater, in the right proportions with performance. I see no evidence that anything like that has been accomplished yet.

Where performance remains, in our society, most transformative, it is hardly an agency of communitas. Think, for instance, of the libertarian dissonance of rock that turned, in punk, into an anarchistic dispersion of music like the mimesis of a primal violence. Which was, as with rock before it, appropriated by the invisible exchange of the trickle-down economy. There is also, inarguably, the transformative power of television. We have mixed feelings about that, as art, as community, since it debases its technical skills and seems to breed isolation in the home which is not exactly Public Solitude. It has, moreover, encouraged a mimetic violence among young people which, after many years of study of the self-evident, has been recently pretty much confirmed. Sports are also transformative for those who play and compete, and they still provide models of emulation for those who watch. We still have nothing in the theater to correspond to the experience you have in a stadium during the play of a double reverse, not to mention the stupendous involvement of spectators all around the world in a championship soccer match. Yet the highest skills of athletics are also caught up in the new ruthlessness of entertainment, which is big business even without the drug traffic, and the community among the spectators is one which is—as with the patriotism of the halftime ceremonies or the violence of a football game during the Vietnam War—something more than suspect. There is an undeniably unifying excitement at a ballgame as at a Broadway musical, where even the most begrudging of us will admire the extraordinary abilities of the performers, but it is not exactly the communitas we have in mind.

We return, then, to the question raised before about not only the means of performance, the technical skills or procedures which we can more or less exchange across cultures, but also the ends of performance: *what for?* As any good performer knows, that also determines the means. As Turner suggests, everything seems open and available to us now, things which were once in the realm of the arcane. But we inevitably have to ask just what the appropriation of any performance technique from an alien culture will mean, not only in the transformations of performance, but in the transformations of power by which all performance is known, even as it reveals that power. The critical question is, as I've remarked, universal in performance, although we are once again in a period where little resembling an answer, or even a possible response, has shown itself persuasively in performance—except for those modes of performance which may look upon the question as a non sequitur, like climbing Mt. Everest, which you do because it is there.

That kind of performance, like orbiting in space, may have lost some of the aura of individual heroism, but it remains an exemplary model of teamwork or ensemble playing. Such teamwork is not necessarily a universal of performance, but that there is something exemplary in performance is still a universal. The problem is that the example, today, may be read in competing ways. Landing on the moon or climbing Mt. Everest may also suggest, though remote from the centers of power, the structure of power which supports the example, and of which we may not entirely approve. It appears to be the same structure in which— amidst the profusion of performances, casual or codified—performance is losing its force *as* example. We can of course hope that a transfusion of power from other cultures will reverse this tendency, but there is nothing so far as I can see which is universal about that. What we may also want to remember in view of that is that performance is the site-specific appearance of local initiative and—whatever it acquires as cultures cross in a worldwide network of appearances—still very much dependent on the discriminating perceptions of individual will, which may be trained to accuracy through performance. As for performing in general, Stanislavski and others have warned against that.

NOTES

1. Sigmund Freud, *Beyond the Pleasure Principle*, trans. James Strachey, intro. Gregory Zilboorg (New York: Norton, 1961), pp. 8–9.

2. Victor Turner, *From Ritual to Theater: The Human Seriousness of Play* (New York: Performing Arts Journal Publications, 1982), pp. 8–9.

3. Richard Schechner, "Actuals: A Look Into Performance Theory (1970)," *Essays on Performance Theory, 1970–1976* (New York: Drama Book Specialists, 1977), pp. 3–35.

4. The line was actually spoken by Azuma to his pupil Katsuko Azuma, who took the Master's name, according to tradition. Quoted by Eugenio Barba, "Theater Anthropology," *The Drama Review*, 26, no. 2 (1982), 20.

5. Quoted by C. G. Jung, "Commentary on *The Secret of the Golden Flower*," in *Psyche and Symbol: A Selection from the Writings of C. G. Jung*, ed. Violet de Laszlo (New York: Anchor, 1958), p. 322.

6. "Restoration of Behavior," *Studies in Visual Communication*, 7, no. 3 (1981), 2.

7. *Theater*, 9, no. 3 (1978), 7–19. The essay is also in Derrida's *Writing and Difference*, trans. and intro. Alan Bass (Chicago: University of Chicago Press, 1978), pp. 232–50.

8. Michel Foucault, *The Order of Things: The Archeology of the Human Sciences* (New York: Vintage, 1973), p. 64.

9. *Of Grammatology*, trans. Gayatri Chakravorty Spivak (Baltimore: Johns Hopkins University Press, 1976), p. 36.

10. Lao Tsu, *Tao Te Ching*, trans Gia-Fu Feng and Jane English (New York: Vintage, 1972), chap. 42 (no page numbers).

11. *Theater*, p. 8.

12. Antonin Artaud, *The Theater and Its Double*, trans. Mary Caroline Richards (New York: Grove, 1958), p. 51.

13. Derrida, *Theater*, p. 9.

14. "Cogito and the History of Madness," *Writing and Difference*, p. 54.

15. Artaud, p. 52.

16. Artaud, p. 93.

17. Derrida, "Freud and the Scene of Writing," *Writing and Difference*, p. 202.

18. Ibid., p. 202.

19. See Barba, p. 19.

20. Turner, pp. 18–19.

21. Toyoichiro Nogami, *Zeami and His Theories on Noh*, trans. Ryozo Matsumoto (Tokyo: Tsunetaro Hinoki, Hinoki Shoten, 1955), pp. 51–61.

22. Barba, pp. 28–29.

23. Quoted by Nogami, p. 51.

NINE

SHADOWING REPRESENTATION

Some of you who have lectured extensively—especially if there has been anything in your thought with an inflection of controversy—will have had something like this experience, which I have had more than once: you will have noticed out there at some quite uninflammatory moment of your talk a sort of brain lesion in attendance, the seething instance of something lethal. Somebody you've never seen before wants to kill you! And when you think it over you realize that he or she will have wanted to kill you not for what you were saying at the moment but for something you may have said many years before, in something you wrote perhaps that you've forgotten. No matter. Your image has gone before you. There is one thing I did write some time ago that I've not forgotten, largely because nothing I've ever written has caused so much immediate outrage, and I will to this day be challenged about it in remote places, where it is also far removed from anything in my talk. It was a remark made in a book published in the sixties, about my work in the theater, where I must admit I wanted to do some killing myself and said so in the book. It may seem rather harmless out of context. The remark was simply this: "Give an audience a chance and it will inevitably be wrong."

I am not remembering that now in order to test this audience, but as a preface to some reflections on the politics of representation and the discourse about it which is by now—though a discourse that has beguiled and much absorbed me—somewhat belabored among us. I realize that some of you have a considerable ideological and professional investment in it, as I do, in theory and in theater. The work I did there was at some methodological level always shadowing representation because always suspicious of theater. For the theater seemed, in all my equivocal years in it, "shaped and undermined," as Derrida has said, following upon Artaud, "by the profound evil of representation. It is that corruption itself." You know the argument: the stage "not threatened by anything but itself, theatrical representation," that deceitful doubling of an originary division which makes of life a deceit to begin with, the contaminated supplement, re-presentation, serving as a model for more of the Same, "inscribed in the structure of representation, in the space of the stage."[1] I'm not sure, as I've already indicated, that that is all the stage is threatened by, but the menacing other might have been satisfied by an implication in the discourse that, so far as the audience is concerned, I was wrong to begin with. You don't have to give the audience a chance, you can't, it will inevitably be wrong anyhow, since its responses occur in a system of reproduction which, even in its dissidence, reproduces the system. That's what Peter Handke apparently realized through the exhaustive enumeration of its responses in the course of *Offending the Audience,* which seems to mirror a system running on alternate currents between the "desiring machine" of the *Anti-Oedipus* and the "debraining machine" of *Ubu Roi.*

Since the reproduction appears to be true of its most reflexive self-criticism, I think we may be dealing with an overstated case, more or less self-evident. I am very much aware that in the demystifications of recent theory it is precisely the self-evident which is ideologically suspect because it looks natural or ordained, coextensive with the real, which is then nothing else but what it appears to be. But what appears to be in theory, if not natural, ordained, is the repetitive enclosure of the discourse, with its doxology of open-endedness, a sort of politics of Derridean deferral of other people's politics. What remains disturbing too—despite attention to representations—is the capitalization of or upon an allegorical figure, the reification of Representation as a selective monolith disfiguring the rest of the world. If it is not so uniform as it has been made to appear in the obsessive critique of the logocentric tradition of Western power, it is far more uniform than it appears in our theoretical deference to other cultures or the discovery of alternative prospects in the indeterminate Other—the alienated, the marginal, the dispossessed—valorizing differences which, with the slightest prompting from chance or history, narrow their own distance to the regrettable Same.

Some of us refuse to believe it or that it's quite the Same or, if it is, that it's merely proof of the globalizing hegemony of the worst, which wants to crush all difference. What it also seems to prove, as in reality testing, is a certain obtuse (as Barthes uses the word on the cinematic still) wiliness of *méconnaissance* which perceives in an otherwise diverse, conflictual, indecipherable, or phantasmic otherness an identity which happens to have the features of its own unnamed assumptions. The motives are not unmixed, and commendably on the side of difference, but if there is a totalizing force in reality, I doubt that it can be adequately described anymore as an agency which is thoroughly bourgeois. Nor can I see an effective resistance in the deconstructive analysis of it as an economy of death, though it may be precisely that—against which the only resistance seems to be, for those of us doing our work in postindustrial cultures, *rhetoric,* which is sometimes conflated with *theater,* all the world becoming a stage, as if by satellite transmission, in a vapor trail of signs.

Signs are taken for wonders, wrote T. S. Eliot before the apotheosis of the signifiers, scorning the illusory apparatus of the newly omniverous media which, no better than a cheap occultism, swaddled the truth in darkness. But in a cybernetic world, the wonder of signs is their almost total mastery of what we take to be truth. "In this passage to a space whose curvature is no longer that of the real, nor of truth," writes Jean Baudrillard, announcing the age of *simulation,* the beginning we are looking for is "the liquidation of all referentials" or, even worse, "their artificial resurrection in systems of signs, a more ductile material than meaning." Neither imitation, representation, nor even parody, it is rather "a question of substituting signs of the real for the real itself," short-circuiting by its operational double-dealing everything biological in the real, all the signs of trouble, so that the real won't ever have to be produced, its place taken by the model or simulacrum in the economy of death.[2]

It may be a powerful rhetoric, the annunciation of this condition, but as Baudrillard suggests only too mordantly in his recent essays—which outdo by bleak light-years the disconsolate vision of *Civilization and Its Discontents*—it is a pretty feeble politics. Or about as effective as Walter Mondale—whom it no doubt thought the Same—against the ductile deficits of Reagan, whose mastery of (the illusion of?) power presumably comes from sophisticated control of the equally ductile material in the apparatus of representation, which nobody told him is dead. Despite the ineptness of the first debate, which reduplicated ineptness they'd seen before, even liberals accede to him as the Great Communicator. Whatever his natural talents, his advisors seem to understand that sophisticated control, given the audience (including, I assume, Baudrillard's Silent Majority), is not only a theoretical mastery of signifying practice, but also its simpler, old-fashioned craft. "The graphic image is not seen; and the acoustic image is not heard," says Derrida of the invisibility which constitutes the difference in the body of the inscription.[3] Not taking chances, however, one of Reagan's advisors was an observer at every one of his talks, doing just about what stage managers do backstage at Broadway plays (with their relatively feudal modes of operation and labor practices), graphing the trace, putting an asterisk in the margin of the text when there was applause, HA when there was a laugh—and it is this signifying practice in the workaday regimen of power which seems, in all its transparency, to be having the last laugh, through all our seductive discourse about representation representing itself, the seditiousness of the self-representative fantasy which remains invisible in the very process of revelation, thereby maintaining the power which enslaves us.

As, it seems at times, the rhetoric does. And I am not speaking of its jargon, which so much disturbs others. *Who speaks?* we ask. Whether or not the enslaved are speaking for themselves, it's questionable that many of us are among them. There is something dubious, at any rate, about the oblates or representatives escalating their own oppression, such as it is, for the purpose of identification or making the identification in order to escalate it, the poverty level of the *mise en abime:* academics ghettoized, women colonized, or all of us in exile; if not exactly *victim,* then invented by evacuation as a signifier through the incursion of the alien discourse that we produce ourselves as it produces us, and in which we now conceive ourselves living, as inhabited Other, the image of the colonized in a death-defying economy of parasitical exchange. It is an ingenious strategy, this new organicism of power-sharing through an inquilinism of rhetoric, but it is a little like playing, I think, at imaginary toads in a real sinkhole. As an aspect of the desire to do away with hierarchies and taxonomies, it seems to siphon out of suffering its grievous particularity as if, even in the embrasure of our partial otherness, in the profession, there were no gradations or distinctions in the indignities or the hurt.

One is reminded of the days when the situation of blacks, to this day bad enough, was being conflated—sometimes too as strategy or rhetoric—with the concentration camps. Well, who can measure suffering? In that poll-taking way that children have, one of mine used to ask with apocalyptic matter-of-factness, would you rather be killed by a snake or an atom bomb? He was dissatisfied if I couldn't answer, or if I put the answer in a context, explaining the wider human loss in the dropping of the bomb. The poll was impatient with that, and I wasn't myself convinced—in this antihumanist age of the end of man—that I was addressing the real down-to-earth eschatological matter. I realize there's a point where pain is pain and that to be dead, given the legions of oblivion, is to be undistinguished. But we have also seen, in our readings of history, a blurring of the brutalities in a kind of confusion of genres which lacks, I'd say, a certain specificity, erasing the difference it wants to sustain. It's like the blurring of history itself in its reported appearance, redoubled in representation, or the history we sometimes invoke as a sort of credential, as if flexing time's factitious muscles in the immateriality of our thought to give it dialectical substance. One methodological assumption not to be lost in the cunning of parasitical exchange: rhetoric *makes* a difference, and *so does its abuse,* one of the surest ways for the colonized to lose their voice, as even through emancipation it leads to the commissars.

While we have a good reason for wanting to politicize academic life, lest it continue to be surreptitiously so on behalf of a repressive pluralism, there is always the liability which Roland Barthes addressed after the exhilarations of May 1968, when he was disturbed by an upsurge of terrorism in the discourse. In trying to mediate things at the time, in the essay on "Writers, Intellectuals, Teachers," he warned us off the line of identification with the proletariat from the vantage point of privilege. Reassessing, too, the psychoanalytical space of the classroom, he placed the student—whom we used to speak of as a *nigger*—in the position of mastery; in Lacan's terms, the one who is supposed to know, since it is the teacher who is being interpreted and judged, the one who speaks while the other maintains a silence. It was a corrective view of that analytical transaction which in the longer historical view of the mutual anxiety of influence, seems like a double misprision. Barthes was writing nervously at the time and offered his reversed perspective, strained through the semiology, with a certain diffidence. But there is too, when literary study becomes politically charged, a "complacency of ideological *recognition,*" as Althusser remarked, which digs in without the diffidence, though the distinction Althusser makes, that "the freedom of men is secured" rather by "the *knowledge* of the laws of their slavery,"[4] remains subject not only to Barthes's reservation about identification from a position of privilege but to Marx's critique of critique at the end of the theses on Feuerbach. If freedom is ever secured, and I doubt it, the laws are those, under the right if unfortunate objective conditions, of concrete and usually violent *action* where there has been—not only theorized but inarguable—oppression or slavery, which are also not always the same.

What is peculiar to our time, and our particular situation, is that there is inordinate analysis and aspiration to mastery of abstract relations, Althusser's objective, though not necessarily in his terms. And it is quite in keeping academically with an advanced technocracy which is itself mastered not only by the network of institutional forces in which the relations are represented by the technocracy, the military, the police, the bureaucratic agencies, and the cultural entrepreneurs who know and assimilate all our strategies, but by the more benign elements of systemic power, including the law and elected officials, social security (shaky as it is), consumer goods (which are not all that bad), and a general feeling of material well-being through a large part of the population, even when they are relatively poor, if the polls were right through the recent election, though they may be programmed to get that response. For Baudrillard, the polls and other devices which statistically try to approximate the will of the masses or Silent Majority might as well be stochastic. For the masses—nothing like a Public, and a miasma as an audience—are no longer a referent, no longer locatable in the dimension of representation; thus Lacan is irrelevant too in pointing out the "*belong to me* aspect of representations, so reminiscent of property,"[5] which permits those who really have it to sustain their property rights while the others are given the representations as compensation, a right to property that does not really exist. The thing is that representation doesn't exist either, and we are far from a body politic into the opaque features of the models in their orbital and imploded circulation, which cancels the social as well. When we try to imagine, therefore, anything like a critical mass we are alluding to a threshold on which, since the power which presumes to control it no longer knows what it is, "the mass is at the same time the death, the end of this political process thought to rule over it. And into it is engulfed the political as will and representation."[6]

There is, perhaps, a perverse wish fulfillment in this vision of a maw of imploded power in the Silent Majority, rather like the delight in the fallout of graffiti in the New York subways as if—though the best artists are now appropriated by the galleries—it were something more than disquieting and messy notes from the underground. Yet there is sufficient truth in what Baudrillard says to suggest how formidable a task it is to develop any reliable, no less masterful, view of the relation between the nature and extent of oppression and the power and limits of representation in complex societies, what people may really think of the system in which, as we dramatize *our* colonization, they may or may not feel like the victims which some of them certainly are.

So far as the mechanisms of identification work through the politics of representation to alleviate fear and anguish caused by an oppressive power, they are seen by Freud as being among the factors which explain the allegiance of oppressed people to the images and cultural ideals, even the crude illusions, of the oppressors, which sometimes improve their lives. It's an irony we don't like to admit, but if we must speak of history, we will have to concede that even the delusions which keep people contented or making the best of a bad job are about as much as history is going to offer in its necessary dialectical time, even when people are not quite so deluded as analysis represents them. There is a doubleness even in misery. That is a complexity to be dealt with when we reflect on displaced populations which think, rightly or wrongly, that they have *chosen* to be where they are—in, say, Miami or Tucson or Bonn or Cologne—exiled in a *freer* situation, with whatever subsequent disenchantments. Or, as we have also seen, prosperity, with some becoming exploiters themselves, which we blame on the system, as if they had no tradition of their own. The freedom of men, and women, is secured only *relatively* even when there *is* revolution, since there appears to be nothing, anywhere, like a Free World—and certainly none so free, imaginable in our time, that would be exempt from, if not the simulacra, the dominion of representation *in all its shadings*.

What is hardest for us to deal with in the effort to master abstract relations are the claims of those who *prefer* the ordinance of established or legitimized power, however it may repel us. In this respect, it is almost harder for those on the Left to defer to the Falwell fundamentalism which supports Reagan than to the even more rabid and retrograde fundamentalism of the followers of Khomeini. At a time when we are deferring in theory to schizophrenia and reappraising the operable space of madness, it would seem to be a problem of thinking through the deconstruction of power a new hierarchy of admissible aberration, which both movements—beyond a shadow of the Silent Majority—certainly are. That too, I know, is a matter of representation. And the matter is particularly complicated in a democracy where the fundamentalism is by no means innocent about the power of the apparatus and uses it now as effectively as any interest group—having made the charge in the past, not altogether unwarranted, that the other side controlled the apparatus and that they *were* being misrepresented. (That they were is now being suggested, atoned for, and generating penitential profits by the liberal follow-up in cinema of what we might have heard in country music if we didn't think it were all merely the same when it was

telling us about real grievances, pain, and outrage that went, when we
didn't believe it, into electing Ronald Reagan for the first time.) One can
still say that their side *and* the other side are not our side, but the
wearisome problem in a democracy is still that for all the accuracy of that
distinction and the excellence of our theory they, with all the invincible
ignorance of their know-nothing delusions, get out the votes as socialism
never did in America, though it has always had—as Lionel Trilling or
Irving Howe or one of those liberal Jewish Eastern intellectuals remarked some time ago—the best ideas.

That exasperating irony, you may remember, led other intellectuals
during the sixties—foremost among them, Herbert Marcuse, in an
aberration of his own—to renounce the liberal establishment and to
propose the hegemony of a more enlightened minority who, in
formulating the precepts of a participatory democracy, would determine
who could participate and who not. This was shortly after Jean-Paul
Sartre gave, in his introduction to Fanon, a mortifying endorsement to a
violence which, however grounded in colonial experience, no intellectual with Danton in his political heritage could ever imagine would
not reach a murderous limit where, inevitably, it turns back murderously
upon itself. One thing has been more than reliably represented in the
politics of our century, and its literature, and that is this warped limit of
a redemptive violence. It is, I would say, just about what it appears to be:
the dumbfounding solution which *is*, not merely part of, the problem;
and that solution is, in the belongingness of representation, by no means
the sole property of the phallocratic order inherited from Oedipus and
ontotheology, though it certainly makes things no better to remember its
full extent. I'm not sufficiently a historian to detail the full evidence, but
who needs to be? It is, like Joyce's snow over Ireland at the end of *The
Dead* or Indira's ashes over India and its dead, appalling all over the
world, and not only because it's faster nowadays from Londonderry to
Trilokpuri, and the bourgeois values can travel. It is all the more appalling when it is seen as some exclusively insidious derivation of the im-
perialistic Logos, as if there *is* a Transcendental Signifier or the Vedas
were pure in heart or Henry Ford was right and history is bunk, and
anthropology as well, as if colonization had no history before it entered
the psyche of the West, achieving a local habitation and a name with the
eminence of the Word—which might just as well have been bunk!

The exclusionary lapse of Marcuse and the unbecoming virulence of
Sartre are vicissitudes of the instincts which might be consigned to

history had they really run their course in the sixties. But they are still very much with us, having (dis)appeared as the radical activism receded into the double sublimation of theory, in which there is nothing more indebted to that period and the "polymorphous perversity" of its counterculture than the current discourse of *desire,* "the non-representative representative,"[7] and nothing more virulent than the desire to *abolish* representation. "Desire, reinvented everywhere," observes Baudrillard in his caustic elegy on the end of the social, "is only the referential of political despair."[8] Maybe yes maybe no. But the trouble with desire in the discourse is that, with *difference* as an honorific signifier, it is articulated on a scale of value allowing for little difference, and thus just about as undistinguished as the washout of representation, even into its seeming plural. That is all the more true of its polysemous plural. What is being conceived there, with more or less radical extremity, is a sort of grid of intensities, a warp of surface with no depth, on which the ductile material of the body, its free enterprise, can play in all directions through a plenum of reciprocal exchange, with momentary arrests, transfers, deferrals, but nothing in arrears or reserve, a semiosis with no meaning except the longitudinal distribution of intensities and affects. Unanchored in origin, it is a conception of economic activity which, indeed, expropriates the expropriators, for it resembles nothing so much as the reversible processes of advanced capitalism whose ideological experience is subject to the law of value, work and money operating as signs and everything a trade-off or write-off.

What is being desired, then, with more or less go-for-broke in the *bricolage* is a deregulation of the libidinal economy, our own supply-side theory. It is an attempt to defray by *dissolving* the cost of energy transfer or displacement in the unconscious, with its bad investments. Good work if you can get it, but even if you can, there is a considerable, crucial, and irreducible difference between doing this in art and doing it in politics even when you try, as the sixties tried, to negate the irreducible difference between the two. And our institutional analyses need to register this: what is imaginable and maybe approachable in art, in paint, light, sound, words, conceptual events, or film is, at some unnegotiable sticking point, not so doable with the human body; or doable at the most execrable human cost, as we discovered exorbitantly in this century, where the synthetic abstractions of modernism and the dismemberments of the postmodern—rupture, fracture, suture, montage—have been quite literally achieved with the body, no mixed-media, by the systematic brutes and torturers and the pieties of fundamentalism as well. Otherwise, we're faking it. Or approaching S/Z through S/M. Which is to say—as Artaud knew in the delirium of Cruelty, wanting a body without organs by burning the body away—that we are not only fastened to a dying animal, but also to representation, as if it were a saving grace.

Grace is grace despite of all controversy, as one of Shakespeare's dissolute characters says, but if the controversy over representation continues, the theater remains pivotal in such reflections because of its carnal investment and—except for rare experiments wanting to disguise or do without it—the ubiquity of the body, an agency of representation even against its will. "It is certainly easier," said Lacan of the expatriates who, bringing Freud to America, yielded to its ahistoricism, "to efface the principles of a doctrine than the stigmata of one's origins."[9] If the desire to abolish representation persists, I have already confessed that I've shared it, that there was such a desire in the grain of my own theaterwork, whose most palpable animus, it appeared, was a sort of giving up of the ghost. But if there seems a certain folly in someone who has spent most of his adult life in the theater entertaining thoughts of its extinction, that is because the desire to do away with *repetition,* and hence representation, has been the most profound and impelling motive in the history of the theater, which is predicated on disappearance, since its emergence from whatever dark backward and abysmal splitting of irrecoverable time. It accounts for the mostly unconscious but omnipresent equivocal feeling in every rehearsal, where the actor is told to do it again and yet not, not *that,* but what *it* is s/he's never sure. As for *who* is doing the telling, that's an archaic problem brought forcibly to attention again in the alchemical manifestos of Artaud, and by Derrida in the continuing dream of the closure of representation. What he tries to reimagine in the two essays on Artaud is the idea of a theater which, execrating repetition, would—in order to remain theater in the nakedly voluminous materialization of its utterly sonorous unconcealment— refuse itself the remainder and, with an excruciating minimalism, barely repeat itself. Nobody has had the power to realize it, but it remains an impelling dream, within the structure of that other power, which exercises itself apparently through, behind, or in *appearance.*

That the representation of power is, today, the major source of power is attested to at every turn, and it seems to be well understood by those in positions of power East and West. To rehearse the self-evident: in an article about loose facts and outright misrepresentation in the second debate of Reagan and Mondale, *Time* magazine—while detailing all the mistakes, more extensively the President's sloppy-mindedness, so morally delinquent it may even be strategic—remarks that there may be some regrettable truth to what George Bush's press secretary told him after the debate with Geraldine Ferraro: " 'You can say anything you want during a debate, and 80 million people hear it. If the press then points out an error, . . . so what? Maybe 200 people read it, or 2,000 or 20,000.' "[10] The article concludes with a confirmation of the power of image-making in presidential politics, now being imitated at practically every level of politics almost anywhere in the world where a candidate has a camera on him—which means, even in the loneliest savannahs and remotest bush, just about everywhere, as everyone knows who has any ethnological awareness or seen films taken of the aborigines. If it is true, as film theoreticians tend to believe, that by reproducing the recidivist code of perspective the camera is an instrument of bourgeois ideology with its sovereignty of the eye, *what* is being reproduced—is it the scopic drive?—when we see those natives develop a self-reflexive consciousness in a matter of spontaneous moments?

At a rather posh workshop and conference at the Asia Society in New York—the culmination of a project where I was involved in swapping performance techniques not only with Japanese Noh actors or Kuttiyatam temple dancers but Shinto priests and Korean shamans—I saw one of the shamans, a woman in her late seventies, maybe eighties, who had apparently never been out of her village before, stake out in an instant the relations of power by the configuration of clicking cameras, as if she'd read Benjamin on Baudelaire and knew that the " 'snapping' of the photographer . . . had the greatest consequences." She was, however, not so much concerned with the way "The camera gave the moment a posthumous shock, as it were";[11] her focus was on the future. She made a point of having herself photographed with the director of the foundation which was paying for this enlightening cross-cultural event within the worldwide hegemony of representation. The shaman soon became one of the more popular figures at the sessions. She seemed to know by the most archaic instincts of an instrumental stateliness what our likable president had to learn through his apprenticeship in Hollywood and salesmanship with General Electric: how to construct a trustworthy image. She was also soon—like the Yaqui chief we worked with in Arizona in another phase of this transcultural project—looking for an offering or (by whatever name) foundation grant to perpetuate her techniques, and since ritual practitioners are measured by efficacity (she is said to be the best), no doubt getting it, as the Yaqui did.

As for the president's technique, summoned up after the calamity of the first debate, due less to debating points than to a seeming calamity of aging, the next time, as one of his aides observed, the president "delivered a couple of good one-liners, stayed close to the podium, looked alert and had a better camera angle. The conclusion is that Reagan won the debate."[12] If not for Tip O'Neill or the 200 or 2000, at least for the 80 million, proving not so much that what I said about the audience is, after all, true or—to avoid a more cynical construction—that you can fool most of the people all of the time, but that, as the aide also observed, the debates are not relevant, only the *look* of them, a widespread opinion which confirms a lot of theory. I am quoting, not incidentally, from the same issue of *Time* whose cover story was concerned with the revival of etiquette and manners; that is, the behavior of appearance. If colonialist discourse is marked by the deployment of appearance in the daemonic fixities of manichean thought, there is an almost demonic iteration in recent discourse of the deceitfulness of appearance—the baseless fabric of invisible power—as if all behavior were theater, with nothing remaining behind. Yet it is the *behavior* of appearance which is, when you look at it, not understood or neglected by the discourse on representation which—in leaving the *articulation* of behavior to the humanistic tradition which it disdains—more often than not suggests, through its decodings, that all appearance is the Same. *As* appearance it surely is. But the word-games of theory leaving it at that also leave something to be desired which is somewhat more than a lack; not only as regards reality but in the theater—the corporeal side of the same etymological coin— which, though it is made of appearance, is not willing to settle for appearance, or at least historically not for very long.

What we see in the theater through its periodic colonizations of the world—which is what happens when it returns to behavior, as it is doing now again—is the *struggle* with representation. *Now you see it now you don't:* no more deceit but a *generic* equivocation, including the refusal to yield finally to either of its major illusions: the dematerialization of reality by drawing it into perspective or the insistence on taking it out and dissolving representation, leaving not a wrack behind. Brecht tried to negotiate the two by taking things out of perspective and restoring them to history, which only complicated the question of illusion. What we rub against in Brecht is the world's body, which is always ideological, clinging to both illusions—*either of which may be humanly serviceable at a particular moment of history.* I am not at all sure, as Artaud was not sure, that the phenomenon we have named representation is a historical accretion or construct like history itself or class or gender or even *yin* and *yang.* And while some of its historical manifestations may be monstrous, I see no point in hardening them all, through suspicion of doubleness, into a one-eyed monster (though I shall return to a related image in the end), since representation may also represent the resistance, and in some sense always does.

As ideological phenomena—phantoms of the brain with material substance—representations go through historical phases or economic admixtures, a repertoire of incongruent forms, partial resolutions, and palpable ruptures in relation to power, whose position of dominance is not always as secure or clear as it appears to be, and sometimes clearer. And because power itself is not without its relation of fantasy and fetish to the subject it occupies—as in the mutually dazzled rites of colonization in Genet's *The Screens*—I am not merely suggesting that representation may be beneficent and liberating in some historical sequence, so that later, elsewhere, it is repressive and malign, or even the reverse, which may very well be. What I am concerned with, rather, are the powers of suasion, allure, absorption, suture, and strangeness whose effects in representation are not easily calculated and which inhabit even its degeneration, and may be inciting there. The always decaying half-life of the atomization of otherness may seem to be in a mutual confusion an antidote to the weakness of power. I should add that one of the risks of our attraction to otherness is a miscalculation of the strength of power, and the attractive sources of that strength.

As for the emphasis on repression in representation, I am not at all convinced by, say, the orthodoxy of film theory—to take one prominent representation of it that has filtered into literary study—which sees the alluring image of woman as empty signifier in a scopophilic space of male desire as a factitious eroticism or negating force in history, seamless, coterminus with the history of woman's exclusion and domination. For that image is coextensive with other images, forces, movements, social and political representations which need assessment in relation to it, not all of them merely submissive to the oedipal underpinnings of bourgeois power. Nor does this take into account the contradictory and almost indecipherable properties of the *dispositif* or technological apparatus on which Baudrillard may not have had the last word, but whose insidious path through the simulacra cannot be read with ideological blinders. There are theorists and practitioners now working in film with a kind of third eye, but I include in the blindness the continuing binocular view of the camera as sustaining the ideological dominion of the sovereign eye. Here, the contradictions are manifold, though there's no denying that the camera seems to have recreated the world as appearance, as it has also modified our ideas of performance.

In the hangup on appearance of the new performative consciousness, not only in Performance Art but in the *theatrum philosophicum* of the human sciences, the old oedipal conventions have been twisting, twisting in the wind. Since character is next to worthless and plot the structural model of the ideologically repressive, a role is a role is a role and a mask is a mask is a mask, as in the transformation exercises of the old Open Theater or—with fewer residues of the older psychology—the autistic serialism of Robert Wilson or the ontological hysteria of Richard Foreman, who has been influenced by both Gertrude Stein and recent French thought. Meanwhile, so far as other modes of behavior are concerned, and their historical particularity, Distinction with its winnowing fan goes begging in abstractions through the combinatory sets. As with the beginnings of a rethought realism in the theater, there is much more to be said in the discourse about the look of the mask, its disposition toward whose specific experience, its nature (forgive the word) and tactile activity, *who* is wearing it, *where, when,* under what circumstances to what end, with what emotional memories, and at what point in the *spectrum* of behavior shifting between indeterminate Master and always already mirroring and strategically parasitical Slave. As for the epistemological and moral implications, I'm not convinced either that they are merely epistemic phantasms or secondary affects of an any more material base. Or, if illusion, then more needs to be said about the heuristic powers of that. (These are, I suppose, among the things at stake in the newer debates about *base* and *superstructure,* and the operational limits of their dialectic. As names for lived phenomena in advanced societies, what they represent is by now as elusive as *karma* or *ikebena,* and the dialectic as fragile as the disappearing figurations of *yin* and *yang*—terms which are, I should note, somewhat indiscriminately referred to, even privileged in the discourse, as in the new ethnology of theater, as if exempt from pernicious ideology or systems of servitude.) Some masks are not only more empowering than others, but also cost more, and not merely when—as some of us did from the Yaquis—you buy a replica to hang on the wall or to play with amidst the *bricolage.*

I mean the cost of its evolution as an enunciation of value or prospect, a signifying practice with promise, still connected in no doubt un-ascertainable ways to representations of (the fiction of?) an origin. I am thinking, too, as William Carlos Williams did of language, of "the poetry of the movements of cost," what it took in intelligence and passion to carve it out of history, as well as historical debts and consequences. If that cost is traced on the mask and, along with historical wear and tear, represented, there is also the *Trieb* or drive which, as Lacan remarks, can only be considered *Trieb*-to-come if "for lack of representation it is not there. . . ."[13] The baneful thing is that which, unrepresented, *never* comes or—in a world polysaturated with image by the technological apparatus of power (for it *is* that, *whose* power we're not sure), swarming with representations—wouldn't be recognized if it did.

If all the world does approach being a stage, I'd rather wear some masks than others and choose the moments when I put them on, without merely playing around with them. That would nevertheless seem to suffer from the double illusion that I am unmasked to begin with and that I have any real choice in the matter, which seems like an over-determined play. Well, despite the stain of theatricalization in reality, I must insist: I can still tell a hawk from a handsaw when the wind is right. If it sometimes appears that the stain is so psychosexually imbedded that we are like the libidinous ladies of Jacobean drama painted indelibly an inch thick, I rather think the image of the face torn with trying to get it off—one of the heroic mimes of modernism—is preferable *as an illusion* to the postmodern one that takes the mask for granted and thinks it can laugh it off. That illusion is attached to a certain negligence of thought about the polysemous devices of the new dispensation of play which, in the structuration of structures, seems to forget now and then that the fort/da is the closet drama of the death drive which amortizes itself, and that play is in due time just about as deadly as the ideological habits it replaces.

Despite these caveats about the discourse, the masque of theory is surely a more necessary if not more honorable one than that of other critical representations which for various historical reasons have lost, for the time being, their urgency. If the cost was originally severe enough out of similar need, that representation will, I suspect, return in some revisionist form, its mask a little chipped and scarred, into the field of representation. There is, with unavoidable reification, no other field. That harrowing realization is the outcome of another play by Genet, *The Balcony*, when through the figurations of Revolution the Allegorical Figures return. There should be something chastening about that to the figure of the Revolutionary rising behind the mask of the newer theory. Meanwhile, one way of appraising the rhetoric of poststructuralist discourse is by the degree to which—at a time when activism on the Left is at loose ends—it displaces the militancy into theory, making for an unseemly melodrama in the language of the discourse. Most of you are, I'm sure, familiar with it, maybe even in your own work.

This is naturally ironic at a time when writing on representation, even the fusion of Marxism with deconstruction, is becoming one of the accrediting exercises in the academic world. There is no real status, in the elitist but widening circle of theory, without a virtual catechistic acceptance of language as being inhabited by relations of power, that imaging is ideological, that women are colonized by language and image and the gaze, and that we enter the Symbolic through the magic mirror as a kind of afterbirth—all of which is largely true, though the litany has turned some who have absorbed it back to the discrepancies, to thoughts of singularity and—with more or less unmanageable transcendence—a materialist Sublime. This is in partial reaction to another cultural production that only repeats itself, differing from the supersaturation of redundancy in the information system with which it is ideologically affiliated in that it poses as *transgression* in order to get through the noise. So far as the talk about transgression is concerned, that merely remains noxious so long as it is part of the noise and not the sort of action which, for the transgressive moment, causes the noise to cease. Which doesn't mean that the action can't be revolting too.

In saying this, I'm not talking as an enemy of the discourse like, say, the hatchet men of the *New York Review of Books* with their assaults on deconstruction, but as one who, with more or less melodrama, has practiced his own subversions and incursions and guerrilla warfare, in the theater and in the guise of *écriture*. When I think, however, of certain ends to which the oppressed feel obliged to go to liberate themselves, taking action which at this critical distance I can only insist is reprehensible, however it may be represented in theory—like the assassination of Mrs. Ghandi (which happened the day before I started to write) or the IRA's attempt on Mrs. Thatcher (some contemptible part of me wishing they hadn't missed)—I realize again how pathetic it all is, the mask of transgression lined with privilege for those of us, male or female, for whom history hasn't provided sufficient misfortune to constitute the material conditions of affiliation with the revolutionary proletariat which, like the fusion of surrealism and socialism, remains for the intellectual one of the century's dreams. If we reflect on the political simulacra in which the fusion seems to have occurred, perhaps that it remains a dream constitutes our better fortune.

". . . it is out of the forfeits and vain oaths, lapses in speech, and unconsidered words, the constellation of which presided at the putting into the world of man," said Lacan, who discerned an originary violence in the vital dehiscence of the mirror, "that is moulded the stone guest who comes, in symptoms, to disturb the banquet of one's desires. . . ."[14] What, in the reformation of reality by desire or politics or the violence we may say is historically justifiable, will stop the forfeits and vain oaths? For all the discourse, I have no idea. The stone guest seems to me the image of representation in all its unmystifiable if not monstrous obduracy, and it is only a vain wish in the vain oaths that dreams it doesn't return, and with a vengeance, as undauntable and unassuageable as the Real. Does that sound too deterministic and keep us from working for change? For those impelled to work, as I learned in the oppressive theater whose only future is illusion, when has reality or the Real ever really impeded that?

NOTES

1. Jacques Derrida, *Of Grammatology,* trans. Gayatri Chakravorty Spivak (Baltimore: Johns Hopkins Univ. Press, 1976), p. 304.

2. Jean Baudrillard, *In the Shadow of the Silent Majority . . . or, The End of the Social,* trans. Paul Foss, Paul Patton, and John Johnston (New York: Semiotext[e], 1983), pp. 3–4.

3. Derrida, p. 65.

4. Louis Althusser, *Lenin and Philosophy and Other Essays,* trans. Ben Brewster (New York: Monthly Review Press, 1971), p. 241.

5. Jacques Lacan, *The Four Fundamental Concepts of Psychoanalysis,* trans. Alan Sheridan (New York: Norton, 1978), p. 81.

6. *Ibid.,* p. 23.

7. *Ibid.,* p. 218.

8. Baudrillard, p. 88.

9. Lacan, *Écrits: A Selection,* trans. Alan Sheridan (New York: Norton, 1977), p. 115.

10. *Time,* no. 45 (Nov. 5, 1984), p. 12.

11. Walter Benjamin, *Illuminations,* ed. Hannah Arendt, trans. Harry Zohn (New York: Schocken, 1977), p. 177.

12. *Time,* p. 13.

13. *Four Concepts,* p. 60.

14. *Écrits,* p. 143.

INDEX

Absence, in Barthes, 100–101; in Beckett, 68, 75; and comedy, 25–27, 36–38; and Freud's *fort/da*, 161; in Genet, 16–17, 19, 124, 125–26, 128, 169, 201; and Imagination, 143, 157; and language, 157–58; and memory, 143, 159

Absurd, and Beckett, 68; and comedy, 24–27, 34–35, 36–38; and counter culture, 22; and history, 23; and language, xv, xix, 17

Adorno, Theodor, 67

Aeschylus, 185

Aging, and appearance, 158; and comedy, 23–24; and death as economy, 151–56; desire in, 150, 158–59; and history, 146–47, 150–51, 153–54, 155; and imagination, 154–57; in James, 146–47; and literary theory, 145; in literature, 154; memory in, 140–41; narcissism in, 137–39, 143–45; and perception, 151–52; and presence, 135–37; in Proust, 135–36, 138, 146–47, 149, 152, 156–57; and repression, 148–49; in Shakespeare, 157; in Stevens, 140, 144, 146, 147, 156, 156–57, 159; and theory, 145; in Tolstoy, 151; in Winters, 154; in Woolf, 158; in Yeats, 145–46, 157

Albee, Edward, 21, 56

Alter, Robert, xxi

Althusser, Louis, 193

Appearance, and aging, 158; in Beckett, 75–76; in performance, 171–72; and politics, 198–200; and power, 169–70; and simulation, 54. *See also* Representation

Artaud, Antonin, xvii, xviii; on the audience, 79–80; on the body, 6, 79–80, 90–91, 107, 169; on the closure of representation, 8, 27, 165–67, 189–90, 198, 201; and Derrida, 6, 8, 79–80, 126, 165–67, 169, 189–90, 198; and desire in language, 15, 126; and Genet, 126–27; and madness, 171; and performance, 173

Ashbery, Jon, xix, 67

Audience, and Artaud, 79–80; and Beckett, 36–37, 74, 79–80, 94; and comedy, 37; and the look, 36–37; and representation, 191, 194; and reproduction, 190; and scopic drive, 36–37, 74, 79–80; and theater, 189

Bahktin, Mikhail, xix

Ball, Hugo, 2

Baraka, Imamu Amiri, 57

Barba, Eugenio, 184

Barth, John, 4

Barthes, Roland, xviii, xix, 6, 185; absence in, 100–101; and Beckett, 88–89, 92–102; and comedy, xv–xvi; on death, 90, 98–99; and desire in language, xxi, 27–28, 93, 96; feminization in, 95; on the gaze, 95; idea of love in, 96–102; and ideological criticism, 10–11; the Imaginary in, 88, 91–95, 97–98; and indeterminacy, xxix–xxx; on *jouissance*, 105; on language, xv–xvi, xxxi, 84–85; on loss, 85–88, 92; pathos in, 85–88, 89–90; on the photograph, 88, 89–91; on the pleasure of the text, 15, 77; on the *punctum*, 86–88, 91–92, 93–94; sentimentality in, 84–85; on the *studium*, 87–88; and the unconscious, 88; and the unconscious as *mise-en-scène*, 91; on writing, 27–28

Baudelaire, Charles, 199; on essence of laughter, 30, 32–33, 39; on the grotesque, 36; on language of comedy, 29

Baudrillard, Jean, and the politics of simulation, 191, 194, 197, 201–202; on simulation, 10, 31

Beckett, Samuel, xv, xviii, xxv, xxxi, xxxv, 16, 20, 25, 30, 37, 38, 39, 90, 149; absence in, 68, 75; and the Absurd, 68; aging in, 157; appearance in, 75–76; and the audience, 36–37, 74, 79–80, 94; and Barthes, 88–89, 92–102; and comedy, 32–34; on death, 94;

The Eye of Prey: Subversions of the Postmodern
is Volume 9 in the series
THEORIES OF CONTEMPORARY CULTURE
Center for Twentieth Century Studies
University of Wisconsin-Milwaukee

General Editor, KATHLEEN WOODWARD